# Fodor's POCKET

# tōkyō

**second edition**

Excerpted from *Fodor's Japan*

**fodor's travel publications**
**new york • toronto • london • sydney • auckland**
www.fodors.com

# contents

# maps

# on the road with fodor's

**THE MORE YOU KNOW BEFORE YOU GO,** the better your trip will be. Tōkyō's most fascinating small museum or its best restaurant could be just around the corner from your hotel, but if you don't know it's there, it might as well be across the globe. That's where this guidebook and our Web site, Fodors.com, come in. Our editors work hard to give you useful, on-target information. Their efforts begin with finding the best contributors—people with good judgment and broad travel experience—the people you'd poll for tips yourself if you knew them.

**Jared Lubarsky** has lived in Japan since 1973. He has worked for cultural exchange organizations, taught at public and private universities, and written extensively for travel publications.

Tennessee-born **James Vardaman** wrote the guidebook *In and Around Sendai* and co-authored *Japanese Etiquette Today* and *Japan from A to Z: Mysteries of Everyday Life Explained*. He has been a professor of English at Surugadai University in Saitama Prefecture and has worked as a translator. James updated the Practical Information chapter.

## Don't Forget to Write

Keeping a travel guide fresh and up-to-date is a big job. So we love your feedback—positive and negative—and follow up on all suggestions. Contact the *Pocket Tōkyō* editor at editors@fodors.com or c/o Fodor's, 280 Park Avenue, New York, New York 10017. And have a wonderful trip!

*Karen Cure*

Karen Cure
Editorial Director

# tokyo

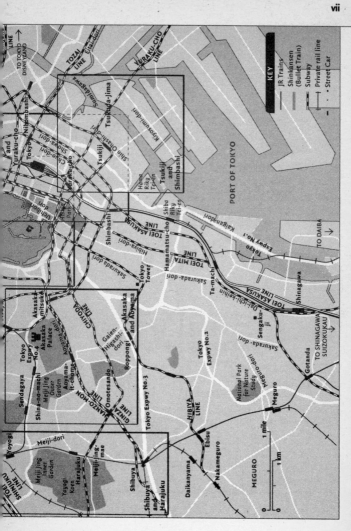

# tokyo subway

Nishi-Takashimadaira · Shin-Takashimadaira · Takashimadaira · Nishidai · Hasune · Shimura-san-chome · Shimura-Sakae · Moto-hasunuma · Itabashi-hon-cho · Itabashi-Kuyakusho-mae · Akabane-Iwabuchi

NAMBOKU

Shimo · Oji-Kamiya · Oji · Nishi-Sugamo · Nish · Sugamo · Komaga

Hikarigaoka · Nerima-Kasugacho · Wakoshi · Eidai-Narimasu · Eidai-Akatsuka · Heiwadai · Hikawadai · Kotake-Mukaihara · Senkawa · Kanamecho

TOEI MITA LINE

Ikebukuro · Otsuka · Shin-Otsuka · Sengoku · Honkomag · Se · Hakusan · Todai

SEIBU IKEBUKURO LINE

Nerima · Toshimaen · Shin-Sakuradai · Nakai · Mejiro · Higashi-Ikebukuro · Takada-no-baba · Gokokuji · Myogadani · Korakuen · Karuga

TOEI LINE NO. 12 · OEDO LINE

Shin · Egota · Ochiai-Minami-Nagasaki · Ochiai · Nishi-Waseda · Waseda · Edogawa-bashi · Kagurazaka

YURAKU-CHO LINE

TOZAI LINE

Mitaka · Ogikubo · Nakano · Nishi-Shinjuku-Gochome · Shinjuku-Nishiguchi · Shinjuku · Hongo-san-chor

Minami-Asagaya · Shin-Koenji · Higashi-Koenji · Shin-Nakano · Nakano-sakaue

MARU-NO-UCHI LINE

Iida-bashi · Suido-bashi

Nakano-shim-bashi · Shinjuku-san-chome · Shinjuku-Gyoen-mae · Yoyogi · Ichigaya · Kudanshita · Jimbo-cho

Nakano-fujimi-cho · Yotsuya-san-chome · Koji-machi · Take-bas

Honan-cho · Sendagaya · Yotsuya · Hanzo-mon

Shinano-machi · Aoyama-itchome · Nagata-cho · Sakura-da-mon

Tama-Senta · Yoyogikoen · Harajuku · Kokuritsu-Kyogijo · Kokkai Gijido-mae · Kasumiga-seki

KEIO LINE

Yoyogi-Uehara · Meiji-jingu-mae · Gaien-mae · Akasaka-mitsuke · Hibiya

CHIYODA LINE

GINZA LINE

Hon-Atsugi · Omotesando · Akasaka · Tameike-Sanno

ODAKYU LINE

HANZO-MON LINE

KEIO INOKASHIRA LINE · Kamiya-cho · Tora-no-mon · Uchisai-wai-cho

TOKYU SHIN-TAMAGAWA LINE · Shibuya · Nogizaka · Roppongi

Chuo-rinkan · Futakotamagawaen

Hiyoshi · Naka-meguro · Ebisu · Hiro-o · Azabu-Juban · Akabane-Bashi · Onari-mon

HIBIYA LINE

TOKYU MEKAMA LINE · Meguro · Shiba-koen

TOKYU IKEGAMI LINE · Gotanda · Sengakuji · Mita · Dai-mon · Shimb

Nishi-Magome · Magome · Nakanobu · Togoshi · Takanawadai · Osaki · Tamachi

TOEI ASAKUSA LINE · Shina-gawa · Hamamatsu-cho

Misakiguchi · KEIHIN-KYUKO LINE

# tōkyō

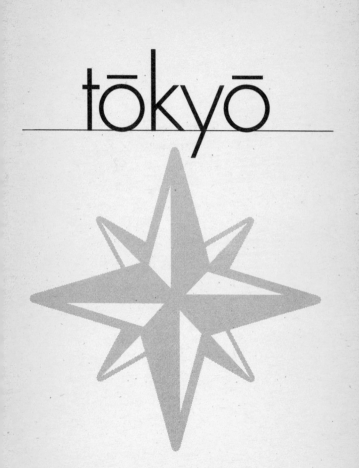

## In This Chapter

*Updated by Jared Lubarsky*

# introducing tōkyō

**OF ALL MAJOR CITIES IN THE WORLD**, Tōkyō is perhaps the hardest to understand or to see in any single perspective. To begin with, consider the sheer, outrageous size of it. Tōkyō incorporates 23 wards, 26 smaller cities, seven towns, and eight villages—altogether sprawling 88 km (55 mi) from east to west and 24 km (15 mi) from north to south. The wards alone enclose an area of 590 square km (228 square mi), which in turn house some 12 million people. More than 3 million of these residents pass through Shinjuku Eki, one of the major hubs in the transportation network, every day.

Space, that most precious of commodities, is so scarce that pedestrians have to weave in and around utility poles as they walk along the narrow sidewalks—yet mile after mile, houses rise only one or two stories, their low uniformity broken here and there by the sore thumb of an apartment building. Begin with that observation, and you discover that the very fabric of life in this city is woven of countless, unfathomable contradictions.

Tōkyō is a state-of-the-art financial marketplace, where billions of dollars are whisked electronically around the globe every day in the blink of an eye—and where automatic teller machines shut down at 9 PM. (There's no service after 5 PM on weekends and holidays, and the machines levy a service charge of ¥105 for withdrawals on Sunday.) A city of astonishing beauty in its small details, Tōkyō also has some of the ugliest buildings on the planet and generates more than 20,000 tons of garbage a day. It installed its first electric light in 1877 yet still has hundreds of thousands of households without a bathtub.

Life was simpler here in the 12th century, when Tōkyō was a little fishing village called Edo (pronounced "*eh*-doh"), near the mouth of the Sumida-gawa on the Kantō Plain. The Kantō was a strategic granary, large and fertile; over the next 400 years it was governed by a succession of warlords and other rulers. One of them, Dōkan Ōta, built the first castle in Edo in 1457. That act is still officially regarded as the founding of the city, but the honor really belongs to Ieyasu ("ee-eh-*ya*-su"), the first Tokugawa shōgun, who arrived in 1590. A key figure in the civil wars of the 16th century, he had been awarded the eight provinces of Kantō in eastern Japan in exchange for three provinces closer to Kyōto, the imperial capital. Ieyasu was a farsighted soldier; the swap was fine with him. On the site of Ōta's stronghold, he built a mighty fortress of his own—from which, 10 years later, he was ruling the whole country.

By 1680 there were more than a million people here, and a great city had grown up out of the reeds in the marshy lowlands of Edo Bay. Tōkyō can only really be understood as a *jō-ka-machi*— a castle town. Ieyasu had fought his way to the shogunate, and he had a warrior's concern for the geography of his capital. Edo-jō (Edo Castle) had the high ground, but that wasn't enough; all around it, at strategic points, he gave large estates to allies and trusted retainers. These lesser lords' villas would also be garrisons, outposts on a perimeter of defense.

Farther out, he kept the barons he trusted least of all—whom he controlled by bleeding their treasuries. He required them to keep large, expensive establishments in Edo; to contribute generously to the temples he endowed; to come and go in alternate years in great pomp and ceremony; and, when they returned to their estates, to leave their families—in effect, hostages—behind.

All this, the Edo of feudal estates, of villas and gardens and temples, lay south and west of Edo-jō. It was called Yamanote— the Bluff, the uptown. Here, all was order, discipline, and ceremony; every man had his rank and duties (very few women were within the garrisons). Almost from the beginning, those duties were less military than bureaucratic. Ieyasu's precautions worked like a charm, and the Tokugawa dynasty enjoyed some 250 years of unbroken peace, during which nothing very interesting ever happened uptown.

But Yamanote was only the demand side of the economy: somebody had to bring in the fish, weed the gardens, weave the mats, and entertain the bureaucrats during their free time. To serve the noble houses, common people flowed into Edo from all over Japan. Their allotted quarters of the city were jumbles of narrow streets, alleys, and cul-de-sacs in the low-lying estuarine lands to the north and east. Often enough, the land assigned to them wasn't even there; they had to make it by draining and filling the marshes (the first reclamation project in Edo dates to 1457). The result was Shitamachi—literally "downtown," the part below the castle, which sat on a hill. Bustling, brawling Shitamachi was the supply side: it had the lumberyards, markets, and workshops; the wood-block printers, kimono makers, and moneylenders. The people here gossiped over the back fence in the earthy, colorful Edo dialect. They went to Yoshiwara—a walled and moated area on the outskirts of Edo where prostitution was under official control. (Yoshiwara was for a time the biggest licensed brothel area in the world.) They supported the bathhouses and Kabuki theaters and reveled in their spectacular summer fireworks festivals. The city and spirit of the Edokko—the people of Shitamachi—have survived, while the great estates uptown are now mostly parks and hotels.

The shogunate was overthrown in 1867. The following year, Emperor Meiji moved his court from Kyōto to Edo and renamed it Tōkyō: the Eastern Capital. By now the city was home to nearly 2 million people, and the geography was vastly more complex. As it grew, it became not one but many smaller cities, with different centers of commerce, government, entertainment, and transportation. In Yamanote rose the commercial emporia, office buildings, and public halls that made up the architecture of an emerging modern state. The workshops of Shitamachi multiplied, some of them to become small jobbers and family-run factories. Still, there was no planning, no grid. The neighborhoods and subcenters were worlds unto themselves, and a traveler from one was soon hopelessly lost in another.

The firebombings of 1945 left Tōkyō, for the most part, in rubble and ashes. That utter destruction could have been an opportunity to rebuild on the rational order of cities like Kyōto, Barcelona, or Washington. No such plan was ever made. Tōkyō reverted to type: it became once again an aggregation of small towns and villages. One village was much like any other; the nucleus was always the *shōten-gai*, the shopping arcade. Each arcade had at least one fishmonger, grocer, rice dealer, mat maker, barber, florist, and a bookstore. You could live your whole life in the neighborhood of the shōten-gai. It was sufficient to your needs.

People seldom moved out of these villages. The vast waves of new residents who arrived after World War II—about three-quarters of the people in the Tōkyō metropolitan area today were born elsewhere—just created more villages. People who lived in the villages knew their way around, so there was no particular need to name the streets. Houses were numbered not in sequence but in the order in which they were built. No. 3 might well share a mailbox with No. 12. And people still take their local geography for granted—the closer you get to the place you're looking for, the harder it is to get coherent directions. Away from main streets and landmarks, even a taxi driver can get hopelessly lost.

Fortunately, there are the *kōban:* small police boxes, or substations, usually with two or three officers assigned to each of them full time, to look after the affairs of the neighborhood. You can't go far in any direction without finding a kōban. The officer on duty knows where everything is and is glad to point the way. (The substation system, incidentally, is one important reason for the legendary safety of Tōkyō: on foot or on white bicycles, the police are a visible presence, covering the beat. Burglaries are not unknown, of course, but street crime is very rare.)

Outsiders, however, rarely venture very far into the labyrinths of residential Tōkyō. Especially for travelers, the city defines itself by its commercial, cultural, and entertainment centers: Ueno, Asakusa, Ginza, Roppongi, Shibuya, Harajuku, and Shinjuku. Megaprojects to develop the waterfront and the Ebisu area in the 1980s and 1990s added yet others to the list. The attention of Tōkyō shifts constantly, seeking new patches of astronomically expensive land on which to realize its enormous commercial energy. Even with the collapse of the speculative bubble in 1992, you can't buy a square yard anywhere in the city's central wards for much less than $1,000.

Tōkyō is still really two areas, Shitamachi and Yamanote. The heart of Shitamachi, proud and stubborn in its Edo ways, is Asakusa; the dividing line is Ginza, west of which lie the boutiques and depāto, the banks and engines of government, the pleasure domes and cafés. Today there are 13 subway lines in full operation that weave the two areas together.

Tōkyō has no remarkable skyline, no prevailing style of architecture, no real context into which a new building can fit. Every new project is an environment unto itself. Architects revel in this anarchy, and so do the designers of neon signs, show windows, and interior spaces. The kind of creative energy you find in Tōkyō could flower only in an atmosphere where there are virtually no rules to break.

Not all of this is for the best. Many of the buildings in Tōkyō are merely grotesque, and most of them are supremely ugly. In the large scale, Tōkyō is not an attractive city—neither is it gracious,

## Your checklist for a perfect journey

### WAY AHEAD

- Devise a trip budget.

- Write down the five things you want most from this trip. Keep this list handy before and during your trip.

- Make plane or train reservations. Book lodging and rental cars.

- Arrange for pet care.

- Check your passport. Apply for a new one if necessary.

- Photocopy important documents and store in a safe place.

### A MONTH BEFORE

- Make restaurant reservations and buy theater and concert tickets. Visit fodors.com for links to local events.

- Familiarize yourself with the local language or lingo.

### TWO WEEKS BEFORE

- Replenish your supply of medications.

- Create your itinerary.

- Enjoy a book or movie set in your destination to get you in the mood.

- Develop a packing list. Shop for missing essentials. Repair and launder or dry-clean your clothes.

### A WEEK BEFORE

- Stop newspaper deliveries. Pay bills.

- Acquire traveler's checks.

- Stock up on film.

- Label your luggage.

- Finalize your packing list— take less than you think you need.

- Create a toiletries kit filled with travel-size essentials.

- Get lots of sleep. Don't get sick before your trip.

### A DAY BEFORE

- Drink plenty of water.

- Check your travel documents.

- Get packing!

### DURING YOUR TRIP

- Keep a journal/scrapbook.

- Spend time with locals.

- Take time to explore. Don't plan too much.

and it is certainly not serene. The pace of life is wedded to the one stupefying fact of population: within a 36-km (22-mi) radius of the Imperial Palace live almost 30 million souls, all of them in a hurry and all of them ferocious consumers—not merely of things but of culture and leisure. Still uncertain about who they are and where they are going, they consume to identify themselves—by what they wear, where they eat, and how they use their spare time.

Sooner or later everything shows up here: Van Gogh's *Sunflowers*, the Berlin Philharmonic, Chinese pandas, Mexican food. Even the Coney Island carousel is here—lovingly restored down to the last gilded curlicue on the last prancing unicorn, back in action at an amusement park called Toshima-en. Tōkyō is a magnet, and now the magnet is drawing you. What follows here is an attempt to chart a few paths for you through this exciting, exasperating, movable feast of a city.

## TŌKYŌ GLOSSARY

Key Japanese words and suffixes in this book include -*bashi* (bridge), *bijutsukan* (art museum), -*chō* (street or block), -*chōme* (street), *chūō* (central), *depāto* ("deh-*pah*-to," department store), *dōri* (avenue), *eki* (train station), *gaijin* (foreigner), -*gawa* (river), -*gū* (Shintō shrine), *guchi* (exit), *hakubutsukan* (museum), *higashi* (east), -*in* (Buddhist temple), *izakaya* (pub), -*ji* (Buddhist temple), -*jima* (island), *jingū* or *jinja* (Shintō shrine), -*jō* (castle), *kita* (north), *kōen* (park), -*ku* (section or ward), *kūkō* (airport), *machi* (town), *matsuri* (festival), *minami* (south), -*mon* (gate), *nishi* (west), *Shinkansen* (bullet train, literally "new trunk line"), *shita* (lower, downward), *torii* ("*to-ree*-ee," gate), -*ya* (shop, as in hon-ya, bookshop), *yama* (mountain), *yamanote* (the hilly part of town).

## In This Chapter

*Updated by Jared Lubarsky*

# here and there

**THE DISTINCTIONS OF SHITAMACHI** (literally "downtown," to the north and east) and Yamanote (literally "uptown," to the south and west) have shaped the character of Tōkyō since the 17th century and will guide you as you explore the city. At the risk of an easy generalization, it might be said that downtown has more to see, uptown more to do. Another way of putting it is that Tōkyō north and east of the Imperial Palace embodies more of the city's history and traditional way of life; the glitzy, ritzy side of contemporary, international Tōkyō generally lies south and west.

The city has been divided into 9 exploring sections in this chapter, 6 in Shitamachi—starting in central Tōkyō with the Imperial Palace District—and 3 uptown in Yamanote. It can be exhausting to walk from one part of Tōkyō to another—you'll look in vain for places outdoors just to sit and rest en route—and bus travel can be particularly tricky. Fortunately, no point on any of these itineraries is very far from a subway station, and you can use the city's efficient subway system to hop from one area to another, to cut a tour short, or to return to a tour the next day. The area divisions in this book are not always contiguous— Tōkyō is too spread out for that—but they generally border each other to a useful degree. As you plan your approach to the city, by all means skip parts of an area that don't appeal or combine parts of one tour with those of another in order to get the best of all worlds.

The listings in this chapter include subway and JR train lines and stops as well as station exit names and numbers in cases where they're most helpful—which is quite often, as several stations have multiple (sometimes more than 15) exits.

## IMPERIAL PALACE DISTRICT

Kōkyo, the Imperial Palace, occupies what were once the grounds of Edo-jō. When Ieyasu Tokugawa chose the site for his castle in 1590, he had two goals in mind. First, it would have to be impregnable; second, it would have to reflect the power and glory of his position. He was lord of the Kantō, the richest fief in Japan, and would soon be shōgun, the military head of state. The fortifications he devised called for a triple system of moats and canals, incorporating the bay and the Sumida-gawa into a huge network of waterways that enclosed both the castle keep (the stronghold, or tower) and the palaces and villas of his court—in all, an area of about 450 acres. The castle had 99 gates (36 in the outer wall), 21 watchtowers (of which 3 are still standing), and 28 armories. The outer defenses stretched from present-day Shimbashi Eki to Kanda. Completed in 1640 and later expanded, it was at the time the largest castle in the world.

The walls of Edo-jō and its moats were made of stone from the Izu Peninsula, about 96 km (60 mi) to the southwest. The great slabs were brought by barge—each of the largest was a cargo in itself—to the port of Edo (then much closer to the castle than the present port of Tōkyō is now) and hauled through the streets on sledges by teams of 100 or more men. Thousands of stonemasons were brought from all over the country to finish the work. Under the gates and castle buildings, the blocks of stone are said to have been shaped and fitted so precisely that a knife blade could not be slipped between them.

The inner walls divided the castle into four main areas, called maru. The hon-maru, the principle area, contained the shōgun's audience halls, his private residence, and, for want of a better word, his seraglio: the ō-oku, where he kept his wife and concubines, with their ladies-in-waiting, attendants, cooks, and servants. At any given time, as many as 1,000 women might be living in the ō-oku. Intrigue, more than sex, was its principal concern, and tales of the seraglio provided a rich source of material for the Japanese literary imagination. Below the hon-maru was the *ni-no-maru*, where the shōgun lived when he transferred his power to an heir and retired. Behind it was the *kita-no-maru*, the northern area, now a public park; south and west was the *nishi-no-maru*, a subsidiary fortress.

Not much of the Tokugawa glory remains. The shogunate was abolished in 1868, and in Emperor Meiji's move from Kyōto to Edo, which he renamed Tōkyō, Edo-jō was chosen as the site of the Imperial Palace. Many of its buildings had been destroyed in the turmoil of the restoration of the emperor, others fell in the fires of 1872, and still others were simply torn down. Of the 28 original *tamon* (armories), only 2 have survived. The present-day Imperial Palace, which dates to 1968, is open to the public only twice a year: on January 2 and December 23 (The Emperor's Birthday), when many thousands of people assemble under the balcony to offer their good wishes to the imperial family. In 1968, to mark the completion of the current palace, the area that once encompassed the hon-maru and ni-no-maru was opened to the public as the Imperial Palace East Garden. There are three entrance gates—Ōte-mon, Hirakawa-mon, and Kita-hane-bashi-mon. You can easily get to any of the three from the Ōte-machi or Takebashi subway station.

*Numbers in the text correspond to numbers in the margin and on the Imperial Palace map.*

## A Good Walk

A good place to start is **Tōkyō Eki** ①. The Ōte-machi subway stop (on the Chiyoda, Marunouchi, Tōzai, Hanzō-mon, and Toei Mita lines) is a closer and handier connection, but the old redbrick Tōkyō Eki building is a more compelling choice. (The Tōkyō Station Hotel, incidentally, which wanders along the west side of Tōkyō Eki on the second and third floors, serves a fairly decent breakfast for ¥1,700.) Leave the station by the Marunouchi Central Exit, cross the street in front at the taxi stand, and walk up the broad divided avenue that leads to the Imperial Palace grounds. To your left is Marunouchi, to your right Ōte-machi: you're in the heart of Japan, Incorporated—the home of its major banks and investment houses, its insurance and trading companies. Take the second right, at the corner of the New Marunouchi Building; walk two blocks, past the gleaming brown-marble fortress of the Industrial Bank of Japan, and turn left. Ahead of you, across Uchibori-dōri (Inner Moat Avenue) from the Palace Hotel, is **Ōte-mon**, one of three entrances to the **Imperial Palace East Garden** ②.

Turn right as you leave the East Garden through Ōte-mon. Where the wall makes a right angle, you will see the Tatsumi, or Ni-jū Yagura (Double-Tiered Watchtower), one of three surviving watchtowers on the original fortifications. Here the sidewalk opens out to a parking lot for tour buses and the beginning of a broad promenade. In the far corner to your right, where the angle of the wall turns again, is the Kikyō-mon, a gate used primarily for deliveries to the palace. At the far end of the parking lot is Sakashita-mon, the gate used by the officials of the Imperial Household Agency itself.

From here to Hibiya Kōen, along both sides of Uchibori-dōri, stretches the concourse of the **Imperial Palace Outer Garden** ③. This whole area once lay along the edge of Tōkyō Bay. Later, the shōgun had his most trusted retainers build their estates here. These in turn gave way to the office buildings of the Meiji government. In 1899 the buildings were relocated, and the promenade was planted with the wonderful stands of pine trees you see today.

Walk along the broad gravel path to **Ni-jū-bashi** ④ (Two-Tiered Bridge) and the Sei-mon (Main Gate). Ni-jū-bashi makes its graceful arch over the moat here from the area inside the gate.

The building in the background, completing the picture, is the Fushimi Yagura, built in the 17th century. It is the last of the three surviving original watchtowers.

Continue on the gravel walk past the Sei-mon, turn right, and pass through the **Sakurada-mon** ⑤. Before you do, turn and look back down the concourse: you will not see another expanse of open space like this anywhere else in Tōkyō.

Look south across the street as you pass through the gate; the broad avenue that begins on the opposite side is Sakurada-dōri. World-renowned architect Kenzō Tange's Metropolitan Police Department building is on the west corner. The stately brick building on the east corner is the old Ministry of Justice. Sakurada-dōri runs through the heart of official Japan; between here and Kasumigaseki are the ministries—from Foreign Affairs and Education to International Trade and Industry—that compose the central government. Turn right at Sakurada-mon and follow the Sakurada Moat uphill along Uchibori-dōri.

A five-minute walk will bring you to where Roppongi-dōri branches in from the left; look in that direction and you will see the approach to the squat pyramid of the **Kokkai-Gijidō** ⑥, which houses the Japanese parliament. You might want to walk in for a closer look. If not, bear right as you continue to follow the moat along Uchibori-dōri to the next intersection, at Miya-zaka. Across the street are the gray-stone slabs of Japan's Supreme Court, the **Saikō Saibansho** ⑦. This and the **Kokuritsu Gekijō** ⑧ (National Theater), next door, are worth a short detour.

Cross back to the palace side of the street and continue north on Uchibori-dōri. At the top of the hill, on your right, a police contingent guards the road to the **Hanzō-mon** ⑨—the western gate to the new Imperial Palace. Here, where the road turns north again, begins the Hanzō Moat.

# imperial palace

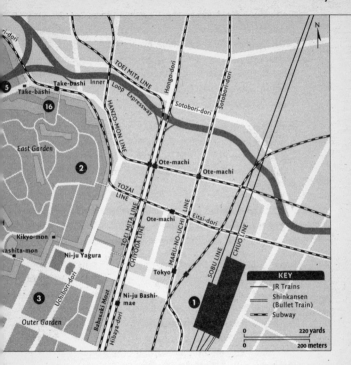

ri-dori

**5** ■ Take-bashi

■ Take-bashi   Inner

TOEI MITA LINE

Hongo-dori

Sotobori-dori

Sotobori-dori

**16**

Loop Expressway

HANZO-MON LINE

East Garden

**2**

Ote-machi

Ote-machi

TOZAI
LINE

Ote-machi   Eitai-dori

Kikyo-mon ■

TOEI MITA LINE

CHIYODA LINE

MARU-NO-UCHI LINE

ashita-mon ■

Ni-ju Yagura

Uchibori-dori

Tokyo

SOBU LINE

CHUO LINE

**3**

Babasaki Moat

Hibaya-dori

Ni-ju Bashi-
mae

**1**

Outer Garden

| KEY |
| --- |
| —— JR Trains |
| ═══ Shinkansen (Bullet Train) |
| ▪▪▪ Subway |

0 — 220 yards

0 — 200 meters

North along the Hanzō Moat is a narrow strip of park; facing it, across the street, is the British Embassy. Along this western edge of his fortress, the shōgun kept his personal retainers, called *hatamoto*, divided by *ban-chō* (district) into six regiments. Today these six ban-chō are among the most sought-after residential areas in Tōkyō, where high-rise apartments commonly fetch ¥100 million or more.

At the next intersection, review your priorities again. You can turn right and complete your circuit of the palace grounds by way of the Inui-mon, or you can continue straight north to the end of Uchibori-dōri to **Yasukuni Jinja** ⑩, the Shrine of Peace for the Nation.

If you do go to Yasukuni Jinja, make time for a short visit on the way to the **Yamatane Bijutsukan** ⑪, a few minutes' walk past the intersection on the east side of Samban-chō.

Leave Yasukuni Jinja the way you came in, cross the street, turn left, and walk down the hill. The entrance to **Chidori-ga-fuchi Kōen** ⑫ is about 50 yards from the intersection, on the right. The green strip of promenade is high on the edge of the moat, lined with cherry trees. Halfway along, it widens, and opposite the Fairmount Hotel a path leads down to the Chidori-ga-fuchi Boathouse. Beyond the boathouse, the promenade leads back in the direction of the Imperial Palace.

If you have the time and stamina for a longer tour, retrace your steps from the boathouse, leave the park the way you came in, turn right, and continue down the hill to the entrance to Kita-no-maru Kōen, through Tayasu-mon, one of the largest and finest of the surviving *masu* (box) gates to the castle. Inside, you come first to the octagonal **Nippon Budōkan** ⑬, site of major rock concerts and martial arts contests.

Opposite the main entrance to the Budōkan, past the parking lot, a pathway leads off through the park back in the direction of the palace. Cross the bridge at the other end of the path, turn right, and then right again before you leave the park on the driveway that leads to the **Kōgeikan** ⑭, a museum devoted to works of traditional craftsmanship by the great modern masters.

Return to the park exit and cross the street to the palace side. Ahead of you is the Inui-mon. This gate is used primarily by members of the imperial family and by the fortunate few with special invitations to visit the palace itself. A driveway here leads to the Imperial Household Agency and the palace. A bit farther down the hill is the Kita-Hane-bashi-mon, one of the entrances to the Imperial Palace East Garden.

At the foot of the hill is Take-bashi—although the name means Bamboo Bridge, the original construction has, of course, long since given way to reinforced concrete. Here, depending on your reserves of time and energy, you might want to cross the street to see the collection of modern Japanese and Western work in the **Tōkyō Kokuritsu Kindai Bijutsukan** ⑮. On the palace side of Take-bashi sits the finely reconstructed **Hirakawa-mon** ⑯, the East Garden's third entrance, which will complete the loop on this walk. From here follow the moat as it turns south again around the garden. In a few minutes you'll find yourself back at Ōte-mon, tired, perhaps, but triumphant.

## TIMING

The Imperial Palace area covers a lot of ground—uphill and down—and even in its shorter versions the walk includes plenty to see. Allow at least an hour for the East Garden and Outer Garden of the palace itself. Plan to visit Yasukuni Jinja after lunch and spend at least an hour there. The Yūshūkan (at Yasukuni Jinja) and Kōgeikan museums are both small and should engage you for no more than half an hour each, but the modern art museum will repay a more leisurely visit—particularly if there's a special exhibit. Set your own pace, but assume that this walk will take you the better part of a full day.

Avoid Monday, when the East Garden and museums are closed; the East Garden is also closed on Friday. In July and August heat will make the palace walk grueling—bring hats, parasols, and bottled water.

## What to See

**⑫ CHIDORI-GA-FUCHI KŌEN.** High on the edge (*fuchi* means "edge") of the Imperial Palace moat, this park is pleasantly arrayed with cherry trees. Long before Edo-jō was built, there was a lovely little lake here, which Ieyasu Tokugawa incorporated into his system of defenses. Now you can rent a rowboat at **Chidori-ga-fuchi Boathouse,** roughly in the middle of the park, and explore it at your leisure. The park entrance is near Yasukuni Jinja, west and downhill from the corner of Yasukuni-dōri and Uchibori-dōri. *tel. 03/3234–1948. Boat rentals ¥300 for 30 mins. Park daily sunrise–sunset; boathouse Apr.–Sept., Tues.–Sun. 9:30–4:30; Oct.–Mar., Tues.–Sun. 9:30–5. Subway: Hanzō-mon and Toei Shinjuku lines, Kudanshita Eki (Exit 2).*

**⑨ HANZŌ-MON.** The house of the legendary Hattori Hanzō once sat at the foot of this small wooden gate. Hanzō was the leader of the shōgun's private corps of spies and infiltrators—and assassins, if need be. They were the menacing, black-clad *ninja*, perennial material for historical adventure films and television dramas. The gate is a minute's walk east from the subway. *Subway: Hanzō-mon Line, Hanzō-mon Eki (Exit 3).*

**⑯ HIRAKAWA-MON.** The approach to this gate crosses the only wooden bridge that spans the Imperial Palace moat. The gate and bridge are reconstructions, but Hirakawa-mon is especially beautiful, looking much as it must have when the shōgun's ladies used it on their rare excursions from the seraglio. Hirakawa-mon is the north gate to the East Garden, southeast of Take-bashi. *Subway: Tōzai Line, Take-bashi Eki (Exit 1A).*

**❷ IMPERIAL PALACE EAST GARDEN.** The entrance to the East Garden, Kōkyo Higashi Gyo-en, is the ☞ **Ōte-mon,** once the main gate of Ieyasu Tokugawa's castle. In lieu of an admission ticket, collect a plastic token at the office on the other side of the gate. As you walk up the driveway you pass, on the left, the National Police Agency *dōjō* (martial arts hall). The hall was built in the Taishō period (1912–25) and is still used for *kendō* (Japanese fencing) practice. On the right is the Ōte Rest House, where for ¥100 you can buy a simple map of the garden.

There was another gate at the top of the driveway, where feudal lords summoned to the palace would descend from their palanquins and proceed on foot. The gate itself is gone, but two 19th-century guardhouses survive, one outside the massive stone supports on the right and a longer one inside on the left. The latter, known as the **Hundred-Man Guardhouse,** was defended by four shifts of 100 soldiers each. Past it, to the right, is the entrance to what was once the *ni-no-maru*, the "second circle" of the fortress. It's now a grove and garden, its pathways defined by rows of perfect rhododendrons, with a pond and a waterfall in the northwest corner. At the far end of the ni-no-maru is the **Suwa Tea Pavilion,** an early 19th-century building relocated here from another part of the castle grounds.

The steep stone walls of the **hon-maru** (the "inner circle"), with the Moat of Swans below (the swans actually swim in the outer waterways), dominate the west side of the garden. Halfway along, a steep path leads to an entrance in the wall to the upper fortress. This is **Shio-mi-zaka,** which translates roughly as "Briny View Hill," so named because in the Edo period the ocean could be seen from here.

Nothing remains on the broad expanse of the hon-maru's lawn to recall the scores of buildings that once stood here, connected by a network of corridors. But you can see the stone foundations of the castle keep at the far end of the grounds. As you enter, turn left and explore the wooded paths that skirt the perimeter.

Here you'll find shade, quiet, and benches where you can sit, rest your weary feet, and listen to birdsong. In the southwest corner, through the trees, you can see the back of the **Fujimi Yagura,** the only surviving watchtower of the hon-maru; farther along the path, on the west side, is the **Fujimi Tamon,** one of the two remaining armories.

The foundations of the keep make a platform with a fine view of **Kita-no-maru Kōen** and the city to the north. The view must have been even finer from the keep itself. Built and rebuilt three times, it soared more than 250 ft over Edo. The other castle buildings were all plastered white; the keep was black, unadorned but for a golden roof. In 1657 a fire destroyed most of the city. Strong winds carried the flames across the moat, where it consumed the keep in a heat so fierce that it melted the gold in the vaults underneath. The keep was never rebuilt.

To the left of the keep foundations there is an exit from the hon-maru that leads northwest to the Kita-Hane-bashi-mon. To the right, another road leads past the **Toka Music Hall**—an octagonal tower faced in mosaic tile, built in honor of the empress in 1966—down to the ni-no-maru and out of the gardens by way of the northern **Hirakawa-mon.** If you decide to leave the hon-maru the way you came in, through the Ōte-mon, stop for a moment at the rest house on the west side of the park before you surrender your token, and look at the photo collection. The pairs of before-and-after photographs of the castle, taken about 100 years apart, are fascinating. *Free. Weekends and Tues.–Thurs. 9–3. Subway: Tōzai, Marunouchi, or Chiyoda line; Ōte-machi Eki (Exit C10).*

**③ IMPERIAL PALACE OUTER GARDEN.** When the office buildings of the Meiji government were moved from this area in 1899, the whole expanse along the east side of the palace was turned into a public promenade and planted with stands of pine. The Outer Garden affords the best view of the castle walls and their Tokugawa-period fortifications: Ni-jū-bashi and the Seï-mon, the 17th-century Fujimi Yagura watchtower, and the Sakurada-mon. *Subway: Chiyoda Line, Ni-jū-bashi-mae Eki (Exit 2).*

**⑭ KŌGEIKAN** (Crafts Gallery of the National Museum of Modern Art). Built in 1910, the Kōgeikan was once the headquarters of the Imperial Guard. It is a rambling redbrick building, Gothic Revival in style, with exhibition halls on the second floor. The exhibits are all too few, but many of the craftspeople represented here— masters in the traditions of lacquerware, textiles, pottery, and metalwork—have been designated by the government as Living National Treasures. The most direct access to the gallery is from the Take-bashi subway station on the Tōzai Line. Walk west and uphill about 10 minutes, on the avenue between Kita-no-maru Kōen and the Imperial Palace grounds; the entrance will be on the right. *1–1 Kita-no-maru Kōen, Chiyoda-ku, tel. 03/3211–7781. ¥420 (includes admission to National Museum of Modern Art); additional fee for special exhibits. Tues.–Sun. 10–4:30. Subway: Hanzō-mon and Toei Shinjuku lines, Kudanshita Eki (Exit 2); Tōzai Line, Takebashi Eki (Exit 1b).*

**⑥ KOKKAI-GIJIDŌ** (National Diet Building). This chunky pyramid houses the Japanese parliament. Completed in 1936 after 17 years of work, it is a building best contemplated from a distance. On a gloomy day it seems as if it might well have sprung from the screen of a German Expressionist movie. *1–7–1 Nagata-chō, Chiyoda-ku. Subway: Marunouchi Line, Kokkai-Gijidō-mae Eki (Exit 2).*

**⑧ KOKURITSU GEKIJŌ** (National Theater). Architect Hiroyuki Iwamoto's winning entry in the design competition for the Kokuritsu Gekijō building (1966) is a rendition in concrete of the ancient *azekura* (storehouse) style, invoking the 8th-century Shōsōin Imperial Repository in Nara. The large hall seats 1,746 and presents primarily Kabuki theater, ancient court music, and dance. The small hall seats 630 and is used mainly for Bunraku puppet theater and traditional music. *4–1 Hayabusa-chō, Chiyoda-ku, tel. 03/ 3265–7411. Varies depending on performance. Subway: Hanzō-mon Line, Hanzō-mon Eki (Exit 1).*

★ **④ NI-JŪ-BASHI** (Two-Tiered Bridge). This is surely the most photogenic spot on the grounds of the former Edo-jō, which you can approach no closer than the head of the short stone bridge called the **Sei-mon Sekkyō**. Cordoned off on the other side is the **Sei-mon,** through which ordinary mortals may pass only on January 2 and December 23. The guards in front of their small, octagonal, copper-roof sentry boxes change every hour on the hour—alas, with nothing like the pomp and ceremony of Buckingham Palace. Ni-jū-bashi arcs over the moat from the area inside Sei-mon. In the background the **Fushimi Yagura** watchtower makes for a picturesque backdrop. The bridge is a minute's walk north of the subway; follow the Imperial Palace moat to the courtyard in front of the gate. *Subway: Chiyoda Line, Ni-jū-bashi-mae Eki (Exit 2).*

**⑬ NIPPON BUDŌKAN.** With its eight-sided plan based on the Hall of Dreams of Hōryū-ji in Nara, the Budōkan was built as a martial arts arena for the Tōkyō Olympics of 1964. It still hosts tournaments and exhibitions of jūdō, karate, and kendō, as well as concerts. Tōkyō promoters are fortunate in their audiences, who don't seem to mind the exorbitant ticket prices and poor acoustics. From the Kudanshita subway stop walk west uphill toward Yasukuni Jinja; the entrance to Kitano Maru Kōen and the Budōkan is a few minutes' walk from the station, on the left. *2–3 Kitano Maru Kōen, Chiyoda-ku, tel. 03/3216–5100. Subway: Tōzai, Hanzō-mon, and Toei Shinjuku lines; Kudanshita Eki (Exit 2).*

**Ōte-mon.** This gate is the main entrance to the Imperial Palace East Garden. In former days it was the principal gate of Ieyasu Tokugawa's castle. The masu style was typical of virtually all the approaches to the shōgun's impregnable fortress: the first portal leads to a narrow enclosure, with a second and larger gate beyond, offering the defenders inside a devastating field of fire upon any would-be intruders. Most of the Ōte-mon was destroyed in 1945 but was rebuilt in 1967 on the original plans. The outer part of the gate, however, survived. *Subway: Tōzai, Marunouchi, and Chiyoda lines; Ōte-machi Eki (Exit C10).*

**⑦ SAIKŌ SAIBANSHO** (Supreme Court). Designed by Shinichi Okada, the Supreme Court building was the last in a series of open architectural competitions sponsored by the various government agencies charged with the reconstruction of Tōkyō after World War II. Its fortresslike planes and angles speak volumes for the role of the law in Japanese society—here is the very bastion of the established order. Okada's winning design was one of 217 submitted. Before the building was finished, in 1968, the open competition had generated so much controversy that the government did not hold another one for almost 20 years. Guided tours are available, but under restrictive conditions: you must be 16 years old or above to take part; tours musts be reserved two weeks in advance; and there is no interpretation in English. Tours are conducted weekdays (except July 20–August 31 and national holidays); they begin at 3 and take about an hour. *4–2 Hayabusa-chō, Chiyoda-ku, tel. 03/3264–8111 for public relations office (Kōhōka) for permission to visit inside. Subway: Hanzō-mon Line, Hanzō-mon Eki (Exit 1).*

**⑤ SAKURADA-MON** (Gate of the Field of Cherry Trees). By hallowed use and custom, the small courtyard between the portals of this masu gate is where joggers warm up for their 5-km (3-mi) run around the palace. *Subway: Yūraku-chō Line, Sakurada-mon Eki (Exit 3).*

**① TŌKYŌ EKI.** The work of Kingo Tatsuno, one of Japan's first modern architects, Tōkyō Eki was completed in 1914. Tatsuno modeled his creation on the railway station of Amsterdam. The building lost its original top story in the air raids of 1945, but it was promptly repaired. More recent plans to tear it down entirely were scotched by a protest movement. Inside, it seems to be in a constant state of redesign and renovation, but the lovely old facade remains untouched. The best thing about the place is the **Tōkyō Station Hotel,** on the west side on the second and third floors. *1–9–1 Marunouchi, Chiyoda-ku, tel. 03/3231–2511.*

**⑮ TŌKYŌ KOKURITSU KINDAI BIJUTSUKAN** (National Museum of Modern Art, Tōkyō). Founded in 1952 and moved to its present site in 1969, this was Japan's first national art museum. It mounts a number of major exhibitions of 20th-century Japanese and Western art throughout the year but tends to be rather stodgy about how it organizes and presents these exhibitions and is seldom on the cutting edge. The second through fourth floors house the permanent collection, which includes the painting, prints, and sculpture of Rousseau, Picasso, Tsuguji Fujita, Ryūzaburo Umehara, and Taikan Yokoyama. *3 Kita-no-maru Kōen, Chiyoda-ku, tel. 03/3561–1400 or 03/3272–8600, www3.momat.go.jp/index_e.html. Subway: Tōzai Line, Take-bashi Eki (Exit 1b); Hanzō-mon and Tōei Shinjuku lines, Kudanshita Eki (Exit 2).*

**⑪ YAMATANE BIJUTSUKAN.** The museum, which specializes in *nihon-ga*—traditional Japanese painting—from the Meiji period and later, has a private collection of masterpieces by such painters as Taikan Yokoyama, Gyoshū Hayami, Kokei Kobayashi, and Gyokudō Kawai. The exhibitions, which sometimes include works borrowed from other collections, change every two months. The decor and display at the Yamatane make it an oasis of quiet and elegance in the surrounding world of high finance, and the chance to buy the lavish catalog of the collection is well worth the visit. An interior garden was designed by architect Yoshio Taniguchi, who also did the Museum of Modern Art. *2 Samban-chō, Chiyoda-ku, tel. 03/3239–5911, fax 03/3239–5913. ¥500. Tues.–Sun. 10–4:30. Subway: Tōzai and Tōei Shinjuku lines, Kudanshita Eki (Exit 2).*

**⑩ YASUKUNI JINJA** (Shrine of Peace for the Nation). Founded in 1869, Yasukuni Jinja is dedicated to the approximately 2.5 million Japanese who have died since then in war or military service. Since 1945 Yasukuni has been the periodic focus of passionate political debate, given that the Japanese constitution expressly renounces both militarism and state sponsorship of religion. Even so, hundreds of thousands of Japanese come here every year, simply to pray for the repose of friends and relatives they have lost.

The shrine is not one structure but a complex of buildings that includes the **Main Hall** and the **Hall of Worship**—both built in the simple, unadorned style of the ancient Shintō shrines at Ise—and the **Yūshūkan,** a museum of documents and war memorabilia. Also here are a **Nō theater** and, in the far western corner, a sumō-wrestling ring. Both Nō and sumō have their origins in religious ritual, as performances offered to please and divert the gods. Sumō matches are held at Yasukuni in April, during the first of its three annual festivals.

Pick up a pamphlet and simplified map of the shrine in English just inside the grounds. Just ahead of you, in a circle on the main avenue, is a statue of Masujiro Omura, commander of the imperial forces that subdued the Tokugawa loyalist resistance to the new Meiji government. From here, as you look down the avenue to your right, you see the enormous steel outer torii of the main entrance to the shrine at Kudanshita; to the left is a bronze inner torii, erected in 1887. (These Shintō shrine arches are normally made of wood and painted red.) Beyond the inner torii is the gate to the shrine itself, with its 12 pillars and chrysanthemums—the imperial crest—embossed on the doors.

Though some of the displays in the Yūshūkan have English labels and notes, the English is not very helpful; fortunately, most objects speak clearly enough for themselves. Rooms on the second floor house an especially fine collection of medieval swords and armor. Perhaps the most bizarre exhibit is the *kaiten* (human torpedo) on the first floor. The kaiten was a black cylinder about 50 ft long and 3 ft in diameter, with 3,400 pounds of high explosives in the nose. The operator, squeezed into a seat with a periscope in the center of the tube, worked the directional vanes with his feet. The kaiten was carried into battle on the deck of a ship and launched, like a kamikaze plane, on its one-way journey.

If time permits, turn right as you leave the Yūshūkan and walk past the other implements of war—cannons, ancient and modern, and a tank, incongruously bright and gay in its green-and-yellow camouflage paint—arrayed in front of the pond at the rear of the shrine. There is, unfortunately, no general admittance to the teahouses on the far side, but the pond is among the most serene and beautiful in Tōkyō, especially in spring, when the irises bloom. *3–1–1 Kudankita, Chiyoda-ku, tel. 03/3261–8326. ¥300. Grounds daily, usually 9–9. Museum Mar.–Oct., daily 9–5; Nov.–Feb., daily 9–4:30. Subway: Hanzō-mon and Toei Shinjuku lines, Kudanshita Eki (Exit 2).*

NEED A BREAK? The specialty at the moderately priced **Tony Roma's**, as it is in this chain's umpteen locations, is charcoal-broiled spareribs. It is on the west side of Uchibori-dōri north of the British Embassy, at the intersection straight west of Inui-mon. *1 Samban-chō, Chiyoda-ku, tel. 03/3222–3440.*

## AKIHABARA

This is it: the greatest sound-and-light show on earth. Akihabara is a merchandise mart for anything—and everything—that runs on electricity, from microprocessors and washing machines to television sets and gadgets that beep when your bathwater is hot. Wherever you go in the world, if people know nothing else about Japan, they recognize the country as a cornucopia of electronics equipment and household appliances. About 10% of what Japan's electronics industry makes for the domestic market passes through Akihabara.

Just after World War II there was a black market here, around the railroad station, where the Yamanote Line and the crosstown Sōbu Line intersect. In time, most of the stalls were doing a legitimate business in radio parts, and in 1951 they were all relocated in one dense clump under the tracks. Retail and wholesale suppliers then spread out into the adjacent blocks and made the area famous for cut-rate prices.

Few visitors to Tōkyō neglect this district; the mistake is to come here merely for shopping. Akihabara may be consumer heaven, but it is also the first stop on a walking tour through the general area known as Kanda—where the true Edokko, the born-and-bred Tōkyōites of the old town, claim their roots—to the bookstalls of Jimbō-chō. In a sense this tour is a journey through time: it's a morning's walk from satellite broadcast antennas to the hallowed precincts of the printed word.

*Numbers in the text correspond to numbers in the margin and on the Akihabara map.*

## A Good Walk

Start at the west exit of JR Akihabara Eki. (There's also a stop, Nakaokachi-machi, nearby on the Hibiya subway line, but the JR provides much easier access.) Come out to the left after you pass through the wicket, head into the station square, turn right, and walk to the main thoroughfare. Ahead of you on the other side of the street you'll see the **LAOX** ⑰ building, one of the district's major discount stores.

Before you get to the corner, on the right is a little warren of stalls and tiny shops that cannot have changed an iota since the days of the black market—except for their merchandise. Wander through the narrow passageways and see an astonishing array of switches, transformers, resistors, semiconductors, printed circuit cards, plugs, wires, connectors, and tools. The labyrinth is especially popular with domestic and foreign techno mavens, the people who know—or want to know—what the latest in Japanese electronic technology looks like from the inside.

If you turn left at the corner and cross the small bridge over the Kanda-gawa, you'll soon come to the **Kōtsū**

# akihabara

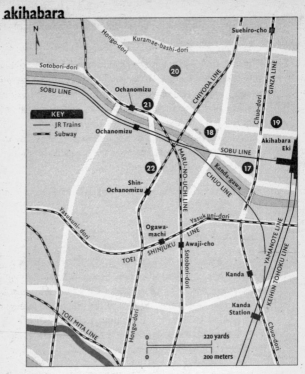

**Hakubutsukan** ⑱—a detour you might want to make if you have children in tow. If not, turn right at the corner and walk north on Chūō-dōri. Music blares at you from hundreds of storefronts as you walk along; this is the heart of the district. Most larger stores on the main drag have one floor—or even an entire annex—of products for the foreign market, staffed by clerks who speak everything from English to Mandarin to Portuguese. Prices are duty free (don't forget to bring your passport). By far the biggest selections are to be found at rival stores **Yamagiwa** and **Minami** ⑲. Yamagiwa is just past the second intersection, on the right, and Minami is at the far end of the block.

At Minami, cross the street, continue north to the Soto Kanda 5-chōme intersection (there's an entrance to the Suehiro-chō subway station on the corner), and turn left onto Kuramae-bashi-dōri. Walk about five minutes—you'll cross one more intersection with a traffic light—and in the middle of the next block you'll see a flight of steps on the left, between two brick buildings. Red, green, and blue pennants flutter from the handrails. This is the back entrance to **Kanda Myōjin** ⑳.

Leave the shrine by the main gate. The seated figures in the alcoves on either side are its guardian gods; carved in camphor wood, they are depicted in Heian costume, holding long bows. From the gate down to the copper-clad torii on Hongo-dōri is a walk of a few yards. On either side are shops that sell the specialties famous in this neighborhood: pickles, miso, and sweet sake laced with ground ginger. On the other side of the avenue are the wall and wooded grounds of the **Yūshima Seidō** ㉑ Confucian shrine.

Cross Hongo-dōri and turn left, following the wall downhill. Turn right at the first narrow side street, and right again at the bottom; the entrance to Yūshima Seidō is a few steps from the corner. As you walk up the path, you'll see a statue of Confucius on your right; where the path ends, a flight of stone steps leads up to the main hall of the shrine—six times destroyed by fire, each time rebuilt. The last repairs date to 1954. The hall could almost be in China: painted black, weathered and somber, it looks like nothing else you're likely to see in Japan.

Retrace your steps, turn right as you leave the shrine, and walk along the continuation of the wall on the side street leading up to Hijiri-bashi (Bridge of Sages), which spans the Kanda-gawa at Ochanomizu Eki on the JR Sōbu Line. Cross the bridge—you're now back on Hongo-dōri—and ahead of you, just beyond the station on the right, you'll see the dome of the Russian Orthodox **Nikolai Cathedral** ㉒.

Continue south to the intersection of Hongo-dōri and Yasukuni-dōri. Surugadai, the area to your right as you walk down the hill, is a kind of fountainhead of Japanese higher education: two of the city's major private universities—Meiji and Nihon—occupy a good part of the hill. Not far from these are a score of elite high schools, public and private. In the 1880s several other universities were founded in this area. They have since moved away, but the student population here is still enormous.

### TIMING

Unless you do a lot of shopping, this walk should take you no more than a morning. Cultural landmarks are few, and you can explore them thoroughly in half an hour each. Getting from place to place will take up much of your time. Keep in mind that most stores in Akihabara do not open until 10 AM. Weekends draw hordes of shoppers, especially on Sunday, when the four central blocks of Chūō-dōri are closed to traffic and become a pedestrian mall.

## What to See

㉠ **KANDA MYŌJIN.** This shrine is said to have been founded in 730 in a village called Shibasaki, where the Ōte-machi financial district stands today. In 1616 it was relocated, a victim of Ieyasu

Tokugawa's ever-expanding system of fortifications. The present site was chosen, in accordance with Chinese geomancy, to afford the best view from Edo-jō and to protect the shrine from evil influences. The shrine itself was destroyed in the Great Kantō Earthquake of 1923, and the present buildings reproduce in concrete the style of 1616. Ieyasu preferred the jazzier decorative effects of Chinese Buddhism to the simple lines of traditional Shintō architecture. This is especially evident in the curved, copper-tile roof of the main shrine and in the two-story front gate.

Three principle deities are enshrined here: Ōkuninushi-no-Mikoto and Sukunohikona-no-Mikoto, both of whom appear in the early Japanese creation myths, and Taira-no-Masakado. The last was a 10th-century warrior whose contentious spirit earned him a place in the Shintō pantheon: he led a revolt against the Imperial Court in Kyōto, seized control of the eastern provinces, declared himself emperor—and in 940 was beheaded for his rebellious ways. The townspeople of Kanda, contentious souls in their own right, made Taira-no-Masakado a kind of patron saint, and even today—oblivious somehow to the fact that he lost—they appeal to him for victory when they face a tough encounter.

Some of the smaller buildings you see as you come up the steps and walk around the main hall contain the *mikoshi*—the portable shrines that are featured in one of Tōkyō's three great blowouts, the **Kanda Festival.** (The other two are the Sannō Festival of Hie Jinja in Nagata-chō and the Sanja Festival of Asakusa Jinja.) The essential shrine festival is a procession in which the gods, housed for the occasion in their mikoshi, pass through the streets and get a breath of fresh air. The Kanda Festival began in the early Edo period. Heading the procession then were 36 magnificent floats, most of which were destroyed in the fires that raged through the city after the earthquake of 1923. The floats that lead the procession today move in stately measure on wheeled carts, attended by the priests and officials of the shrine dressed in Heian-period (794–1185) costume. The mikoshi, some 70 of them, follow behind, bobbing and weaving, carried on the shoulders of the townspeople. Shrine festivals like Kanda's are a peculiarly competitive form of worship: piety is a matter of who can shout the loudest, drink the most beer, and have the best time. The festival takes place in August in odd-numbered years. Kanda Myōjin is on Kuramae-bashi-dōri, about a five-minute walk west from the Suehiro-chō stop (Exit 3) on the Ginza Line. 2–16–2 Soto Kanda, Chiyoda-ku, tel. 03/3254–0753.

**KŌTSŪ HAKUBUTSUKAN** (Transportation Museum). This is a fun place to take children. Displays explain the early development of the railway system and include a miniature layout of the rail services, as well as Japan's first airplane, which lifted off in 1903. To get here from JR Akihabara Eki, take the Denki-gai Exit, cross the bridge on Chūō-dōri over the Kanda-gawa, and turn right at the next corner. 1–25 Kanda Sudachō, Chiyoda-ku, tel. 03/3251–8481. ¥310. Tues.–Sun. 9:30–5.

**LAOX.** Of all the discount stores in Akihabara, LAOX has the largest and most comprehensive selection, with four buildings in this area—one exclusively for musical instruments, another for duty-free appliances—and outlets in Yokohama and Narita. This is a good place to find cameras, watches, and pearls. 1–2–9 Soto Kanda, Chiyoda-ku, tel. 03/3255–9041. Mon.–Sat. 10–8, Sun. 10–7:30. JR Akihabara Eki (Nishi-guchi/West Exit).

**NIKOLAI CATHEDRAL.** Formally, this is the Holy Resurrection Cathedral. The more familiar name derives from its founder, St. Nikolai Kassatkin (1836–1912), a Russian missionary who came to Japan in 1861 and spent the rest of his life here propagating the Russian Orthodox faith. The building, planned by a Russian engineer and executed by a British architect, was completed in 1891. Heavily damaged in the earthquake of 1923, the cathedral was restored with a dome much more modest than the original.

Even so, it endows this otherwise featureless part of the city with the charm of the unexpected. 4–1 Surugadai, Kanda, Chiyoda-ku, tel. 03/3295–6879. Free. Tues.–Fri. 1–4. Subway: Chiyoda Line, Shin-Ochanomizu Eki (Exit B1).

**(19) YAMAGIWA AND MINAMI.** These rival giants have whole floors devoted to computer hardware, software, fax machines, and copiers. Yamagiwa has a particularly good selection of lighting fixtures, most of them—alas—for 220 volts. Both stores, however, have annexes with English-speaking staff for export models of the most popular appliances and devices. You should be able to bargain prices down a bit—especially if you are buying more than one big-ticket item. Yamagiwa: 4–1–1 Soto Kanda, Chiyoda-ku, tel. 03/3253–2111. Weekdays 10:30–7:30, weekends 10–7:30. Minami: 4–3–3 Soto Kanda, Chiyoda-ku, tel. 03/3255–3730. Weekdays 10:30–7, weekends 10–7. JR Akihabara Eki (Nishi-guchi/West Exit).

**(21) YŪSHIMA SEIDŌ.** The origins of this shrine date to a hall, founded in 1632, for the study of the Chinese Confucian classics. The original building was in Ueno, and its headmaster was Hayashi Razan, the official Confucian scholar to the Tokugawa government. The shogunal dynasty found these Chinese teachings—with their emphasis on obedience and hierarchy—attractive enough to make Confucianism a kind of state ideology. Moved to its present site in 1691, the hall became an academy for the ruling elite. In a sense, nothing has changed: In 1872 the new Meiji government established the country's first teacher-training institute here, and that, in turn, evolved into Tōkyō University—the graduates of which still make up much of the ruling elite. 1–4–25 Yūshima, Bunkyō-ku, tel. 03/3251–4606. Free. Apr.–Sept., Fri.–Wed. 10–5; Oct.–Mar., Fri.–Wed. 10–4. Subway: Marunouchi Line, Ochanomizu Eki (Exit B2).

# UENO

JR Ueno Eki is Tōkyō's version of the Gare du Nord: the gateway to and from Japan's northeast provinces. Since 1883, when the station was completed, it has served as a terminus in the great migration to the city by villagers in pursuit of a better life.

Ueno was a place of prominence long before the coming of the railroad. When Ieyasu Tokugawa established his capital here in 1603, it was merely a wooded promontory, called Shinobu-ga-oka (Hill of Endurance), overlooking the bay. Ieyasu gave a large tract of land on the hill to one of his most important vassals, Takatora Toda, who designed and built Edo-jō. Ieyasu's heir, Hidetada, later commanded the founding of a temple on the hill. Shinobu-ga-oka was in the northeast corner of the capital. In Chinese geomancy, the northeast approach required a particularly strong defense against evil influences.

That defense was entrusted to Tenkai (1536–1643), a priest of the Tendai sect of Buddhism and an adviser of great influence to the first three Tokugawa shōguns. The temple he built on Shinobu-ga-oka was called Kanei-ji, and he became the first abbot. The patronage of the Tokugawas and their vassal barons made Kanei-ji a seat of power and glory. By the end of the 17th century it occupied most of the hill. To the magnificent Main Hall were added scores of other buildings—including a pagoda and a shrine to Ieyasu—and 36 subsidiary temples. The city of Edo itself expanded to the foot of the hill, where Kanei-ji's main gate once stood. And most of what is now Ueno was called Monzen-machi: "the town in front of the gate."

The power and glory of Kanei-ji came to an end in just one day: April 11, 1868. An army of clan forces from the western part of Japan, bearing a mandate from Emperor Meiji, arrived in Edo and demanded the surrender of the castle. The shogunate was by then a tottering regime; it capitulated, and with it went everything that had depended on the favor of the Tokugawas. The Meiji Restoration began with a bloodless coup.

A band of some 2,000 Tokugawa loyalists assembled on Ueno Hill, however, and defied the new government. On May 15 the imperial army attacked. The *Shōgitai* (loyalists), outnumbered and surrounded, soon discovered that right was on the side of modern artillery. A few survivors fled; the rest committed ritual suicide—and took Kanei-ji with them—torching the temple and most of its outbuildings.

The new Meiji government turned Ueno Hill into one of the nation's first public parks. The intention was not merely to provide a bit of greenery but to make the park an instrument of civic improvement and to show off the achievements of an emerging modern state. It would serve as the site of trade and industrial expositions; it would have a national museum, a library, a university of fine arts, and a zoo. The modernization of Ueno still continues, but the park is more than the sum of its museums. The Shōgitai failed to take everything with them: some of the most important buildings in the temple complex survived or were restored and should not be missed.

*Numbers in the text correspond to numbers in the margin and on the Ueno map.*

## A Good Walk

The best way to begin is to come to JR Ueno Eki on the JR Yamanote Line and leave the station by the *Kōen-guchi* (Park Exit), upstairs. Directly across from the exit is the Tōkyō Bunka Kaikan, one of the city's major venues for classical music.

Follow the path to the right of the Bunka Kaikan to the information booth, where you can pick up a useful detailed map of the park in English; northwest of the booth (turn left, away from Ueno Eki) is the **Kokuritsu Seiyō Bijutsukan** ㉓. The Rodins in the courtyard—*The Gate of Hell*, *The Thinker*, and the magnificent *Burghers of Calais*—are authentic castings from Rodin's original molds.

Turn right at the far corner of the Seiyō and walk along a stretch of wooded park; you come next to the museum of science, the

# ueno

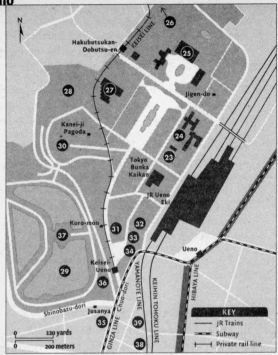

**Kokuritsu Kagaku Hakubutsukan** ㉔; at the next corner is the main street that cuts through the park. Turn left on this street, and cross at the traffic signal some 50 yards west to the main entrance of the **Tōkyō Kokuritsu Hakubutsukan** ㉕, which has one one of the world's greatest collections of East Asian art and archaeology.

Turn right as you leave the museum complex, walk west, and turn right at the first corner; this road dead-ends in about five minutes in the far northwest corner of the park, opposite the gate to **Kanei-ji** ㉖. (The gate is usually locked; use the side entrance to the left.) The only remarkable remaining structure here is the ornately carved vermilion gate to what was the mausoleum of Tsunayoshi, the fifth shōgun. Tsunayoshi is famous in the annals of Tokugawa history for his disastrous fiscal mismanagement and his *Shōrui Awaremi no Rei* (Edicts on Compassion for Living Things), which, among other things, made it a capital offense for a human being to kill a dog. Stretching away to the right is the cemetery of Kanei-ji, where several Tokugawa shōguns had their mausoleums. These were destroyed in the air raids of 1945, but the gate that led to the tomb of the fourth shōgun, Ietsuna, remains.

Retrace your steps to the main gate of the Tōkyō Kokuritsu Hakubutsukan, and cross the street to the long esplanade, with its fountain and reflecting pool. Keep to the right as you walk south. The first path to the right brings you to the **Tōkyō-to Bijutsukan** ㉗ and its small but impressive permanent collection of modern Japanese painting.

At the south end of the esplanade is the central plaza of the park. (Look to your left for the police substation, a small steel-gray building of futuristic design.) To the right is the entrance to the **Ueno Zoo** ㉘. Opened in 1882, the zoo gradually expanded to its present 35 acres, and the original section here on the hill was connected to the one below, along the edge of **Shinobazu Pond** ㉙, by a bridge and a monorail. The process of the zoo's expansion somehow left within its confines the 120-ft, five-story Kanei-ji Pagoda, built in 1631 and rebuilt after a fire in 1639.

A few steps farther south, on the continuation of the esplanade, is the path that leads to **Tōshō-gū** ㉚—the shrine to the first Tokugawa shōgun, Ieyasu. The entrance to the shrine is marked by a stone torii built in 1633.

From Tōshō-gū, return to the avenue, turn right, and continue walking south. Shortly you'll see a kind of tunnel of red-lacquered torii, with a long flight of stone steps leading down to the shrine to Inari, a Shintō deity of harvests and family prosperity. Shrines of this kind are found all over the downtown part of Tōkyō, tucked away in alleys and odd corners, always with their guardian statues of foxes—the mischievous creatures with which the god is associated. Just below the Inari shrine is a shrine to Sugawara Michizane (854–903), a Heian-period nobleman and poet worshiped as the Shintō deity Tenjin. Because he is associated with scholarship and literary achievement, Japanese students visit his various shrines by the hundreds of thousands in February and March to pray for success on their college entrance exams.

Return to the avenue and continue south. On the left side is a flight of stone steps to **Kiyomizu Kannon-dō** ㉛, one of the important temple structures that survived the Meiji-Tokugawa battle of 1868.

Leave Kiyomizu by the front gate, on the south side. As you look to your left, you will see a two-story brick administration building, on the other side of which is the **Ueno-no-Mori Bijutsukan** ㉜. After a stop in the museum, continue south, and you soon come to where the park narrows to a point. Two flights of steps lead down to the main entrance on Chūō-dōri. Before you reach the steps, you'll see the **Shōgitai Memorial** ㉝ on the left, and a few steps away, with its back to the gravestone, the **statue of Takamori Saigō** ㉞.

Leave the park and walk south, keeping to the west side of Chūō-dōri until you get to the corner where Shinobazu-dōri comes in on the right. About a block beyond this corner, you'll see a building hung with banners; this is **Suzumoto** ㉟, a theater specializing in a traditional narrative comedy called *rakugo*.

Turn right at the Shinobazu-dōri intersection and walk west. A few doors from the corner is Jusan-ya, a nearly three-century-old family-run shop that sells handmade boxwood combs. Directly across the avenue is an entrance to the grounds of Shinobazu Pond; just inside, on the right, is the small black-and-white building that houses the **Shitamachi Hakubutsukan** ㊱. Japanese society in the days of the Tokugawa shōguns was rigidly stratified. In Tōkyō—then called Edo—the common people lived "below the castle," most of them in long, single-story tenements called *nagaya*, one jammed up against the next along the narrow alleys and unplanned streets of Ueno and the areas nearby. They developed a unique culture and way of life, which this museum celebrates.

From in front of the museum, a path follows the eastern shore of Shinobazu Pond. On the island in the middle of the pond is **Benzaiten** ㊲, a shrine to the patron goddess of the arts. You can walk up the east side of the embankment to the causeway and cross to the shrine. Then cross to the other side of the pond, turn left in front of the boathouse, and follow the embankment back to Shinobazu-dōri. Off to your right as you walk, a few blocks away and out of sight, begin the precincts of Tōkyō University, the nation's most prestigious seat of higher learning, alma mater to generations of bureaucrats. Turn left as you leave the park and walk back in the direction of the Shitamachi Hakubutsukan.

When you reach the intersection, cross Chūō-dōri and turn right; walk past the ABAB clothing store and turn left at the second corner. At the end of this street is **Tokudai-ji** ㊳, a temple over a supermarket, and the bustling heart of **Ame-ya Yoko-chō**

Market ㊱. There are more than 500 little shops and stalls in this market, which stretches from the beginning of Shōwa-dōri at the north end to Ōkachi-machi at the south end. Ōkachi-machi means "Ōkachi Town"; the *ōkachi*—the "honorable infantry," the samurai of lowest rank in the shōgun's service—lived in the area.

From here follow the JR tracks as you wander north. In a few minutes you'll find yourself back in front of Ueno Eki.

### TIMING

Exploring Ueno can be one excursion or two: an afternoon of cultural browsing or a full day of discoveries in one of the great centers of the city. Avoid Monday, when most of the museums are closed. Ueno out of doors is no fun at all in February or the rainy season of late June to mid-July; mid-August can be brutally hot and muggy. In April, the cherry blossoms of Ueno Kōen are glorious.

## What to See

㊵ **AME-YA YOKO-CHŌ MARKET.** The history of Ame-ya Yoko-chō (often shortened to Ameyoko) begins in the desperate days immediately after World War II. Ueno Eki had survived the bombings—virtually everything around it was rubble—and anyone who could make it here from the countryside with rice and other small supplies of food could sell them at exorbitant black-market prices. Sugar was a commodity that couldn't be found at any price in postwar Tōkyō. Before long, there were hundreds of stalls in the black market selling various kinds of *ame* (confections), most of them made from sweet potatoes. These stalls gave the market its name: Ame-ya Yoko-chō means "Confectioners' Alley."

Shortly before the Korean War, the market was legalized, and soon the stalls were carrying a full array of watches, chocolate, ballpoint pens, blue jeans, and T-shirts that had somehow been "liberated" from American PXs. In years to come the merchants of Ameyoko diversified still further—to fine Swiss timepieces and French designer luggage of dubious authenticity, cosmetics, jewelry, fresh fruit, and fish. The market became especially famous for the traditional prepared foods of the New Year, and during the last few days of December, as many as half a million people crowd into the narrow alleys under the railroad tracks to stock up for the holiday. *Ueno 4-chōme, Taitō-ku. Most shops and stalls daily 10–7. JR Ueno Eki (Hirokō-ji Exit).*

**③⑦ BENZAITEN.** Perched in the middle of Shinobazu Pond, this shrine is for the goddess Benten. She is one of the Seven Gods of Good Luck, a pantheon that emerged some time in the medieval period from a jumble of Indian, Chinese, and Japanese mythology. As matron goddess of the arts, she is depicted holding a lutelike musical instrument called a *biwa*. The shrine, with its distinctive octagonal roof, was destroyed in the bombings of 1945. The present version is a faithful copy. You can rent rowboats and pedal boats at a nearby boathouse. *tel. 03/3828–9502 for boathouse. Boathouse daily 9:30–5. Rowboats ¥600 for 1 hr, pedal boats ¥600 for 30 mins. JR Ueno Eki; Keisei private rail line, Keisei-Ueno Eki (Ikenohata Exit).*

**②⑥ KANEI-JI.** In 1638 the second Tokugawa shōgun, Hidetada, commissioned the priest Tenkai to build a temple on Shinobu-ga-oka Hill in Ueno to defend his city from evil spirits. Tenkai turned for his model to the great temple complex of Enryaku-ji in Kyōto, established centuries earlier on Mt. Hiei to protect the imperial capital. The main hall of Tenkai's temple, called Kanei-ji, was moved to Ueno from the town of Kawagoe, about 40 km (25 mi) away, where he had once been a priest; it was moved again, to its present site, in 1879, and looks a bit weary of its travels. *1–14–11 Ueno Sakuragi, Taitō-ku, tel. 03/3821–1259. Free, contributions welcome. Daily 9–5. JR Ueno Eki (Kōen-guchi/Park Exit).*

**③① KIYOMIZU KANNON-DŌ** (Kannon Hall). This National Treasure was a part of Abbot Tenkai's grand attempt to echo in Ueno the grandeur of Kyōto, but the echo is a little weak. The model for it was Kyōto's magnificent Kiyomizu-dera, but where the original rests on enormous wood pillars over a gorge, the Ueno version merely perches on the lip of a little hill. And the hall would have a grand view of Shinobazu Pond—which itself was landscaped to recall Biwa-ko (Lake Biwa), near Kyōto—if the trees in front of the terrace were not too high and too full most of the year to afford any view at all. The principal Buddhist image of worship here is the Senjū Kannon (Thousand-Armed Goddess of Mercy). Another figure, however, receives greater homage. This is the Kosodate Kannon, who is believed to answer the prayers of women having difficulty conceiving children. If their prayers are answered, they return to Kiyomizu and leave a doll, as both an offering of thanks and a prayer for the child's health. In a ceremony held every September 25, the dolls that have accumulated during the year are burned in a bonfire. *1–29 Ueno Kōen, Taitō-ku, tel. 03/ 3821–4749. Free. Daily 7–5. JR Ueno Eki (Kōen-guchi/Park Exit).*

**24 KOKURITSU KAGAKU HAKUBUTSUKAN** (National Science Museum). This conventional natural history museum displays everything from dinosaurs to moon rocks, but it provides relatively little in the way of hands-on learning experiences. Kids seem to like it anyway—but otherwise this is not a place to linger if your time is short. *7–20 Ueno Kōen, Taitō-ku, tel. 03/3822–0111. ¥420; additional fees for special exhibits. Tues.–Sun. 9–4:30. JR Ueno Eki (Kōen-guchi/Park Exit).*

**23 KOKURITSU SEIYŌ BIJUTSUKAN** (National Museum of Western Art). Along with castings from the original molds of Rodin's *Gate of Hell, The Burghers of Calais,* and *The Thinker,* the wealthy businessman Matsukata Kojiro acquired some 850 paintings, sketches, and prints by such masters as Renoir, Monet, and Cézanne. He kept the collection in Europe. The French government sent it to Japan after World War II—Matsukata left it to the country in his will—and it opened to the public in 1959 in a building designed by Swiss-born architect Le Corbusier. Since then, the museum has diversified a bit and ushered in the new millennium with a luxurious special exhibition hall; more recent acquisitions include works by Reubens, Tintoretto, El Greco, Max Ernst, and Jackson Pollock. The Seiyō is one of the best-organized, most pleasant museums to visit in Tōkyō. *7-7 Ueno Kōen, Taitō-ku, tel. 03/3828–5131. ¥420; additional fee for special exhibits. Tues.–Thurs. and weekends 9:30–4:30, Fri. 9:30–7:30. JR Ueno Eki (Kōen-guchi/Park Exit).*

**29 SHINOBAZU POND.** Shinobazu was once an inlet of Tōkyō Bay. When the area was reclaimed, it became a freshwater pond. The abbot Tenkai, founder of Kanei-ji on the hill above the pond, had an island made in the middle of it, on which he built ☞ **Benzaiten** for the goddess of the arts. Later improvements included a causeway to the island, embankments, and even a racecourse (1884–93). Today the pond is in three sections. The first, with its famous lotus plants, is a sanctuary for about 15 species of birds, including pintail ducks, cormorants, great egrets, and grebes. Some 5,000 wild ducks migrate here from as far away as Siberia, sticking around from September to April. The second section, to the north, belongs to Ueno Zoo; the third, to the west, is a small lake for boating.

During the first week of June, the path is lined on both sides with the stalls of the annual All-Japan Azalea Fair, a spectacular display of flowering bonsai shrubs and trees. Nurserymen in *happi* (workmen's) coats sell a variety of plants, seedlings, bonsai vessels, and ornamental stones. *Shinobazu-dōri, Ueno, Taitō-ku. Free. Daily sunrise–sunset. Keisei private rail line, Keisei-Ueno Eki (Higashi-guchi/East Exit); JR Ueno Eki (Kōen-guchi/Park Exit).*

**★ 36 SHITAMACHI HAKUBUTSUKAN.** Shitamachi (literally, the "Lower Town") lay originally between Ieyasu's fortifications, on the west, and the Sumida-gawa, on the east. As it expanded, it came to include what today constitutes the Chūō, Taitō, Sumida, and Kōtō wards. During the Edo period some 80% of the city was allotted to the warrior class and to temples and shrines. In

Shitamachi—the remaining 20% of the space—lived the common folk, who made up more than half the population. The people here were hardworking, short-tempered, free-spending, quick to help a neighbor in trouble—and remarkably stubborn about their way of life. The Shitamachi Museum preserves and exhibits what remained of that way of life as late as 1940.

The two main displays on the first floor are a merchant house and a tenement, intact with all their furnishings. This is a hands-on museum: you can take your shoes off and step up into the rooms. On the second floor are displays of toys, tools, and utensils donated, in most cases, by people who had grown up with them and used them all their lives. There are also photographs of Shitamachi and video documentaries of craftspeople at work. Occasionally various traditional skills are demonstrated, and you're welcome to take part. This don't-miss museum makes great use of its space, and there's even a passable brochure in English. 2–1 Ueno Kōen, Taitō-ku, tel. 03/3823–7451. ¥300. Tues.– Sun. 9:30–4:30. Keisei private rail line, Keisei-Ueno Eki (Higashi- guchi/East Exit); JR Ueno Eki (Kōen-guchi/Park Exit).

**33 SHŌGITAI MEMORIAL.** Time seems to heal wounds very quickly in Japan. Only six years after they had destroyed most of Ueno Hill, the Meiji government permitted the Shōgitai to be honored with a gravestone, erected on the spot where their bodies had been cremated. JR Ueno Eki (Kōen-guchi/Park Exit); Keisei private rail line, Keisei-Ueno Eki (Higashi-guchi/East Exit).

**34 STATUE OF TAKAMORI SAIGŌ.** As chief of staff of the Meiji imperial army, Takamori Saigō (1827–77) played a key role in forcing the surrender of Edo and the overthrow of the shogunate. Ironically, Saigō himself fell out with the other leaders of the new Meiji government and was killed in an unsuccessful rebellion of his own. The sculptor Takamura Kōun's bronze, made in 1893, sensibly avoids presenting him in uniform. JR Ueno Eki (Kōen- guchi/Park Exit); Keisei private rail line, Keisei-Ueno Eki (Higashi- guchi/East Exit).

**㉟ SUZUMOTO.** Originally built around 1857 for Japanese comic monologue performances called rakugo and since rebuilt, Suzumoto is the oldest theater operation of its kind in Tōkyō. A rakugo comedian sits on a purple cushion, dressed in a kimono, and tells stories that have been handed down for centuries. Using only a few simple props—a fan, a pipe, a handkerchief—the storyteller becomes a whole cast of characters, with all their different voices and facial expressions. The audience may have heard his stories 20 times already and still laughs in all the right places. There is no English interpretation, and even for the Japanese themselves, the monologues are difficult to follow, filled with puns and expressions in dialect—but don't let that deter you. For a slice of traditional pop culture, rakugo at Suzumoto is worth seeing, even if you don't understand a word. The theater is on Chūō-dōri, a few blocks north of the Ginza Line's Ueno Hirokō-ji stop (Exit 3). 2–7–12 Ueno, Taitō-ku, tel. 03/3834–5906. ¥2,500. Continual performances daily 12:20–4:30 and 5:20–9.

**㉚ TOKUDAI-JI.** This is a curiosity in a neighborhood of curiosities: a temple on the second floor of a supermarket. Two deities are worshiped here. One is the bodhisattva Jizō, and the act of washing this statue is believed to help safeguard your health. The other, principal image is of the Indian goddess Marishi, a daughter of Brahma, usually depicted with three faces and four arms. She is believed to help worshipers overcome various sorts of difficulties and to help them prosper in business. 4–6–2 Ueno, Taitō-ku. JR Yamanote and Keihin-tōhoku lines, Ōkachi-machi Eki (Higashi-guchi/East Exit) or Ueno Eki (Hirokō-ji Exit).

**★ ㉕ TŌKYŌ KOKURITSU HAKUBUTSUKAN** (Tōkyō National Museum). This complex of four buildings grouped around a courtyard is one of the world's great repositories of East Asian art and archaeology. The Western-style building on the left, with its bronze cupolas, is the **Hyōkeikan.** Built in 1909, it was devoted to archaeological exhibits; it was closed in 1999 and the greater part of the collection transferred to the new, larger **Heiseikan,** behind it. Look especially for the flamelike sculpted rims and elaborate markings of Middle Jōmon–period pottery (circa 3500 BC–2000 BC), so different from anything produced in Japan before or since. Also look for the terra-cotta figures called *haniwa*, unearthed at burial sites dating from the 4th to the 7th century. The figures are deceptively simple in shape and mysterious and comical at the same time in effect.

In the far left corner of the museum complex is the **Hōryū-ji Hōmotsukan** (Gallery of Hōryū-ji Treasures). In 1878 the 7th-century Hōryū-ji in Nara presented 319 works of art in its possession—sculpture, scrolls, masks, and other objects—to the Imperial Household. These were transferred to the National Museum in 2000 and now reside in this gallery designed by Yoshio Taniguchi. There is a useful guide to the collection in English, and the exhibits are well explained. Don't miss the hall of carved wooden *gigaku* (Buddhist processional) masks.

The central building in the complex, the **Honkan**, was built in 1937 and houses Japanese art exclusively: paintings, calligraphy, sculpture, textiles, ceramics, swords, and armor. The more attractive **Tōyōkan**, on the right, completed in 1968, is devoted to the art of other Asian cultures. Altogether, the museum has some 87,000 objects in its permanent collection, with several thousand more on loan from shrines, temples, and private owners. Among these are 84 objects designated by the government as National Treasures. The Honkan rotates the works on display several times during the year; it also hosts two special exhibitions a year, April–May or June and October–November, which feature important collections from both Japanese and foreign museums. These, unfortunately, can be an ordeal: the lighting in the Honkan is not particularly good, the explanations in English are sketchy at best, and the hordes of visitors make it impossible to linger over a work you especially want to study. *13–9 Ueno Kōen, Taitō-ku, tel. 03/3822–1111, www.tnm.go.jp. ¥420. Tues.–Sun. 9:30–4:30. JR Ueno Eki (Kōen-guchi/Park Exit).*

**㉗ TŌKYŌ-TO BIJUTSUKAN** (Tōkyō Metropolitan Art Museum). The museum displays its own collection of modern Japanese art on the lower level and rents out the remaining two floors to various art institutes and organizations. At any given time, there will be at least five exhibits in the building: work by promising young painters, for example, or new forms and materials in sculpture or modern calligraphy. Completed in 1975, the museum was designed by Maekawa Kunio, who also did the nearby Metropolitan Festival Hall. *8–36 Ueno Kōen, Taitō-ku, tel. 03/3823–6921, www.tef.or.jp/tmm/eng/index.html. Permanent collection free, fees vary for other exhibits (usually ¥300–¥800). Daily (except 3rd Mon. of month) 9–4:30. JR Ueno Eki (Kōen-guchi/Park Exit).*

★ **㉚ TŌSHŌ-GŪ.** Ieyasu, the first Tokugawa shōgun, died in 1616 and the following year was given the posthumous name Tōshō-Daigongen (The Great Incarnation Who Illuminates the East). The Imperial Court declared him a divinity of the first rank, thenceforth to be worshiped at Nikkō, in the mountains north of his city, at a shrine he had commissioned before his death. That shrine is the first and foremost Tōshō-gū. The one here, built in the ornate style called *gongen-zukuri*, dates from 1627. Miraculously, it survived the disasters that destroyed most of the other original buildings on the hill—the fires, the 1868 revolt, the 1923 earthquake, the 1945 bombings—making it one of the few early Edo-period buildings in Tōkyō. The shrine and most of its art are designated National Treasures.

Two hundred *ishidoro* (stone lanterns) line the path from the stone entry arch to the shrine itself. One of them, just outside the arch to the left, is more than 18 ft high—one of the three largest in Japan. This particular lantern is called *obaketoro* (ghost lantern) because of a story connected with it: it seems that one night a samurai on guard duty slashed at the ghost—*obake*—that was believed to haunt the lantern. His sword was so good it left a nick in the stone, which can still be seen. Beyond these lanterns is a double row of 50 copper lanterns, presented by the feudal lords of the 17th century as expressions of their piety and loyalty to the regime.

The first room inside is the **Hall of Worship**; the four paintings in gold on wooden panels are by Tan'yū, one of the famous Kano family of artists who enjoyed the patronage of emperors and shōguns from the late 15th century to the end of the Edo period. Tan'yū was appointed *goyō eshi* (official court painter) in 1617. His commissions included the Tokugawa castles at Edo and Nagoya as well as the Nikkō Tōshō-gū. The framed tablet between the walls, with the name of the shrine in gold, is in the calligraphy of Emperor Go-Mizuno-o (1596–1680). Other works of calligraphy are by the abbots of Kanei-ji. Behind the Hall of Worship, connected by a passage called the *haiden*, is the sanctuary, where the spirit of Ieyasu is said to be enshrined.

The real glories of Tōshō-gū are its so-called **Chinese Gate**, which you reach at the end of your tour of the building, and the fence on either side. Like its counterpart at Nikkō, the fence is a kind of natural history lesson, with carvings of birds, animals, fish, and shells of every description; unlike the one at Nikkō, this fence was left unpainted. The two long panels of the gate, with their dragons carved in relief, are attributed to Hidari Jingoro— a brilliant sculptor of the early Edo period whose real name is unknown (*hidari* means "left"; Jingoro was reportedly left-handed). The lifelike appearance of his dragons has inspired a legend. Every morning they were found mysteriously dripping with water. Finally it was discovered that they were sneaking out at night to drink from the nearby Shinobazu Pond, and wire cages were put up around them to curtail this disquieting habit. *9–88 Ueno Kōen, Taitō-ku, tel. 03/3822–3455. ¥200. Daily 9–5. JR Ueno Eki (Kōen-guchi/Park Exit).*

**32 UENO-NO-MORI BIJUTSUKAN.** Although the museum has no permanent collection of its own, it makes its galleries available to various groups, primarily for exhibitions of modern painting and calligraphy. *1–2 Ueno Kōen, Taitō-ku, tel. 03/3833–4191. Prices* *vary depending on exhibition, but usually ¥400–¥500. Sun.–Wed. 10–5:30, Thurs.–Sat. 10–7:30. JR Ueno Eki (Kōen-guchi/Park Exit).*

☝ ㉘ **UENO ZOO.** The zoo houses some 900 different species, most of which look less than enthusiastic about being here. First built in 1882 and several times expanded without really modernizing, Ueno is not among the most attractive zoos in the world. But it does have a giant panda (quartered near the main entrance), and you might decide the zoo is worth a visit on that score alone. On a pleasant Sunday afternoon, however, upwards of 20,000 Japanese are likely to share your opinion; don't expect to have a leisurely view. *9–83 Ueno Kōen, Taitō-ku, tel. 03/3828–5171. ¥600; free on Mar. 20, Apr. 29, and Oct. 1. Tues.–Sun. 9:30–4. JR Ueno Eki (Kōen-guchi/Park Exit); Keisei private rail line, Ueno Eki (Dōbutsu-en Exit).*

## ASAKUSA

In the year 628, so the legend goes, two brothers named Hamanari and Takenari Hikonuma were fishing on the lower reaches of the Sumida-gawa when they dragged up a small, gilded statue of Kannon—an aspect of the Buddha worshiped as the goddess of mercy. They took the statue to their master, Naji-no-Nakamoto, who enshrined it in his house. Later, a temple was built for it in nearby Asakusa. Called Sensō-ji, the temple was rebuilt and enlarged several times over the next 10 centuries—but Asakusa itself remained just a village on a river crossing a few hours' walk from Edo.

Then Ieyasu Tokugawa made Edo his capital and Asakusa blossomed. Suddenly, it was the party that never ended, the place where the free-spending townspeople of the new capital came to empty their pockets. For the next 300 years it was the wellspring of almost everything we associate with Japanese popular culture.

The first step in that transformation came in 1657, when Yoshiwara—the licensed brothel quarter not far from

Nihombashi—was moved to the countryside farther north: Asakusa found itself square in the road, more or less halfway between the city and its only nightlife. The village became a suburb and a pleasure quarter in its own right. In the narrow streets and alleys around Sensō-ji, there were stalls selling toys, souvenirs, and sweets; acrobats, jugglers, and strolling musicians; sake shops and teahouses—where the waitresses often provided more than tea. (The Japanese have never worried much about the impropriety of such things; the approach to a temple is still a venue for very secular enterprises of all sorts.) Then, in 1841, the Kabuki theaters—which the government looked upon as a source of dissipation second only to Yoshiwara—moved to Asakusa.

Highborn and lowborn, the people of Edo flocked to Kabuki. They loved its extravagant spectacle, its bravado, and its brilliant language. They cheered its heroes and hissed its villains. They bought wood-block prints, called *ukiyo-e*, of their favorite actors. (*Ukiyo* means "the floating world" of everyday life; *e* means "picture." The genre flourished in the 18th and 19th centuries.) Asakusa was home to the Kabuki theaters for only a short time, but that was enough to establish it as the entertainment quarter of the city—a reputation it held unchallenged until World War II.

When Japan ended its long, self-imposed isolation in 1868, where else would the novelties and amusements of the outside world first take root but in Asakusa? The country's first photography studios appeared here in 1875. Japan's first skyscraper, a 12-story mart called the Jū-ni-kai, was built in Asakusa in 1890 and filled with shops selling imported goods. The area around Sensō-ji had by this time been designated a public park and was divided into seven sections; the sixth section, called Rok-ku, was Tōkyō's equivalent of 42nd Street and Times Square. The nation's first movie theater opened here in 1903—to be joined by dozens more, and these in turn were followed by music halls, cabarets, and revues. The first drinking establishment in Japan to call itself a "bar" was started in Asakusa in 1880; it still exists.

Most of this area was destroyed in 1945. As an entertainment district, it never really recovered, but Sensō-ji was rebuilt almost immediately. The people here would never dream of living without it—just as they would never dream of living anywhere else. This is the heart and soul of Shitamachi, where you can still hear the rich, breezy downtown Tōkyō accent of the 17th and 18th centuries. Where, if you sneeze in the middle of the night, your neighbor will demand to know the next morning why you aren't taking better care of yourself. Where a carpenter will refuse a well-paid job if he doesn't think the client has the mother wit to appreciate good work when he sees it. Where you can still go out for a good meal and not have to pay through the nose for a lot of uptown pretensions. Even today the temple precinct embraces an area of narrow streets, arcades, restaurants, shops, stalls, playgrounds, and gardens. It is home to a population of artisans and small entrepreneurs, neighborhood children and their grandmothers, and hipsters and hucksters and mendicant priests. In short, if you have any time at all to spend in Tōkyō, you really have to devote at least a day of it to Asakusa.

*Numbers in the text correspond to numbers in the margin and on the Asakusa map.*

## A Good Walk

For more information on depāto and individual shops mentioned in this walk, *see* Shopping, *below.*

Start at Asakusa Eki, at the end of the Ginza Line. This was in fact Tōkyō's first subway, opened from Asakusa to Ueno in 1927; it became known as the Ginza Line when it was later extended through Ginza to Shimbashi and Shibuya. When you exit the station, take a minute to check out the Asahi Beer headquarters, complete with a golden flame atop the building, across the Sumda-gawa; Philippe Starck designed the unique structure. Follow the signs, clearly marked in English, to Exit 1. When you come up to the street level, turn right and walk west along Kaminari-mon-dōri. In a few steps you will come to a gate, on your right, with two huge red lanterns hanging from it: this is **Kaminari-mon** ⑩, the main entrance to the grounds of Sensō-ji.

Another way to get to Kaminari-mon is via the "river bus" ferry from Hinode Pier (☞ Boat & Ferry Travel, *below*), which stops in Asakusa at the southwest corner of the park, called Sumida Kōen. Walk out to the three-way intersection, cross two sides of the triangle, and turn right. Kaminari-mon is in the middle of the second block.

Take note of the Asakusa Bunka Kankō Center (Asakusa Tourist Information Center; 03/3842–5566), across the street from Kaminari-mon. A volunteer staff with some English is on duty here daily 10–5 and will happily load you down with maps and brochures.

From Kaminari-mon, Nakamise-dōri—a long, narrow avenue lined on both sides with small shops—leads to the courtyard of Sensō-ji. One shop worth stopping at is Ichiban-ya, about 100 yards down on the right, for its handmade, toasted *sembei* (rice crackers) and its seven-pepper spices in gourd-shape bottles of zelkova wood. At the end of Nakamise-dōri, on the right, is Sukeroku, which specializes in traditional handmade dolls and models clothed in the costumes of the Edo period. Just beyond Sukeroku is a two-story gate called Hozō-mon.

At this point, take an important detour. Look to your left as you pass through the gate. Tucked away in the far corner is a vermilion-color building in the traditional temple style (just to the left of the pagoda, behind an iron railing) that houses the Sensō-ji administrative offices: walk in, go down the corridor on

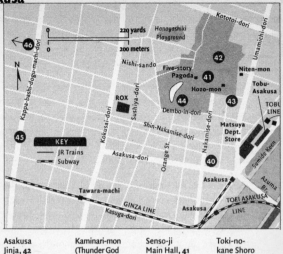

| Asakusa Jinja, 42 | Kaminari-mon (Thunder God Gate), 40 | Senso-ji Main Hall, 41 | Toki-no-kane Shoro (belfry), 43 |
| Dembo-in, 44 | Kappa-bashi, 45 | Sogen-ji, 46 | |

the right to the third door on the left, and ask for permission to see the Garden of Dembō-in. There is no charge. You simply enter your name and address in a register and receive a ticket. Hold on to the ticket: you'll need it later.

Return to Hozō-mon and walk across the courtyard to **Senso-ji Main Hall** ④. To the left of the Main Hall is the Five-Story Pagoda. To the right is **Asakusa Jinja** ④—a shrine to the Hikonuma brothers and their master, Naji-no-Nakatomo. Near the entrance to the shrine is the east gate to the temple grounds, Niten-mon.

From Niten-mon, walk back in the direction of Kaminari-mon to the southeast corner of the grounds. On a small plot of ground here stands the shrine to Kume-no-Heinai, a 17th-century outlaw who repented and became a priest of one of the subsidiary temples of Sensō-ji. Late in life he carved a stone statue of himself and buried it where many people would walk over it. In his will, he expressed the hope that his image would be trampled upon forever. Somehow, Heinai came to be worshiped as the patron god of lovers—as mystifying an apotheosis as you will ever find in Japanese religion.

Walk south again from Heinai's shrine along the narrow street that runs back to Kaminari-mon-dōri, parallel to Nakamise-dōri. On the left you pass a tiny hillock called Benten-yama and the **Toki-no-kane Shōrō** ㊸, a 17th-century belfry. Opposite Benten-yama is a shop called Naka-ya, which sells all manner of regalia for Sensō-ji's annual Sanja Festival.

Next door is Kuremutsu, a tiny ramshackle *nomiya* (Japanese pub) dating back nearly 100 years and open only in the evening. Just up the street from Kuremutsu is Hyaku-suke, the last place in Tōkyō to carry government-approved skin cleanser made from powdered nightingale droppings. Ladies of the Edo period—especially the geisha—swore by the cleanser. The wonderful variety of handcrafted combs and cosmetic brushes, intended for actors and dancers in traditional Japanese theater, makes for interesting gifts and souvenirs. The shop is closed on Tuesday.

Three doors up, on the same side of the street, is Fuji-ya, a shop that deals exclusively in *tenugui*—printed cotton hand towels. Owner Keiji Kawakami designs and dyes all of the tenugui himself. They unfold to about 3 ft, and many people buy them for framing. When Kawakami feels he has made enough of one pattern, he destroys the stencil.

Turn right at the corner past Fuji-ya and walk west on Dembō-in-dōri until you cross Nakamise-dōri. On the other side of the intersection, on the left, is Yono-ya, purveyor of pricey handmade boxwood combs for traditional Japanese coiffures and wigs. Some combs are carved with auspicious motifs, like peonies, hollyhocks, or cranes, and all are engraved with the family benchmark.

Now it's time to cash in the ticket you've been carrying around. Walk west another 70 yards or so, and on the right you will see an old dark wooden gate; this is the side entrance to **Dembō-in** ㊹, the living quarters of the abbot of Sensō-ji. The only part of the grounds you can visit is the garden: go through the small door in the gate, across the courtyard and through the door on the opposite side, and present your ticket to the caretaker in the house at the end of the alley. The entrance to the garden is down a short flight of stone steps to the left.

Turn right as you leave Dembō-in and continue walking west on Dembō-in-dōri. You'll pass a small Shintō shrine with a number of small statues of the bodhisattva Jizō; this is a shrine for prayers for the repose of the souls of *mizuko*—literally "water children"—those who were aborted or miscarried.

Farther on, in the row of knockdown clothing stalls along the right side of the street, is the booth of calligrapher Kōji Matsumaru, who makes *hyōsatsu*, the Japanese equivalent of doorplates. A hyōsatsu is a block of wood, preferably cypress, hung on a gatepost or an entranceway, with the family name on it in India ink. The hyōsatsu is the first thing people will learn about a home, and the characters on it must be felicitous and well formed—so one comes to Matsumaru. Famous in Asakusa for his fine hand, he will also render Western names in the *katakana* syllabic alphabet reserved for foreign words, should you decide to take home a hyōsatsu of your own.

Opposite the row of clothing stalls, on the corner of Orange-dōri, is the redbrick Asakusa Public Hall; performances of Kabuki and traditional dance are sometimes held here, as well as exhibitions of life in Asakusa before World War II. Across the street is Nakase, one of the best of Asakusa's many fine tempura restaurants.

Now review your options. If you have the time and energy, you might want to explore the streets and covered arcades on the south and west sides of Dembō-in. Where Dembō-in-dōri meets Sushiya-dōri, the main avenue of the Rok-ku entertainment district, there is a small flea market. Turn right here, and you are in what remains of the old movie-theater district. Nishi-Sandō—an arcade where you can find kimonos and yukata (cotton kimono) fabrics, traditional accessories, fans, and festival costumes at very reasonable prices—runs east of the movie theaters, between Rok-ku and Sensō-ji. If you turn to the left at the flea market, you soon come to the ROX Building, a misplaced attempt to endow Asakusa with a glitzy vertical mall. Just beyond it, you can turn left again and stroll along Shin-Nakamise-dōri (New Street of Inside Shops). This arcade and the streets that cross it north–south are lined with stores selling clothing and accessories; purveyors of crackers, seaweed, and tea; and restaurants and coffee shops. This is Asakusa's answer to the suburban shopping center.

Turn south, away from Dembō-in on any of these side streets; return to Kaminari-mon-dōri; turn right, and walk to the end of the avenue. Cross Kokusai-dōri, turn left, and then right at the next major intersection onto Asakusa-dōri; on the corner is the entrance to Tawara-machi Eki on the Ginza subway line. Head west on Asakusa-dōri; at the second traffic light, you'll see the Niimi Biru building across the street, on the right. Atop the Niimi Biru is the guardian god of Kappa-bashi: an enormous chef's head in plastic, 30 ft high, beaming, mustached, and crowned, as every chef in Japan is crowned, with a tall white hat. Turn right onto Kappa-bashi-dōgu-machi-dōri to explore the shops of **Kappa-bashi** ㊺, Tōkyō's wholesale restaurant supply district.

At the second intersection, on the right, is the main showroom of the Maizuru Company, virtuosos in the art of counterfeit cuisine: the plastic models of food you see in the front windows of most popularly priced Japanese restaurants. In 1960 models by Maizuru were included in the Japan Style Exhibition at London's Victoria and Albert Museum. Here you can buy individual pieces of plastic sushi or splurge on a whole Pacific lobster, perfect in coloration and detail down to the tiniest spines on its legs. A few doors down is Biken Kōgei, a good place to look for the folding red-paper lanterns that grace the front of inexpensive bars and restaurants.

Across the street from Maizuru is Nishimura, a shop specializing in *noren*—the short divided curtains that hang from bamboo rods over the doors of shops or restaurants to announce that they are open for business. Nishimura also carries ready-made noren with motifs of all sorts, from white-on-blue landscapes to geisha and sumō wrestlers in polychromatic splendor. They make wonderful wall hangings and dividers.

In the next block, on the right (east) side of the street, is Kondo Shōten, which sells all sorts of bamboo trays, baskets, scoops, and containers. A block farther, look for Iida Shōten, which stocks a good selection of embossed cast-iron kettles and casseroles, called *nambu* ware.

On the far corner is Union Company, which sells everything you need to run a coffee shop (or the make-believe one in your own kitchen): roasters, grinders, beans, flasks, and filters of every description.

The intersection here is about in the middle of Kappa-bashi. Turn left and walk about 100 yards to the next traffic light; just past the light, on the right, is **Sōgen-ji** ㊻—better known as the Kappa Temple, with its shrine to the imaginary creature that gives this district its name.

From Sōgen-ji retrace your steps to the intersection. There is more of Kappa-bashi to the north, but you can safely ignore it; continue east, straight past Union Company down the narrow side street. In the next block, on the left, look for Tsubaya

Hōchōten. Tsubaya sells cutlery for professionals—knives of every length and weight and balance for every imaginable use, from slicing sashimi to turning a cucumber into a paper-thin sheet to making decorative cuts in fruit.

Continue on this street east to Kokusai-dōri and then turn right (south). As you walk, you'll see several shops selling *butsudan*, Buddhist household altars. The most elaborate of these, hand-carved in ebony and covered with gold leaf, are made in Toyama Prefecture and can cost as much as ¥1 million. No proper Japanese household is without at least a modest butsudan; it's the spiritual center of the family, where reverence for ancestors and continuity of the family traditions are expressed. In a few moments, you will be back at Tawara-machi Eki—the end of the Asakusa walk.

### TIMING

Unlike most of the other areas to explore on foot in Tōkyō, Sensō-ji is admirably compact. You can easily see the temple and environs in a morning. The garden at Dembō-in is worth half an hour. If you decide to include Kappa-bashi, allow yourself an hour more. Some of the shopping arcades in this area are covered, but Asakusa is essentially an outdoor experience. Be prepared for rain in June, heat and humidity in July and August.

## What to See

### THE SENSŌ-JI COMPLEX

Dedicated to the goddess Kannon, ★**Sensō-ji** is the heart and soul of Asakusa. Come for its local and historical importance, its garden, its 17th-century Shintō shrine, and the wild Sanja Matsuri in May. *2–3–1 Asakusa, Taitō-ku, tel. 03/3842–0181. Free. Temple grounds daily 6–sundown. Subway: Ginza Line, Asakusa Eki (Exit 1/Kaminari-mon Exit).*

**㊷ ASAKUSA JINJA.** Several structures in the temple complex survived the bombings of 1945. The largest, to the right of the Main Hall, is a Shintō shrine to the putative founders of Sensō-ji. In Japan, Buddhism and Shintoism have enjoyed a comfortable coexistence since the former arrived from China in the 6th century. It's the rule, rather than the exception, to find a Shintō shrine on the same grounds as a Buddhist temple. The shrine, built in 1649, is also known as Sanja Sanma (Shrine of the Three Guardians). The Sanja Festival, held every year on the third weekend in May, is the biggest, loudest, wildest party in Tōkyō. Each of the neighborhoods under Sanja Sanma's protection has its own mikoshi, and on the second day of the festival, these palanquins are paraded through the streets of Asakusa to the shrine, bouncing and swaying on the shoulders of the participants all the way. Many of the "parishioners" take part naked to the waist, or with the sleeves of their tunics rolled up, to expose fantastic red-and-black tattoo patterns that sometimes cover their entire backs and shoulders. These are the tribal markings of the Japanese underworld.

Near the entrance to Asakusa Jinja is another survivor of World War II: the east gate to the temple grounds, **Niten-mon,** built in 1618 for a shrine to Ieyasu Tokugawa (the shrine itself no longer exists) and designated by the government as an Important Cultural Property.

★ ㊹ **DEMBŌ-IN.** Believed to have been made in the 17th century by Kōbori Enshū, the genius of Zen landscape design, the garden of Dembō-in, part of the living quarters of the abbot of Sensō-ji, is the best-kept secret in Asakusa. Anyone can see the front entrance to Dembō-in from Nakamise-dōri—behind an iron fence in the last block of shops—but the thousands of Japanese visitors passing by seem to have no idea what it is. (And if they do, it somehow never occurs to them to visit it themselves.) The garden of Dembō-in is usually empty and always utterly serene, an island of privacy in a sea of pilgrims. Spring, when the wisteria blooms, is the ideal time to be here. As you walk along the path that circles the pond, a different vista presents itself at every turn. The only sounds are the cries of birds and the splashing of carp.

A sign in English on Dembō-in-dōri, about 150 yards west of the intersection with Naka-mise-dōri, indicates the entrance, through the side door of a large wooden gate. For permission to see the abbot's garden, apply at the temple administration building, between Hozō-mon and the Five-Story Pagoda, in the far corner. *tel. 03/3842–0181 for reservations. Free. Daily 9–4; may be closed if abbot has guests.*

---

**NEED A BREAK?** The tatami-mat rooms in **Nakase,** a fine tempura restaurant, look out on a perfect little interior garden—hung, in May, with great fragrant bunches of white wisteria. Carp and goldfish swim in the pond; you can almost lean out from your room and trail your fingers in the water as you listen to the fountain. Nakase is expensive: lunch (11–3) at the tables inside starts at ¥3,000; more elaborate meals by the garden start at ¥7,000. It's across Orange Street from the redbrick Asakusa Public Hall. *1–39–13 Asakusa, Taitō-ku, tel. 03/3841–4015. No credit cards. Closed Tues.*

---

**40 KAMINARI-MON** (Thunder God Gate). This is the proper Sensō-ji entrance, with its huge red-paper lantern hanging in the center. The original gate was destroyed by fire in 1865. The replica that stands here now was built after World War II. Traditionally, two fearsome guardian gods are installed in the alcoves of Buddhist temple gates to ward off evil spirits. The Thunder God (Kaminari-no-Kami) of the Sensō-ji main gate is on the left. He shares his duties with the Wind God (Kaze-no-Kami) on the right. Few Japanese visitors neglect to stop at **Tokiwa-dō,** the shop on the west side of the gate, to buy some of Tōkyō's most famous souvenirs: *kaminari okoshi* (thunder crackers), made of rice, millet, sugar, and beans.

Kaminari-mon also marks the southern extent of **Nakamise-dōri**, the Street of Inside Shops. The area from Kaminari-mon to the inner gate of the temple was once composed of stalls leased to the townspeople who cleaned and swept the temple grounds. The rows of redbrick buildings now technically belong to the municipal government, but the leases are, in effect, hereditary: some of the shops have been in the same families since the Edo period.

**41 SENSŌ-JI MAIN HALL.** The **Five-Story Pagoda** and the **Main Hall** of Sensō-ji are both faithful copies in concrete of originals that burned down in 1945. It took 13 years, when most of the people of Asakusa were still rebuilding their own bombed-out lives, to raise money for the restoration of their beloved Sensō-ji. To them—and especially to those involved in the world of entertainment—it is far more than a tourist attraction: Kabuki actors still come here before a new season of performances; sumō wrestlers come before a tournament to pay their respects; the large lanterns in the Main Hall were donated by the geisha associations of Asakusa and nearby Yanagi-bashi. Most Japanese stop at the huge bronze incense burner, in front of the Main Hall, to bathe their hands and faces in the smoke—it's a charm to ward off illnesses—before climbing the stairs to offer their prayers.

The Main Hall, about 115 ft long and 108 ft wide, is not an especially impressive piece of architecture. Unlike in many other temples, however, part of the inside has a concrete floor, so you can come and go without removing your shoes. In this area hang the Sensō-ji's chief claims to artistic importance: a collection of votive paintings on wood, from the 18th and 19th centuries. Plaques of this kind, called *ema*, are still offered to the gods at shrines and temples, but they are commonly simpler and smaller. The worshiper buys a little tablet of wood with the picture already painted on one side and inscribes a prayer on the other. The temple owns more than 50 of these works, which were removed to safety in 1945 and so escaped the air raids.

Only eight of them, depicting scenes from Japanese history and mythology, are on display. A catalog of the collection is on sale in the hall, but the text is in Japanese only.

Lighting is poor in the Main Hall, and the actual works are difficult to see. This is also true of the ceiling, done by two contemporary masters of Nihon-ga (traditional Japanese-style painting); the dragon is by Ryūshi Kawabata, and the motif of angels and lotus blossoms is by Inshō Dōmoto. One thing that visitors cannot see at all is the holy image of Kannon itself, which supposedly lies buried somewhere deep under the temple. Not even the priests of Sensō-ji have ever seen it, and there is in fact no conclusive evidence that it actually exists.

**Hozō-mon,** the gate to the temple courtyard, serves as a repository for sutras (Buddhist texts) and other treasures of Sensō-ji. This gate, too, has its guardian gods; should either of them decide to leave his post for a stroll, he can use the enormous pair of sandals hanging on the back wall—the gift of a Yamagata Prefecture village famous for its straw weaving.

**43 TOKI-NO-KANE SHŌRŌ** (belfry). The tiny hillock Benten-yama, with its shrine to the goddess of good fortune, is the site for this 17th-century belfry. The bell here used to toll the hours for the people of the district, and it was said that you could hear it anywhere within a radius of some 6 km (4 mi). The bell still sounds at 6 AM every day, when the temple grounds open. It also rings on New Year's Eve—108 strokes in all, beginning just before midnight, to "ring out" the 108 sins and frailties of humankind and make a clean start for the coming year. Benten-yama and the belfry are at the beginning of the narrow street that parallels Nakamise-dōri.

NEED A **Kuremutsu,** formerly a tiny old teahouse, has been turned into a
BREAK? fairly expensive *nomiya*—literally, a "drinking place," the drink of choice in this case being sake. It's open evenings, Friday–Wednesday. 2–2–13 Asakusa, Taitō-ku, tel. 03/3842–0906.

### ELSEWHERE IN ASAKUSA

★ **45** **KAPPA-BASHI.** The more than 200 wholesale dealers in this area sell everything the city's restaurant and bar trade could possibly need to do business, from paper supplies to steam tables, from signs to soup tureens. In their wildest dreams the Japanese themselves would never have cast Kappa-bashi as a tourist attraction, but indeed it is.

For one thing, it is the place to buy plastic food. From the humblest noodle shop or sushi bar to neighborhood restaurants of middling price and pretension, it's customary in Japan to stock a window with models of what can be eaten inside. The custom began, according to one version of the story, in the early days of the Meiji Restoration, when anatomical models made of wax first came to Japan as teaching aids in the new schools of Western medicine. A businessman from Nara decided that wax models would also make good point-of-purchase advertising for restaurants. He was right: the industry grew in a modest way at first, making models mostly of Japanese food, but in the boom years after 1960, restaurants began to serve all sorts of cookery ordinary people had never seen before, and the models offered much-needed reassurance: "So that's a cheeseburger. It doesn't look as bad as it sounds. Let's go in and try one." By the mid-1970s, the makers of plastic food were turning out creations of astonishing virtuosity and realism, and foreigners had discovered in them a form of pop art. Nishi-Asakusa 1-chōme and 2-chōme, Taitō-ku. Most shops daily 9–6. Subway: Ginza Line, Tawara-machi Eki (Exit 1).

**46** **SŌGEN-JI.** In the 19th century, so the story goes, there was a river in the present-day Kappa-bashi district and a bridge. The surrounding area was poorly drained and was often flooded. A local shopkeeper began a project to improve the drainage, investing all his own money, but met with little success until a troupe of kappa—mischievous green water sprites—emerged from the river to help him. The local people still come to the shrine at Sōgen-ji to leave offerings of cucumber and sake—the kappa's favorite food and drink.

A more prosaic explanation for the name of the district points out that the lower-ranking retainers of the local lord used to earn extra money by making straw raincoats, also called kappa, that they spread to dry on the bridge. To get here, walk north on Kappa-bashi-dōgu-machi-dōri from the Niimi Biru to the fifth intersection and turn left. *3–7–2 Matsugaya, Taitō-ku, tel. 03/ 3841–2035. Free. Temple grounds sunrise–sunset. Subway: Ginza Line, Tawara-machi Eki (Exit 1).*

## TSUKIJI

Tsukiji is a reminder of the awesome disaster of the great fire of 1657. In the space of two days, it leveled almost 70% of Ieyasu Tokugawa's new capital and killed more than 100,000 people. Ieyasu was not a man to be discouraged by mere catastrophe, however; he took it as an opportunity to plan an even bigger and better city, one that would incorporate the marshes east of his castle. Tsukiji, in fact, means "reclaimed land," and a substantial block of land it was, laboriously drained and filled, from present-day Ginza to the bay.

The common people of the tenements and alleys, who had suffered most in the great fire, benefited not at all from this project; land was first allotted to feudal lords and to temples. After 1853, when Japan opened its doors to the outside world, Tsukiji became Tōkyō's first foreign settlement—the site of the American legation and an elegant two-story brick hotel, and home to missionaries, teachers, and doctors. Today this area is best known for the largest fish market in Asia.

*Numbers in the text correspond to numbers in the margin and on the Tsukiji map.*

# A Good Walk

## TSUKIJI

Take the Tōei Ōedo Line subway to Tsukiji-shijō Eki, leave the station by Exit A1 onto Shin-Ōhashi-dōri, and turn right. After walking about 30 paces, you will come to the back gate of the fish market, which extends from here southeast toward the bay. Alternatively, take the Hibiya Line subway to Tsukiji Eki (signs in English to the FISH MARKET are posted in the station), come up on Shin-Ōhashi-dōri (Exit 1), and turn southeast. Cross Harumi-dōri, walk along the covered sidewalk for about 110 yards to the traffic light, and turn left. Walk to the end of the street (you'll will see the stone torii of a small shrine), and turn right. If you reach this point at precisely 5 AM, you'll hear a signal for the start of Tōkyō's greatest ongoing open-air spectacle: the fish auction at the **Tōkyō Chūō Oroshiuri Ichiba** ㊼, the Central Wholesale Market.

By 9 AM the business of the Central Market is largely finished for the day, but there is still plenty to do and see. You'll have missed the auctions, but you can still explore the maze of alleys between the market and Harumi-dōri, where you'll come across the **Backstreet Shops of Tsukiji** ㊽. You'll find all kinds of eateries, as well as food and cookware stores. For a close-up shot of Japanese daily life, this is one of the best places in Tōkyō to visit.

From the Central Market, go back to Shin-Ōhashi-dōri; turn right; and walk to the next block, past Harumi-dōri. On the right, as you approach the Hibiya subway line's Tsukiji Eki, are the grounds of **Tsukiji Hongan-ji** ㊾. Looking much like a transplant from India, this temple is the main branch in Tōkyō of Kyōto's Nishi Hongan-ji. Continue northeast on Shin-Ōhashi-dōri, and turn right at the next corner. When you come to a small park, turn left and follow the path through it. At the end of the path, turn right, keeping St. Luke's International Hospital on your immediate left. About 30 yards down this street, in a traffic island on the right, are two unassuming stone **Tsukiji**

# tsukiji

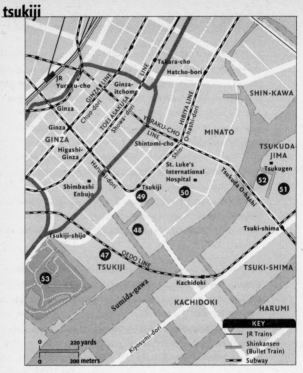

**memorials** ⑤⓪ that mark the true importance of the area in the modern history of Japan.

St. Luke's International Hospital, across the street, was founded in 1900 by Dr. Rudolf Teusler, an American medical missionary. The chapel on the second floor of the charming brick-and-granite old wing of the hospital is quite lovely. Covering the several square blocks north of the hospital was the foreign settlement created after the signing of the U.S.-Japan Treaty of Commerce in 1858. Among the residents here in the latter part of the 19th century was a Scottish surgeon and missionary named Henry Faulds. Intrigued by the Japanese custom of putting their thumbprints on documents for authentication, he began the research that established for the first time that no two people's fingerprints are alike. In 1880 he wrote a paper for *Nature* magazine suggesting that this fact might be of some use in criminal investigation.

After you've seen the hospital, review your priorities. From here you can retrace your steps to the Hibiya Line station on Shin-Ōhashi-dōri and take the subway to Higashi-Ginza and Shimbashi. Or you can take a longish but rewarding detour to **Tsukuda-jima** ⑤①. If you choose the latter, walk north from the hospital, parallel to the Sumida-gawa and one block west of it, for two blocks. Cross the main intersection here and turn right. The street rises to become the Tsukuda Ōhashi (Tsukuda Bridge). Just before it crosses the water, you'll find a flight of steps up to the pedestrian walkway that brings you to the island.

Tsukugen, a shop on the first street along the breakwater as you leave the bridge, is famous for its delicious *tsukudani*—whitebait boiled in soy sauce and salt—the island's most famous product. At the end of the breakwater, turn right. From here it's a short walk to the gate of the **Sumiyoshi Jinja** ⑤②, a shrine established by fishermen from Ōsaka when they first settled on the island in the 17th century.

If you've opted not to visit Tsukuda-jima, retrace your steps from St. Luke's to the Tsukiji subway station and walk southwest again on Shin-Ōhashi-dōri. Pass the turnoff to the Central Market on your left and the Asahi Newspapers Building on your right. The avenue curves and brings you to an elevated walkway. The entrance to the gardens of **Hama Rikyū Tei-en** ⑤③ is on the left. (The path to the left as you enter the garden leads to the "river bus" ferry landing, from which you can leave this excursion and begin another: up the Sumida to Asakusa.)

On your way to Hama Rikyū Tei-en, as you walk west on Shin-Ōhashi-dōri, keep on the right side of the street. After you cross Harumi-dōri, take the first narrow street on the right; just past the next corner, on the left, is Edo-Gin, a venerable sushi bar that serves sizable portions of market-fresh sushi. Lunchtime set menus are bargains.

## TIMING

The Tsukiji walk offers few places to spend time in; backtracking and getting from point to point, however, can consume most of a morning—especially if you decide to devote an hour or so to Tsukuda-jima. The backstreet shops will probably require no more than half an hour. Allow yourself an hour or more to explore the Central Market and the nearby shops; if fish in all its diversity holds a special fascination for you, take two or three hours. Remember that in order to see the fish auction in action, you'll need to get to the Central Market before 6:30 AM; by 9 AM the business of the market is largely finished for the day.

This part of the city can be brutally hot and muggy in August; during the O-bon holiday, in the middle of the month, Tsukiji is comparatively lifeless. Mid-April and early October are best for strolls in the Hama Rikyū Garden.

# What to See

★ **48** **BACKSTREET SHOPS OF TSUKIJI.** Because of the area's proximity to the fish market, there are scores of fishmongers here—but also sushi bars, restaurants, and stores for pickles, tea, crackers, kitchen knives, baskets, and crockery. Markets like these provide a vital counterpoint to the museums and monuments of conventional sightseeing; they bring you up close to the way people really live in the city. If you have time on your itinerary for just one market, this is the one to see. The area that these shops occupy is between the Tōkyō fish market and Harumi-dōri. 5–2–1 Tsukiji, Chūō-ku. Subway: Tōei Ōedo Line, Tsukiji-shijō Eki (Exit A1); Hibiya Line, Tsukiji Eki (Exit 1).

**53** **HAMA RIKYŪ TEI-EN** (Detached Palace Garden). The land here was originally owned by the Owari branch of the Tokugawa family from Nagoya, and it extended to part of what is now the fish market. When one of the family became shōgun in 1709, his residence was turned into a shogunal palace—with pavilions, ornamental gardens, pine and cherry groves, and duck ponds. The garden became a public park in 1945, although a good portion of it is fenced off as a nature preserve. None of the original buildings survive, but on the island in the large pond is a reproduction of the pavilion where former U.S. president Ulysses S. Grant and Mrs. Grant had an audience with the emperor Meiji in 1879. The building can now be rented for parties. The path to the left as you enter the garden leads to the "river bus" ferry landing, from which you can leave this excursion and begin another: up the Sumida to Asakusa. 1–1 Hamarikyū–Teien, Chūō–ku, tel. 03/3541–0200. ¥300. Daily 9–4:30. Subway: Tōei Ōedo Line, Tsukiji-shijō Eki (Exit A1); Hibiya Line, Tsukiji Eki (Exit 1).

**52** **SUMIYOSHI JINJA.** A few steps from the breakwater at the north end of Tsukuda-jima, this shrine dates from the island's earliest period, when Ōsaka fishermen settled here. The god enshrined here is the protector of those who make their livelihood from the sea. Once every three years (2002, 2005, 2008), on the first weekend in August, the god is brought out for his procession in an eight-sided palanquin, preceded by huge, golden lion heads carried high in the air, their mouths snapping in mock ferocity to drive any evil influences out of the path. As the palanquin passes, the people of the island douse it with water, recalling the custom, before the breakwater was built, of carrying it to the river for a high-spirited dunking. *1–1 Tsukuda, Chūō-ku, tel. 03/3531–6525. Free. Daily dawn–sunset. Subway: Yūraku-chō and Tōei Ōedo lines, Tsukishima Eki (Exit 6).*

★ ㊼ **TŌKYŌ CHŪŌ OROSHIURI ICHIBA** (Tōkyō Central Wholesale Market). The city's fish market used to be farther uptown, in Nihombashi. It was moved to Tsukiji after the Great Kantō Earthquake of 1923, and it occupies the site of what was once Japan's first naval training academy. Today the market sprawls over some 54 acres of reclaimed land. Its warren of buildings houses about 1,200 wholesale shops, supplying 90% of the fish consumed in Tōkyō every day and employing some 15,000 people. Most of the seafood sold in Tsukiji comes in by truck, arriving through the night from fishing ports all over the country.

What makes Tsukiji a great show is the auction system. The catch—more than 100 varieties of fish in all, including whole frozen tuna, Styrofoam cases of shrimp and squid, and crates of crabs—is laid out in the long covered area between the river and the main building. Then the bidding begins. Only members of the wholesalers' association can take part. Wearing license numbers fastened to the front of their caps, they register their bids in a kind of sign language, shouting to draw the attention of the auctioneer and making furious combinations in the air with their fingers. The auctioneer keeps the action moving in a hoarse croak that sounds like no known language, and spot quotations change too fast for ordinary mortals to follow.

Different fish are auctioned off at different times and locations, and by 6:30 AM or so, this part of the day's business is over, and the wholesalers fetch their purchases back into the market in barrows. Restaurant owners and retailers arrive about 7, making the rounds of favorite suppliers for their requirements. Chaos seems to reign, but everybody here knows everybody else, and they all have it down to a system.

A word to the wise: the 52,000 or so buyers, wholesalers, and shippers who work at the Central Market may be a lot more receptive to casual visitors than they were in the past, but they are not running a tourist attraction. They're in the fish business, moving some 636,000 tons of it a year to retailers and restaurants all over the city, and this is their busiest time of day. The cheerful banter they use with each other can turn snappish if you get in their way. Also bear in mind that you are not allowed to take photographs while the auctions are under way (flashes are a distraction). The market is kept spotlessly clean, which means the water hoses are running all the time. Boots are helpful, but if you don't want to carry them, bring a pair of heavy-duty trash bags to slip over your shoes and secure them above your ankles with rubber bands. 5–2–1 Tsukiji, Chūō-ku, tel. 03/3542–1111. Free. Business hrs Mon.–Sat. (except 2nd and 4th Wed. of month) 5–4. Subway: Tōei Ōedo Line, Tsukiji-shijō Eki (Exit A1); Hibiya Line, Tsukiji Eki (Exit 1).

**49 TSUKIJI HONGAN-JI.** Disaster seemed to follow this temple since it was first located here in 1657: it was destroyed at least five times thereafter, and reconstruction in wood was finally abandoned after the Great Kantō Earthquake of 1923. The present stone building dates from 1935. It was designed by Chūta Ito, a pupil of Tatsuno Kingo, who built Tōkyō Eki. Ito's other credits include the Meiji Jingū in Harajuku; he also lobbied for Japan's first law for the preservation of historic buildings. Ito traveled extensively in Asia; the evocations of classical Hindu architecture in the temple's domes and ornaments were his homage to India as the cradle of Buddhism. 3–15–1 Tsukiji, Chūō-ku, tel. 03/3541–1131. Free. Daily 6–4. Subway: Hibiya Line, Tsukiji Eki (Exit 1).

NEED A
BREAK? **Edo-Gin,** one of the area's older sushi bars, founded in 1924, is
legendary for its portions—slices of raw fish that almost hide
the balls of rice on which they sit. Dinner is pricey, but the set
menu at lunch is a certifiable *bāgen* (bargain) at ¥1,000. Walk
southwest on Shin-Ōhashi-dōri from its intersection with
Harumi-dōri. Take the first right and look for Edo-Gin just past
the next corner, on the left. *4–5–1 Tsukiji, Chūō-ku, tel. 03/3543–
4401. AE, MC, V. Closed Sun. Subway: Hibiya Line, Tsukiji Eki (Exit 1).*

**⑤⓪ TSUKIJI MEMORIALS.** The taller of the two unassuming stone
memorials pays tribute to Ryōtaku Maeno and Gempaku Sugita.
With a group of colleagues, these two men translated the first
work of European science into Japanese. Maeno and his
collaborators were samurai and physicians. Maeno himself was
in the service of the Lord Okudaira, whose mansion was one of
the most prominent in Tsukiji. In 1770 Maeno acquired a Dutch
book on human anatomy in Nagasaki. It took his group four
years to produce its translation. At this time Japan was still
officially closed to the outside world, and the trickle of scientific
knowledge accessible through the Dutch trading post at
Nagasaki—the only authorized foreign settlement—was
enormously frustrating to the eager young scholars who wanted
to modernize their country. Maeno and his colleagues began
with barely a few hundred words of Dutch among them and had
no reference works or other resources on which to base their
translation, except the diagrams in the book. It must have been
an agonizing task, but the publication in 1774 of *Kaitai Shinsho*
(New Book of Anatomy) had a tremendous influence. From this
time on, Japan would turn away from classical Chinese scholarship
and begin to take its lessons in science and technology from the
West.

The other stone memorial commemorates the founding of Keiō
University by Yūkichi Fukuzawa (1835–1901), the most
influential educator and social thinker of the Meiji period. The
son of a low-ranking samurai, Fukuzawa was ordered by his lord

to start a school of Western learning, which he opened in Tsukiji in 1858. Later the school was moved west to Mita, where the university is today. Engraved on the stone is Fukuzawa's famous statement: HEAVEN CREATED NO MAN ABOVE ANOTHER, NOR BELOW. Uttered when the feudal Tokugawa regime was still in power, this was an enormously daring thought. It took Japan almost a century to catch up with Fukuzawa's liberal and egalitarian vision.

**51 TSUKUDA-JIMA.** In 1613 the shogunate ordered a group of fishermen from the village of Tsukuda, now part of Ōsaka, to relocate here, on an island reclaimed from mudflats at the mouth of the Sumida-gawa. Officially, they were brought here to provide the castle with whitebait; unofficially, their role was to keep watch and report on any suspicious maritime traffic in the bay. Over the years more and more land has been reclaimed from the bay, more than doubling the size of the island and adding other areas to the south and west. The part to explore is the original section: a few square blocks just west and north of the Tsukuda Ōhashi. This neighborhood—with its maze of narrow alleys, its profusion of potted plants and bonsai, its old houses with tile roofs—could almost have come straight out of the Edo period. 1–1 Tsukuda, Chūō-ku. Subway: Yūraku-chō and Ōedo lines, Tsukishima Eki (Exit 6).

# NIHOMBASHI, GINZA, AND YŪRAKU-CHŌ

Tōkyō is a city of many centers. The municipal administrative center is in Shinjuku. The national government center is in Kasumigaseki. For almost 350 years Japan was ruled from Edo Castle, and the great stone ramparts still define—for travelers, at least—the heart of the city. History, entertainment, fashion, traditional culture: every tail you could want to pin on the donkey goes in a different spot. Geographically speaking, however, there is one and only one center of Tōkyō: a tall, black iron pole on the north side of Nihombashi—and if the tail you were holding represented high finance, you would have to pin that one right here as well.

When Ieyasu Tokugawa had the first bridge constructed at Nihombashi, he designated it the starting point for the five great roads leading out of his city, the point from which all distances were to be measured. His decree is still in force: the black pole on the present bridge, erected in 1911, is the Zero Kilometer marker for all the national highways.

In the early days of the Tokugawa Shogunate, Edo had no port; almost everything the city needed was shipped here. The bay shore was marshy and full of tidal flats, so heavily laden ships would come only as far as Shinagawa, a few miles down the coast, and unload to smaller vessels. These in turn would take the cargo into the city through a network of canals to wharves and warehouses at Nihombashi. The bridge and the area south and east became a wholesale distribution center, not only for manufactured goods but also for foodstuffs. The city's first fish market, in fact, was established at Nihombashi in 1628 and remained here until the Great Earthquake of 1923.

All through the Edo period, this was part of Shitamachi. Except for a few blocks between Nihombashi and Kyō-bashi, where the city's deputy magistrates had their villas, it belonged to the common people—not all of whom lived elbow to elbow in poverty. There were fortunes to be made in the markets, and the early millionaires of Edo built their homes in the Nihombashi area. Some, like the legendary timber magnate Bunzaemon Kinokuniya, spent everything they made in the pleasure quarters of Yoshiwara and died penniless. Others founded the great trading houses of today—Mitsui, Mitsubishi, Sumitomo— which still have warehouses nearby.

It was appropriate, then, that when Japan's first corporations were created and the Meiji government developed a modern system of capital formation, the Tōkyō Stock Exchange (Shōken

Torihikijo) would go up on the west bank of the Nihombashi-gawa. A stone's throw from the exchange now are the home offices of most of the country's major securities companies, which in the hyperinflated bubble economy of the 1980s and early '90s were moving billions of yen around the world electronically—a far cry from the early years of high finance, when the length of a trading day was determined by a section of rope burning on the floor of the exchange. Trading finished when the rope had smoldered down to the end.

A little farther west, money—the problems of making it and of moving it around—shaped the area in a somewhat different way. In the Edo period there were three types of currency in circulation: gold, silver, and copper, each with its various denominations. Determined to unify the system, Ieyasu Tokugawa started minting his own silver coins in 1598 in his home province of Suruga, even before he became shōgun. In 1601 he established a gold mint; the building was only a few hundred yards from Nihombashi, on the site of what is now the Bank of Japan. In 1612 he relocated the Suruga plant to a patch of reclaimed land west of his castle. The area soon came to be known informally as Ginza (Silver Mint).

The value of these various currencies fluctuated. There were profits to be made in the changing of money, and this business eventually came under the control of a few large merchant houses. One of the most successful of these merchants was a man named Takatoshi Mitsui, who had a dry-goods shop in Kyōto and opened a branch in Edo in 1673. The shop, called Echigo-ya, was just north of Nihombashi. By the end of the 17th century it was the base of a commercial empire—in retailing, banking, and trading—known today as the Mitsui Group. Not far from the site of Echigo-ya stands its direct descendant: Mitsukoshi depāto.

*Rui wa tomo wo yobu* goes the Japanese expression: "Like calls to like." From Nihombashi through Ginza to Shimbashi is the domain of all the noble houses that trace their ancestry back to the dry-goods and kimono shops of the Edo period: Mitsukoshi, Takashimaya, Matsuzakaya, Matsuya. All are intensely proud of being at the top of the retail business, as purveyors of an astonishing range of goods and services.

The district called Yūraku-chō lies west of Ginza's Sukiya-bashi, stretching from Sotobori-dōri to Hibiya Kōen and the Outer Garden of the Imperial Palace. The name derives from one Urakusai Oda, younger brother of the warlord who had once been Ieyasu Tokugawa's commander. Urakusai, a Tea Master of some note—he was a student of Sen no Rikyū, who developed the tea ceremony—had a town house here, beneath the castle ramparts, on land reclaimed from the tidal flats of the bay. He soon left Edo for the more refined comforts of Kyōto, but his name stayed behind, becoming Yūraku-chō—the Pleasure (yūraku) Quarter (chō)—in the process. Sukiya-bashi was the name of the long-gone bridge near Urakusai's villa that led over the moat to the Silver Mint.

The "pleasures" associated with this district in the early postwar period stemmed from the fact that a number of the buildings here survived the air raids of 1945 and were requisitioned by the Allied forces. Yūraku-chō quickly became the haunt of the so-called pan-pan women, who provided the GIs with female company. Because it was so close to the military post exchange in Ginza, the area under the railroad tracks became one of the city's largest black markets. Later, the black market gave way to clusters of cheap restaurants, most of them little more than counters and a few stools, serving yakitori and beer. Office workers on meager budgets and journalists from the nearby Mainichi, Asahi, and Yomiuri newspaper headquarters would gather here at night. Yūraku-chō-under-the-tracks was smoky, loud, and friendly—a kind of open-air substitute for the local taproom. The area has long since become upscale, and no more than a handful of the yakitori stalls remains.

*Numbers in the text correspond to numbers in the margin and on the Nihombashi, Ginza, and Yūraku-chō map.*

## A Good Walk

For more information on depāto and individual shops mentioned in this walk, *see* Shopping, *below*.

### NIHOMBASHI

Begin at Tōkyō Eki. Take the Yaesu Central Exit on the east side of the building, cross the broad avenue in front of you (Sotobori-dōri), and turn left. Walk north until you cross a bridge under the Shuto Expressway and turn right at the second corner, at the **Nihon Ginkō** ⑤④. From here walk east two blocks to the main intersection at Chūō-dōri. On your left is the Mitsui Bank, on your right **Mitsukoshi** ⑤⑤ depāto. The small area around the store, formerly called Suruga-chō, is the birthplace of the Mitsui conglomerate.

Turn right on Chūō-dōri. As you walk south, you'll see on the left a shop founded in 1849, called Yamamoto Noriten, which specializes in *nori*, the ubiquitous dried seaweed used to wrap *maki* (sushi rolls) and *onigiri* (rice balls); nori was once the most famous product of Tōkyō Bay.

At the end of the next block is the **Nihombashi** ⑤⑥ (this is name of the bridge itself, as well as the neighborhood), shaken but not stirred by the incessant rumbling of the expressway overhead. Before you cross the bridge, notice on your left the small statue of a sea princess seated by a pine tree: a monument to the fish market that stood here before the 1923 quake. To the right is the Zero Kilometer marker, from which all highway distances are measured. On the other side, also to the right, is a plaque depicting the old wooden bridge. In the Edo period the south end of the bridge was set aside for posting public announcements—and for displaying the heads of criminals.

# nihombashi, ginza, and yuraku-cho

**KEY**

- JR Trains
- Shinkansen (Bullet Train)
- Subway

**Nihombashi**

Burijisuton Bijutsukan (Bridgestone Museum of Art), 59

Kabuto Jinja, 57

Kite Museum, 58

Mitsukoshi, 55

Nihombashi, 56

Nihon Ginko (Bank of Japan), 54

**Ginza**

Ginza, 60

Sukiya-bashi, 61

**Yuraku-cho**

Dai-ichi Mutual Life Insurance Company Building, 64

Idemitsu Bijutsukan, 63

Tokyo International Forum, 62

Turn left as soon as you cross the bridge and walk past the Nomura Securities Building to where the expressway loops overhead and turns south. This area is called Kabuto-chō, after the small **Kabuto Jinja** ⑤⑦ here on the left, under the loop. Just across the street from the shrine is the Tōkyō Stock Exchange.

At the main entrance to the Stock Exchange, turn right. Walk south two blocks to the intersection at Eitai-dōri and turn right again. Walk west on Eitai-dōri, turn right onto Shōwa-dōri, and then left on the first small street behind the Bank of Hiroshima. Just off the next corner is a restaurant called Taimeiken. On the fifth floor of this building is the delightful little private **Kite Museum** ⑤⑧—well worth the detour for visitors of all ages.

Retrace your steps to Eitai-dōri, continue west, and turn left onto Chūō-dōri. One block south, on the left, is the Takashimaya depāto; on the right is Maruzen, one of Japan's largest booksellers.

Look right at the next intersection; you'll see that you've come back almost to Tōkyō Eki. Below the avenue from here to the station runs the Yaesu Underground Arcade, with hundreds of shops and restaurants. The whole area here, west of Chūō-dōri, was named after Jan Joosten, a Dutch sailor who was shipwrecked on the coast of Kyūshū with William Adams—hero of James Michener's novel *Shōgun*—in 1600. Like Adams, Joosten became an adviser to Ieyasu Tokugawa, took a Japanese wife, and was given a villa near the castle. "Yaesu" (originally Yayosu) was as close as the Japanese could come to the pronunciation of his name. Adams, an Englishman, lived out his life in Japan; Joosten drowned off the coast of Indonesia while attempting to return home.

On the southeast corner of the intersection is the **Burijisuton Bijutsukan** ⑤⑨, one of Japan's best private collections of early modern painting and sculpture, both Western and Japanese.

### GINZA

Consider your feet. By now they may be telling you that you'd really rather not walk to the next point on this excursion. If so, get on the Ginza Line—there's a subway entrance right in front of the Burijisuton Bijutsukan—and ride one stop to **Ginza** ⑥⓪. Take any exit directing you to the 4-chōme intersection (yon-*chō*-me kō-sa-ten). When you come up to the street level, orient yourself by the Ginza branch of the Mitsukoshi depāto, on the northeast corner, and the round Sanai Building on the southwest.

From Ginza 4-chōme, walk west on Harumi-dōri in the direction of the Imperial Palace. From Chūō-dōri to the intersection called **Sukiya-bashi** ⑥①, named for a bridge that once stood here, your exploration should be free-form: the side streets and parallels north–south are ideal for wandering, particularly if you are interested in art galleries—of which there are 300 or more in this part of Ginza.

### YŪRAKU-CHŌ

From the Sukiya-bashi intersection, walk northwest on the right side of Harumi-dōri. Pass the curved facade of the Mullion Building depāto complex and cross the intersection. You'll go through a tunnel under the JR Yamanote Line tracks, and then turn right. Walk two long blocks east, parallel to the tracks, until you come to the gleaming white expanse of the **Tōkyō International Forum** ⑥②.

The plaza of the Tōkyō International Forum is that rarest of Tōkyō rarities—civilized open space: a long, tree-shaded central courtyard with comfortable benches to sit on and things to see. Freestanding sculpture, triumphant architecture, and people strolling—actually *strolling*—past in both directions are all here. Need a refreshment? Café Wien, next to the Plaza Information Center, serves pastry and coffee.

From the southwest corner of the Forum, turn left and walk halfway down the block to the main entrance of the International Building. On the ninth floor you'll find the **Idemitsu Bijutsukan** ⑥. After a stop inside, continue west along the side of the International Building toward the Imperial Palace to Hibiya-dōri.

Turn left, and less than a minute's walk along Hibiya-dōri will bring you to the **Dai-ichi Mutual Life Insurance Company Building** ⑥. Across the avenue is Hibiya Kōen, Japan's first Western-style public park, which dates to 1903. Its lawns and fountains make a pretty place for office workers from nearby buildings to have lunch on a warm spring afternoon, but it doesn't provide compelling reasons for you to make a detour. Press on, past the Hibiya police station, across the Harumi-dōri intersection, and at the second corner, just before you come to the Imperial Hotel, turn left.

At the end of the block, on the corner, is the Takarazuka Theater, where all-female casts take the art of musical review to the highest levels of camp. Continue southeast, and in the next block, on both sides of the street (just under the railroad bridge), are entrances to the International Shopping Arcade (☞ Shopping, *below*), the last point of interest on this walk. Stores here sell kimonos and happi coats, pearls and cloisonné, prints, cameras, and consumer electronics: one-stop shopping for presents and souvenirs.

Turn left down the narrow side street that runs along the side of the arcade to the Hankyū depāto—the horned monstrosity in the pocket park on the corner is by sculptor Taro Okamoto— and you will find yourself back on Harumi-dōri, just a few steps from the Sukiya-bashi crossing. From here you can return to your hotel by subway, or a minute's walk will bring you to JR Yūraku-chō Eki.

## TIMING

There's something about this part of Tōkyō—the traffic, the numbers of people, the way it exhorts you to keep moving—that can make you feel you've covered a lot more ground than you really have. Take this walk in the morning; when you're done, you can better assess the energy you have left for the rest of the day. None of the stops along the way, with the possible exception of the Bridgestone and Idemitsu museums, should take you more than 45 minutes. The time you spend shopping, of course, is up to you. In summer make a point of starting early, even though many stores and attractions do not open until 10 or 11: by midday the heat and humidity can be brutal. On weekend afternoons (October–March, Saturday 3–6 and Sunday 12–5; April–September, Saturday 3–7 and Sunday 3–6), Chūo-dōri is closed to traffic from Shimbashi all the way to Kyō-bashi and becomes a pedestrian mall with tables and chairs set out along the street. That's great if you plan only to shop, but keep in mind that some of the museums and other sights in the area close on Sundays.

## What to See

🟢 **BURIJISUTON BIJUTSUKAN** (Bridgestone Museum of Art). This is one of Japan's best private collections of French Impressionist art and sculpture and of post-Meiji Japanese painting in Western styles by such artists as Shigeru Aoki and Tsuguji Fujita. The collection, assembled by Bridgestone Tire Company founder Shōjiro Ishibashi, includes work by Rembrandt, Picasso, Utrillo, and Modigliani as well. The Bridgestone also puts on major exhibits from private collections and museums abroad. 1–10–1 Kyō-bashi, Chūo-ku, tel. 03/3563–0241. ¥700. Tues.–Sun. 10–5:30. Subway: Ginza Line, Kyō-bashi Eki (Meijiya Exit), Nihombashi Eki (Takashimaya Exit).

🟢 **DAI-ICHI MUTUAL LIFE INSURANCE COMPANY BUILDING.** Built like a fortress, the edifice survived World War II virtually intact and was taken over by the Supreme Command of the Allied powers. From his office here, General Douglas MacArthur directed the affairs of Japan from 1945 to 1951. The room is kept exactly as it was then. It can be visited by individuals and small groups without appointment; you need only to sign in at the reception desk in the lobby. *1–13–1 Yūraku-chō, Chiyoda-ku, tel. 03/3216–1211. Free. Weekdays 10–4:30. Subway: Hibiya Line, Hibiya Eki (Exit B1).*

**60 GINZA.** Ieyasu's Silver Mint moved out of this area in 1800. The name *Ginza* remained, but only much later did it begin to acquire any cachet for wealth and style. The turning point was 1872, when a fire destroyed most of the old houses here, and the main street of Ginza, together with a grid of parallel and cross streets, was rebuilt as a Western quarter. It had two-story brick houses with balconies, the nation's first sidewalks and horse-drawn streetcars, gaslights, and, later, telephone poles. Before the turn of the 20th century, Ginza was already home to the great mercantile establishments that still define its character. The **Wako** depāto, for example, on the northwest corner of the 4-chōme intersection, established itself here as Hattori, purveyors of clocks and watches. The clock on the present building was first installed in the Hattori clock tower, a Ginza landmark, in 1894.

Many of the nearby shops have lineages almost as old, or older, than Wako's. A few steps north of the intersection, on Chūō-dōri, **Mikimoto** (4–5–5 Ginza) sells the famous cultured pearls first developed by Kokichi Mikimoto in 1883. His first shop in Tōkyō dates to 1899. South of the intersection, next door to the Sanai Building, **Kyūkyodō** (5–7–4 Ginza) carries a variety of handmade Japanese papers and related goods. Kyūkyodō has been in business since 1663 and on Ginza since 1880. Across the street and one block south is **Matsuzakaya** depāto, which began as a kimono shop in Nagoya in 1611. Exploring this area—there's even a name for browsing: Gin-bura, or "Ginza wandering"—is best on Sunday from noon to 5 or 6 (depending on the season), when Chūō-dōri is closed to traffic between

Shimbashi and Kyō-bashi. *Subway: Ginza and Hibiya lines, Ginza Eki.*

**63 IDEMITSU BIJUTSUKAN.** With its four spacious rooms, the Idemitsu is one of the largest and best designed private museums in Tōkyō. The strength of the collection lies in its Tang and Song dynasty Chinese porcelain and in Japanese ceramics—including works by Ninsei Nonomura and Kenzan Ōgata, and masterpieces of Old Seto, Oribe, Old Kutani, Karatsu, and Kakiemon ware. The museum also houses an outstanding examples of Zen painting and calligraphy, wood-block prints, and genre paintings of the Edo period. Of special interest to scholars is the resource collection of shards from virtually every pottery-making culture of the ancient world. *3–1–1 Marunouchi, Chiyoda-ku, tel. 03/3213–9402. ¥800. Tues.–Sun. 10–4:30. Subway: Yūraku-chō Line, Yūraku-chō Eki (Exit A1).*

**57 KABUTO JINJA.** This shrine, like the Nihombashi itself, is another bit of history lurking in the shadows of the expressway. Legend has it that a noble warrior of the 11th century, sent by the Imperial Court in Kyōto to subdue the barbarians of the north, stopped here and prayed for assistance. His expedition was successful, and on the way back he buried a *kabuto,* a golden helmet, on this spot as an offering of thanks. Few Japanese are aware of this legend, and the monument of choice in Kabuto-chō today is the nearby Tōkyō Stock Exchange. *1–8 Kabuto-chō, Nihombashi, Chūō-ku. Subway: Tōzai Line, Kayaba-chō Eki (Exit 10).*

**58 KITE MUSEUM.** Kite flying is an old tradition in Japan. The Motegi collection includes examples of every shape and variety from all over the country, hand-painted in brilliant colors with figures of birds, geometric patterns, and motifs from Chinese and Japanese mythology. Call ahead, and the museum will arrange a kite-making workshop (in Japanese) for groups of children. *1–12–10 Nihombashi, Chūō-ku, tel. 03/3271–2465, www.tako.gr.jp. ¥200. Mon.–Sat. (except national holidays) 11–5. Subway: Tōzai Line, Nihombashi Eki (Exit C5).*

**55 MITSUKOSHI.** Takatoshi Mitsui made his fortune by revolutionizing the retail system for kimono fabrics. The drapers of his day usually did business on account, taking payments semiannually. In his store (then called Echigo-ya), Mitsui started the practice of unit pricing, and his customers paid cash on the spot. As time went on, the store was always ready to adapt to changing needs and merchandising styles: garments made to order, home delivery, imported goods, and even—as the 20th century opened and Echigo-ya changed its name to Mitsukoshi—the hiring of women to the sales force. The emergence of Mitsukoshi as Tōkyō's first depāto, also called *hyakkaten* (hundred-kinds-of-goods emporium), actually dates to 1908, with a three-story Western building modeled on Harrods of London. This was replaced in 1914 by a five-story structure with Japan's first escalator. The present flagship store is vintage 1935. *1–4–1 Nihombashi Muro-machi, Chūō-ku, tel. 03/3241–3311. Daily 10–7. Subway: Ginza and Hanzō-mon lines, Mitsukoshi-mae Eki.*

**56 NIHOMBASHI** (Bridge of Japan). Why, back in 1962, the expressway *had* to be routed directly over this lovely old landmark is one of the mysteries of Tōkyō and its city planning—or lack thereof. There were protests and petitions, but they had no effect—planners argued the high cost of alternative locations. At that time Tōkyō had only two years left to prepare for the Olympics, and the traffic congestion was already out of hand. So the bridge, with its graceful double arch and ornate lamps, its bronze Chinese lions and unicorns, was doomed to bear the perpetual rumble of trucks overhead—its claims overruled by concrete ramps and pillars. *Subway: Tōzai and Ginza lines, Nihombashi Eki (Exits B5 and B6); Ginza and Hanzō-mon lines, Mitsukoshi-mae Eki (Exits B5 and B6).*

**54 NIHON GINKŌ** (Bank of Japan). The older part of the Bank of Japan is the work of Tatsuno Kingo, who also designed Tōkyō Eki. Completed in 1896, the bank is one of the very few surviving Meiji-era Western buildings in the city. *2–2–1 Nihombashi Hongoku-chō, Chūō-ku, tel. 03/3279–1111, www.boj.or.jp. Subway: Ginza (Exit A5) and Hanzō-mon (Exit B1) lines, Mitsukoshi-mae Eki.*

**61 SUKIYA-BASHI.** The side streets of the Sukiya-bashi area are full of art galleries, several hundred in fact. The galleries operate a bit differently here than they do in most of the world's art markets: A few, like the venerable **Nichidō** (5–3–16 Ginza), **Gekkōso** (7–2–8 Ginza), **Yoseidō** (5–5–15 Ginza), **Yayoi** (7–6–16 Ginza), and **Kabuto-ya** (8–8–7 Ginza), actually function as dealers, representing particular artists, as well as acquiring and selling art. The majority, however, are rental spaces. Artists or groups pay for the gallery by the week, publicize their shows themselves, and in some cases even hang their own work. It's not unreasonable to suspect that a lot of these shows, even in so prestigious a venue as Ginza, are vanity exhibitions by amateurs with money to spare—but that's not always the case. The rental spaces are also the only way for serious professionals, independent of the various art organizations that might otherwise sponsor their work, to get any critical attention; if they're lucky, they can at least recoup their expenses with an occasional sale. *Subway: Ginza, Hibiya, and Marunouchi lines, Ginza Eki (Exit C4).*

**62 TŌKYŌ INTERNATIONAL FORUM.** This postmodern masterpiece, the work of Uruguay-born American architect Raphael Viñoly, is the first major convention and art center of its kind in Tōkyō. Viñoly's design was selected in a 1989 competition that drew nearly 400 entries from 50 countries. Opened in January 1997, the forum is really two buildings. On the east side of the plaza is Glass Hall, the main exhibition space—an atrium with an 180-ft ceiling, a magnificent curved wooden wall, and 34 upper-floor conference rooms. The west building has six halls for international conferences, exhibitions, receptions, and concert performances— the largest with seating for 5,012.

The **Cultural Information Lobby** (tel. 03/5221–9084), in the west building, has the latest schedules of conventions and events in the forum itself; it also has an English-speaking staff and an excellent audiovisual library on tourist attractions, festivals, and events all over Japan—making this a worthwhile first stop when you come to town. Another useful resource is the information office of the **JNTO** (Japan National Tourist Organization; tel. 03/3201–3331), at the north end of the lower concourse. *3–5–1 Marunouchi, Chiyoda-ku, tel. 03/5221–9000, www.tif.or.jp. Cultural Information Lobby daily 10–6:30; JNTO weekdays 9–5, Sat. 9–noon. Subway: Yūraku-chō Line, Yūraku-chō Eki (Exit A-4B).*

..........................................................................

NEED A  Amid all of Tōkyō's bustle and crush, you actually can catch your
BREAK?  breath in the open space of the plaza of the Tōkyō International Forum. If you also feel like having coffee and a bite of pastry, stop in at **Café Wien,** next to the Plaza Information Center. *3–5–1 Marunouchi, Chiyoda-ku, tel. 03/3211–3111. Daily 9 AM–10 PM. Subway: Yūraku-chō Line, Yūraku-chō Eki (Exit A-4B).*

## AOYAMA, HARAJUKU, AND SHIBUYA

Who would have known? As late as 1960, this was as unlikely a candidate as any area in Tōkyō to develop into anything remotely chic. True, there was the Meiji Jingū, which gave the neighborhood a certain solemnity and drew the occasional festival crowd. Between the Shrine and the Aoyama Cemetery to the east, however, the area was so unpromising that the municipal government designated a substantial chunk of it for low-cost public housing. Another chunk, called Washington Heights, was being used by U.S. occupation forces—who spent their money elsewhere. The few young Japanese people in Harajuku and Aoyama were either hanging around Washington Heights to practice their English or attending the Methodist-founded Aoyama Gakuin (Aoyama University)—and seeking their leisure farther south in Shibuya.

Then Tōkyō won its bid to host the 1964 Olympics, and Washington Heights was turned over to the city for the construction of the Olympic Village. Aoyama-dōri, the avenue through the center of the area, was improved; under it ran the extension of the Ginza Line subway, and later the Hanzō-mon Line. Public transportation is the chief ingredient in Tōkyō's commercial alchemy; suddenly, people could get to Aoyama and Harajuku easily, and they did—in larger and larger numbers, drawn by the Western-style fashion houses, boutiques, and design studios that decided this was the place to be. By the 1980s the area was positively smart. Two decades have passed since then, and parts of the area have gone a bit downhill, but it should still be high on your list of places to explore in Tōkyō.

On weekends the heart of Harajuku belongs to high school and junior high school shoppers, who flock here with hoarded sums of pocket money and for whom last week was ancient history. Harajuku is where the market researchers come, pick 20 teenagers off the street at random, give them ¥2,000, and ask them to buy a tote bag. Whole industries convulse themselves to keep pace with those adolescent decisions. Stroll through Harajuku—with its outdoor cafés, its designer ice cream and Belgian waffle stands, its ever-changing profusion of mascots and logos—and you may find it impossible to believe that Japan is in fact the most rapidly aging society in the industrial world.

Shibuya is south and west of Harajuku and Aoyama. Two subway lines, three private railways, the JR Yamanote Line, and two bus terminals move about a million people a day through Shibuya. The hub's commercial character is shaped by the fierce battle for supremacy between the Seibu and Tōkyū depāto. As fast as one of them builds a new branch, vertical mall, or specialty store, its rival counters with another. Shops, restaurants, and amusements in this area target a population of university students, young office workers, and consumers younger still.

*Numbers in the text correspond to numbers in the margin and on the Aoyama, Harajuku, and Shibuya map.*

## A Good Walk

For more information on depāto and individual shops mentioned in this walk, see Shopping, below.

### AOYAMA

Begin outside of the Gaien-mae subway station on Aoyama-dōri. This is also the stop for the Jingū Baseball Stadium, home field of the Yakult Swallows. You'll see it across the street from the Chichibu-no-miya Rugby and Football Ground. The stadium is actually within the **Meiji Jingū Gai-en** ⑥⑤ (Outer Garden). The National Stadium—Japan's largest stadium, with room for 75,000 people, and the seat from which the city hosted the 1964 Summer Olympics—sits on the other side of this park.

From Gaien-mae, continue west some five blocks toward Shibuya, and turn left at the intersection where you see the Omotesandō subway station on the right-hand side of the avenue. Hold tight to your credit cards here: This is the east end of Omotesandō, Tōkyō's premier fashion boulevard, lined on both sides with the boutiques of couturiers like Issey Miyake, Missoni, Calvin Klein, and Comme des Garçons. At the far end of the street (a 15-minute walk at a brisk pace), across the intersection to the right, you'll see the walls of the **Nezu Institute of Fine Arts** ⑥⑥.

From the Nezu Institute of Fine Arts, retrace your steps to Aoyama-dōri. If you turned left here, you would come in due course (it's a longish walk) to Shibuya, by way of the Aoyama Gakuin University campus on the left. **Aoyama Kodomo-no-Shiro** ⑥⑦, for the child with you (or in you), is also to the left on Aoyama-dōri. To make your way to Harajuku, continue straight across Aoyama-dōri northwest on Omotesandō.

### HARAJUKU

On the north side of Aoyama-dōri, Omotesandō becomes a broad divided boulevard lined with ginko trees, sloping gently downhill—and down-market—to the intersection of Meiji-dōri.

# aoyama, harajuku, and shibuya

**KEY**

| | |
|---|---|
| —— | JR Trains |
| ══ | Subway |
| ┼┼┼ | Private rail line |

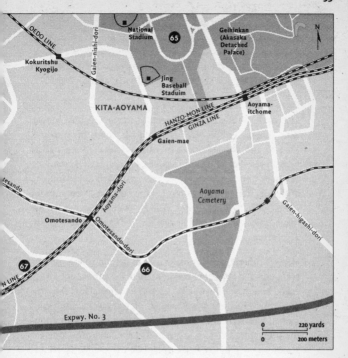

True, a few conservative fashion houses dot the west boulevard, like Mori Hanae and Ralph Lauren. But the pulse of Harajuku beats at the rate of the adolescents who—with less to spend, perhaps, than a couturier's clientele—still take their apprenticeship as consumers very seriously indeed.

On the left side of the boulevard as you approach the Meiji-dōri intersection is the Oriental Bazaar, a store especially popular with foreign visitors for its extensive stock of Japanese, Korean, and Chinese souvenirs at reasonable prices; browse here for scroll paintings and screens, kimono fabrics, antiques, ceramics, and lacquerware. A few doors down is Kiddyland, one of the city's largest toy stores. On the northwest corner of the intersection itself is La Foret. With some 110 boutiques on five floors, this was one of the earliest of Tōkyō's characteristic vertical malls.

Here you might want to make a brief detour, to the right on Meiji-dōri and left at the corner of the third narrow side street, called Takeshita-dōri, which rises to JR Harajuku Eki at the other end. This is where the youngest of Harajuku's consumers gather, from all over Tōkyō and the nearby prefectures, packing the street from side to side and end to end, filling the coffers of stores with names like Rap City and Octopus Army. If Japanese parents ever pause to wonder where their offspring might be on a Saturday afternoon, Takeshita-dōri is the likely answer.

Retrace your steps to La Foret, turn right, and walk uphill on the right side of Omotesandō to the first corner. Turn right again, and a few steps from the corner on this small street you'll find the **Ōta Kinen Bijutsukan** ⑥⑧—an unlikely setting for an important collection of traditional wood-block prints. Return to Omotesandō and walk up to the intersection at the top. Across the street to your right look for JR Harajuku Eki; straight ahead is the entrance to the Meiji Jingū Inner Garden and the **Meiji Jingū** ⑥⑨ itself.

When you have finished exploring the grounds of the shrine, you have two options. You can leave the Inner Garden on the northwest side and walk west about five minutes from Sangū-bashi Eki on the private Odakyū railway line to the **Tōken Hakubutsukan** ⑦ to see its collection of swords. From there you can return to Sangū-bashi Eki and take the train two stops north to Shinjuku, the next major exploring section. The other possibility is to return to Harajuku Eki and take the JR Yamanote Line one stop south to Shibuya.

## SHIBUYA

Begin your exploration of this area at JR Shibuya Eki.; use the **Statue of Hachiko** ⑦, in the plaza on the north side of the station, as a starting point. Cross the intersection and walk southwest on Dōgen-zaka. In a minute the street will fork at a vertical mall called the 109 Fashion Community; bear right on Bunka-mura-dōri and walk about four blocks to where the street suddenly narrows. Ahead of you will be the main branch of the Tōkyū depāto chain. Cross to the entrance and turn left to the **Bunka-mura** ⑦ complex of theaters, exhibition halls, shops, and restaurants on the next corner. Les Deux Magots, in the sunken courtyard of the complex is a good place for a light meal.

Return to Bunka-mura-dōri and walk back toward Shibuya station on the left side of the street to the second corner. Turn left at the first traffic light and walk north, crossing Sentā-gai, a street lined with fast-food shops, down-market clothing stores, and game centers, to Inogashira-dōri. Ahead of you, across the street, will be the entrance to Supein-dōri, the heart of Shibuya's appeal to young consumers: a narrow brick-paved passageway, climbing to a flight of steps at the other end, supposedly inspired by the Spanish Steps in Rome. Spain-dōri leads to Kōen-dōri, the smartest street in the neighborhood, by way of Parco (on the left), a vertical mall developed by the Seibu depāto conglomerate. The Parco Theater, on the top floor, has an interesting calendar of plays and art films. Farther up Kōen-dōri, on the right, is the **Tobako to Shio Hakubutsukan** ⑦, an interesting paean of sorts to the uses of tobacco and salt.

Turn left at the top of Kōen-dōri, and you'll see the **NHK Broadcasting Center** ⑦ across the street on your right. The building next to it, at the far north corner, is the 4,000-seat NHK Hall, the pride of which is a 7,640-pipe organ, the foremost of its kind in the world. West of the NHK Hall, across the street, is the **National Yoyogi Sports Center** ⑦. From here you can finish off Shibuya in either of two ways: Retrace your steps to JR Shibuya Eki, or walk through **Yoyogi Kōen** ⑦ along the extension of Omotesandō to Harajuku and the JR station there.

## TIMING

Aoyama and Harajuku together make a long walk, with considerable distances between the sights. Ideally, you should devote an entire day to it, giving yourself plenty of time to browse in shops. You can see Meiji Jingū in less than an hour; the Nezu Institute warrants a leisurely two-hour visit. Don't be afraid to come on weekends; there are more people on the streets, of course, but people-watching is a large part of the experience of Harajuku. Spring is the best time of year for the Meiji Inner Garden; as with any other walk in Tōkyō, the June rainy season is horrendous, and the humid heat of midsummer can quickly drain your energy and add hours to the time you need for a comfortable walk.

Shibuya is fairly compact; you can easily cover it in about two hours. Unless you switch into shopping mode, no particular stop along the way should occupy you for more than half an hour; allow a full hour for the NHK Broadcasting Center, however, if you decide to take the guided tour. Spring is the best time of year for Yoyogi Kōen, and Sunday the best day. The area will be crowded, of course, but Sunday affords the best opportunity to observe Japan's younger generation on display.

# What to See

⊙ 67 **AOYAMA KODOMO-NO-SHIRO** (National Children's Castle). This complex includes a swimming pool, a gym, and an audiovisual library. The 1,200-seat theater presents a range of concerts, plays, and other performances regularly throughout the year, especially for kids. At the Omotesandō subway station on the Ginza, Hanzō-mon, and Chiyoda lines, take the exit for Aoyama Gakuin and walk southwest on Aoyama-dōri about five minutes. Aoyama Kodomo-no-Shiro is on the right side of the avenue. 5–53–1 Jingū-mae, Shibuya-ku, tel. 03/3797–5666. ¥500. Tues.–Fri. 12:30–5, weekends 10–5. Subway: Omotesandō Eki (Exit B2).

72 **BUNKA-MURA.** This six-story theater and gallery complex is a venture of the next-door Tōkyū depāto and one of the liveliest venues in Tōkyō for music and art, hosting everything from science-fiction film festivals to opera, from ballet to big bands. The design of the building would be impressive if there were any vantage point from which to see it whole. The museum on the lower-level Garden Floor often has well-planned, interesting exhibits on loan from major European museums. 2–2–4–1 Dōgen-zaka, Shibuya-ku, tel. 03/3477–9111; 03/3477–9999 for ticket center. Theater admission and exhibit prices vary with events. Ticket counter in lobby open daily 10–7. Subway, JR, and private rail lines: Shibuya Eki (Kita-guchi/North Exit for JR Yamanote Line, Ginza subway line, and private rail lines; Exits 5 and 8 for Hanzō-mon subway line).

NEED A
BREAK?
**Les Deux Magots,** sister of the famed Paris café, in the Bunka-mura complex, serves a good selection of beers and wines, sandwiches, salads, quiches, tarts, and coffee. There's a fine art bookstore next door, and the tables in the courtyard are perfect for people-watching. Bunka-mura, lower courtyard, 2–24–1 Dōgen-zaka, Shibuya-ku, tel. 03/3477–9124. Subway, JR, and private rail lines: Shibuya (Kita-guchi/North Exit for JR Yamanote Line, Ginza subway line, and private rail lines; Exits 5 and 8 for Hanzō-mon subway line).

**69 MEIJI JINGŪ.** The Meiji shrine honors the spirits of the emperor Meiji, who died in 1912, and the empress Shōken. It was established by a resolution of the Imperial Diet the year after the emperor's death to commemorate his role in ending the long isolation of Japan under the Tokugawa Shogunate and setting the country on the road to modernization. Completed in 1920 and virtually destroyed in an air raid in 1945, it was rebuilt in 1958 with funds raised in a nationwide public subscription.

The two torii at the entrance to the grounds of the jingū, made from 1,700-year-old cypress trees from Mt. Ari in Taiwan, tower 40 ft high; the crosspieces are 56 ft long. Torii are meant to symbolize the separation of the everyday secular world from the spiritual world of the Shintō shrine. The buildings in the shrine complex, with their curving green copper roofs, are also made of cypress wood. The surrounding gardens have some 100,000 flowering shrubs and trees, many of which were donated by private citizens.

The annual festival at Meiji Jingū takes place on November 3, the emperor's birthday, which is a national holiday. On the festival day and at New Year's, as many as a million people come to offer prayers and pay their respects. A variety of other festivals and ceremonial events are held at Meiji Jingū throughout the year; check by phone or on the shrine Web site to see what's scheduled during your visit. Even on a normal weekend the shrine draws thousands of visitors, but this seldom disturbs its mood of quiet gravitas: the faster and more unpredictable the pace of modern life, the more respectable the Japanese seem to find the certainties of the Meiji era.

The **Jingū Nai-en** (Inner Garden), where the irises are in full bloom in the latter half of June, is on the left as you walk in from the main gates, before you reach the shrine. Beyond the shrine is the **Treasure House,** a repository for the personal effects and clothes of Emperor and Empress Meiji—perhaps of less interest to gaijin than to the Japanese. 1–1 *Kamizono-chō, Yoyogi, Shibuya-*

*ku, tel. 03/3379–5511, www.meijijingu.or.jp. Shrine free, Treasure House ¥500, Inner Garden ¥500. Shrine daily sunrise–sunset. Inner Garden Mar.–Oct., daily 9–4:30; Nov.–Feb., daily 9–4. Treasure House daily 10–4 (closed 3rd Fri. of month). Subway: Chiyoda Line, Meiji-jingū-mae Eki; JR Yamanote Line, Harajuku Eki (Exit 2).*

**65 MEIJI JINGŪ GAI-EN** (Meiji Outer Garden). This park is little more than the sum of its parts. The Yakult Swallows play at **Jingū Baseball Stadium** (13 Kasumigaoka, Shinjuku-ku, tel. 03/3404–8999); the Japanese baseball season runs between April and October. The **National Stadium** (10 Kasumigaoka, Shinjuku-ku, tel. 03/3403–1151) was the main venue of the 1964 Summer Olympics and now hosts soccer matches. Some World Cup matches will be played here when Japan cohosts the event with Korea in autumn 2002. and East across the street from the National Stadium is the **Kaigakan** (Meiji Memorial Picture Gallery; 9 Kasumigaoka, Shinjuku-ku, tel. 03/3401–5179), open daily 9–4:30 (¥500), which you needn't plan to see unless you are a particular fan of the emperor Meiji and don't want to miss some 80 otherwise undistinguished paintings depicting events in his life. *Subway: Ginza and Hanzō-mon lines, Gai-en-mae Eki (Exit 2); JR Chūō Line, Shina-no-machi Eki.*

**75 NATIONAL YOYOGI SPORTS CENTER.** The center consists of two paired structures created by Kenzō Tange for the 1964 Olympics. Tange's design, of flowing ferroconcrete shell structures and cable-and-steel suspension roofing, successfully fuses traditional and modern Japanese aesthetics. The stadium, which can accommodate 15,000 spectators for swimming and diving events, and the annex, which houses a basketball court with a seating capacity of 4,000, are open to visitors when there are no competitions. *2–1–1 Jinnan, Shibuya-ku, tel. 03/3468–1171. Pool ¥550. Daily noon–4. JR Yamanote Line, Harajuku Eki (Exit 2).*

★ **66 NEZU INSTITUTE OF FINE ARTS.** This museum houses the private art collection of Meiji-period railroad magnate and politician Kaichirō Nezu. The permanent display in the main building (1955) and the annex (1990) includes superb examples of Japanese painting, calligraphy, and ceramics—some of which are registered as National Treasures—and Chinese bronzes, sculpture, and lacquerware. The institute also has one of Tōkyō's finest gardens, with more than 5 acres of shade trees and flowering shrubs, ponds, and waterfalls, and seven tea pavilions. Walk southeast on Omotesandō-dōri from the intersection of Aoyama-dōri about 10 minutes, where the street curves away to the left. The Nezu Institute is opposite the intersection, on the right, behind a low sandstone-gray wall. 6–5–1 Minami-Aoyama, Minato-ku, tel. 03/ 3400–2536, www.nezu-muse.or.jp/index_e.html. ¥1,000. Tues.–Sun. 9–4. Subway: Ginza and Hanzō-mon lines, Omotesandō Eki (Exit A5).

---

**NEED A BREAK?** How can you resist a café with a name like **Yoku Moku**? As you approach, you'll probably notice a steady stream of very smartly dressed young people on their way in and out. Tables alfresco in the tree-shaded courtyard continue to make Yoku Moku, which established itself as Japan's primo confectionery just after World War II, an Aoyama favorite. Its blue-tile front is on Omotesandō-dōri near the Nezu Institute. The café is open daily 10:30–6. 5–3–3 Minami-Aoyama, Shibuya-ku, tel. 03/5485–3340. Subway: Ginza, Chiyoda, and Hanzō-mon lines, Omotesandō Eki (Exit A4).

---

⓻ **NHK BROADCASTING CENTER.** The 23-story Japanese National Public Television facility was built as the Olympic Information Center in 1964. NHK (Nippon Hōsō Kyōkai) runs a "Studio Park" tour, in Japanese only, in the main building, during which you can see the latest developments in broadcast technology. The center is a 15-minute walk on Kōen-dōri from JR Shibuya Eki. 2–2–1 Jinnan, Shibuya-ku, tel. 03/3465–1111. ¥200. Daily 10–5. Closed 3rd Mon. of month, except Aug.

★ ⓺ **ŌTA KINEN BIJUTSUKAN** (Ōta Memorial Museum of Art). The gift of former Tōhō Mutual Life Insurance chairman Seizō Ōta, this is probably the city's finest private collection of ukiyo-e, traditional ·

Edo-period wood-block prints. The works on display are selected and changed periodically from the 12,000 prints in the collection, which includes some extremely rare work by artists such as Hiroshige, Sharaku, and Utamaro. From JR Harajuku Eki, walk southwest downhill on Omotesandō-dōri and turn left on the narrow street before the intersection of Meiji-dōri. The museum is less than a minute's walk from the corner, on the left. *1–10–10 Jingū-mae, Shibuya-ku, tel. 03/3403–0880. ¥500, special exhibitions ¥800. Tues.–Sun. 10:30–5. Closed from 1st to 4th of each month for new installations.*

**71 STATUE OF HACHIKO.** The subject of at least one three-hanky motion picture, Hachiko is Japan's version of the archetypal faithful dog. Hachiko's master, a professor at the University of Tōkyō, would take the dog with him every morning as far as Shibuya Eki on his way to work, and Hachiko would go back to the station every evening to greet him on his return. One day in 1925 the professor failed to appear; he had died that day of a stroke. Every evening for the next seven years, Hachiko would go to Shibuya and wait there hopefully until the last train had pulled out of the station. Then the dog died, too, and his story made the newspapers. A handsome bronze statute of Hachiko was installed in front of the station, funded by thousands of small donations from readers all over the country. The present version is a replica; the original was melted down for its metal in World War II—but it remains a familiar landmark where younger people, especially, arrange to meet. *JR Shibuya Eki, West Plaza.*

**73 TOBAKO TO SHIO HAKUBUTSUKAN** (Tobacco and Salt Museum). A museum that displays examples of every conceivable artifact associated with tobacco and salt since the days of the Maya might not seem, at first, to serve a compelling social need, but the existence of the T&S reflects one of the more interesting facts of Japanese political life. Tobacco and salt were both made government monopolies at the beginning of the 20th century. Sales and distribution were eventually liberalized, but production remained under exclusive state control, through the Japan Tobacco and Salt Public Corporation, until 1985. The corporation was then privatized. Renamed Nihon Tabako Sangyō (Japan Tobacco, Inc.), it continues to provide comfortable, well-paying second careers—called *amakudari* (literally, "descent from Heaven")—for retired public officials. It remains Japan's exclusive producer of cigarettes, still holds a monopoly on the sale of salt, and dabbles in real estate, gardening supplies, and pharmaceuticals—ringing up sales of some $17 billion a year. Japan Tobacco, Inc., in short, has more money than it knows what to do with: so why not put up a museum? What makes this museum noteworthy is the special exhibit on the fourth floor of ukiyo-e on the themes of smoking and traditional salt production. T&S is a 10-minute walk on Kōen-dōri from Shibuya Eki. *1–16–8 Jinnan, Shibuya-ku, tel. 03/3476–2041, www.jtnet.ad.jp. ¥100. Tues.–Sun. 10–5:30. Subway, JR, and private rail lines: Shibuya Eki (Kita-guchi/North Exit).*

**⑳ TŌKEN HAKUBUTSUKAN** (Japanese Sword Museum). It's said that in the late 16th century, before Japan closed its doors to the West, the Spanish tried to establish a trade here in weapons of their famous Toledo steel. The Japanese were politely uninterested; they had already been making blades of incomparably better quality for more than 600 years. Early Japanese sword smiths learned the art of refining steel from a pure iron sand called *tamahagane*, carefully controlling the carbon content by adding straw to the fire in the forge. The block of steel was repeatedly folded, hammered, and cross-welded to an extraordinary strength, then "wrapped" around a core of softer steel for flexibility. At one time there were some 200 schools of sword making in Japan; swords were prized not only for their effectiveness in battle but for the beauty of the blades and fittings and as symbols of the higher spirituality of the warrior caste. There are few inheritors of this art today. The Japanese Sword Museum offers a unique opportunity to see the works of noted sword smiths, ancient and modern—but don't expect any detailed explanations of them in

English. *4–25–10, Yoyogi, Shibuya-ku, tel. 03/3379–1386. ¥525. Tues.–Sun. 9–4. Odakyū private rail line, Sangū-bashi Eki.*

**76 YOYOGI KŌEN.** Once a parade ground for the Imperial Japanese Army, this area was known in the immediate postwar period—when it was appropriated by the occupying forces for military housing—as Washington Heights. During the Tōkyō Games of 1964, it served as the site of the Olympic Village, and in 1967 it became a public park. On Sunday and holidays, a flea market takes place in the park, along the main thoroughfare that runs through it, opposite the National Yoyogi Sports Center. *Jinnan 2-chōme. Subway: Chiyoda Line, Meiji Jingū-mae Eki (Exit 2); JR Yamanote Line, Harajuku Eki (Omotesandō exit).*

## SHINJUKU

If you have a certain sort of love for big cities, you're bound to love Shinjuku. Come here, and for the first time Tōkyō begins to seem *real*. Shinjuku is where all the celebrated virtues of Japanese society—its safety and order, its grace and beauty, its cleanliness and civility—fray at the edges.

To be fair about all this, the area has been at the fringes of respectability for centuries. When Ieyasu, the first Tokugawa shōgun, made Edo his capital, Shinjuku was at the junction of two important arteries leading into the city from the west. It became a thriving post station, where travelers would rest and refresh themselves for the last leg of their journey; the appeal of this suburban pit stop was its "teahouses," where the waitresses dispensed a good bit more than sympathy with the tea.

When the Tokugawa dynasty collapsed in 1868, the 16-year-old emperor Meiji moved his capital to Edo, renaming it Tōkyō, and modern Shinjuku became the railhead connecting it to Japan's western provinces. As the haunt of artists, writers, and students, it remained on the fringes of respectability; in the 1930s Shinjuku was Tōkyō's bohemian quarter. The area was virtually leveled during the firebombings of 1945—a blank slate on which developers could write, as Tōkyō surged west after the war. By the 1970s property values in Shinjuku were the nation's highest, outstripping even those of Ginza. Three subways and seven railway lines converge here. Every day more than 3 million commuters pass through Shinjuku Eki, making this the city's busiest and most heavily populated commercial center. The hub at Shinjuku—a vast, interconnected complex of tracks and terminals, depāto and shops—divides that property into two distinctly different subcities, Nishi-Shinjuku (West Shinjuku) and Higashi-Shinjuku (East Shinjuku).

After the Great Kantō Earthquake of 1923, Nishi-Shinjuku was virtually the only part of Tōkyō left standing; the whims of nature had given this one small area a gift of better bedrock. That priceless geological stability remained largely unexploited until the late 1960s, when technological advances in engineering gave architects the freedom to soar. Some 20 skyscrapers have been built here since then, including the Tōkyō Tochō complex, and Nishi-Shinjuku has become Tōkyō's 21st-century administrative center.

By day the quarter east of Shinjuku Eki is an astonishing concentration of retail stores, vertical malls, and discounters of every stripe and description. By night it is an equally astonishing collection of bars and clubs, strip joints, hole-in-the-wall restaurants, pinball parlors, and peep shows—just about anything that amuses, arouses, alters, or intoxicates is for sale in Higashi-Shinjuku, if you know where to look. Drunken fistfights are hardly unusual here; petty theft is not unknown. Not surprisingly, Higashi-Shinjuku has the city's largest—and busiest—police substation.

*Numbers in the text correspond to numbers in the margin and on the Shinjuku map.*

# A Good Walk

## NISHI-SHINJUKU

JR trains and subways will drop you off belowground at Shinjuku Eki; head for the west exit. You'll need to get up to the street level, in front of the Odakyū depāto, with the Keiō depāto on your left, to avoid the passageway under the plaza. Walk across the plaza, through the bus terminal, or take the pedestrian bridge on the north side. Traffic in front of the station is rather confusing—what you're looking for is the wide divided avenue on the other side, called Chūō-dōri (YON-GŌ GAIRO on some street markers) between the Fuji Bank on the left and the Dai-ichi Kangyō Bank on the right. Walk west on Chūō-dōri one block to the Shinjuku Center Building, cross at the traffic light, and turn right. In the next block is the tapering shape of the Yasuda Fire and Marine Insurance Building; the **Seiji Tōgō Museum** ⑦ is on the 42nd floor.

Retrace your steps to Chūō-dōri, turn right, and walk west to where the avenue dead-ends at Kyū-gō Gairo, also called Higashi-dōri. You'll see the 52-story Shinjuku Sumitomo Building, ahead of you to the right, and to the left the unmistakable shape of the Tōkyō Tochō complex—but you'll need to make a slight detour to reach it. Cross Kyū-gō Gairo, turn left, and walk south past the front of the Keiō Plaza Inter-Continental, the first of the high-rise hotels to be built in the area, to the next corner.

Across the street you'll see the blue phallic shape of the sculpture in front of the Shinjuku Monolith Building. Turn right and walk downhill on Fureai-dōri. In the middle of this next block, on the left, is the Shinjuku NS Building. Opposite the NS Building, to the right, are the steps to the Citizens' Plaza of the adored and reviled **Tōkyō Tochō** ⑱.

From here you have two options. You can turn east and walk back along any of the streets parallel to Chūō-dōri that return

# shinjuku

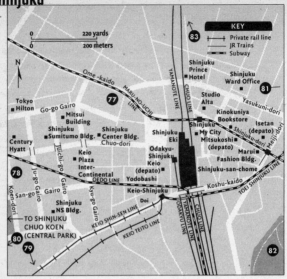

**KEY**
┤├ Private rail line
── JR Trains
▬▬ Subway

220 yards
200 meters
N

Ome-kaido
MARU-NO-UCHI LINE
YAMANOTE LINE
CHUO LINE

(83)
(81)
(77)
(78)
(80)
(79)
(82)

Shinjuku Prince Hotel
Shinjuku Ward Office
Studio Alta
Yasukuni-dori
Kinokuniya Bookstore
Isetan (depato)
Shinjuku-dori
Meiji-dori
Tokyo Hilton
Go-go Gairo
Mitsui Building
Shinjuku Sumitumo Bldg.
Shinjuku Center Bldg.
Chuo-dori
Shinjuku Eki
My City
Shinjuku
Mitsukoshi (depato)
Century Hyatt
Ju-ichi-go Gairo
Keio Plaza Inter-Continental
OEDO LINE
Odakyu-Shinjuku
Keio (depato)
Yodobashi
Marui
Fashion Bldg.
Shinjuku-san-chome
Ju-go Gairo
Koshu-kaido
TOEI SHINJUKU LINE
koen-dori
San-go Gairo
Kyu-go Gairo
Shinjuku NS Bldg.
Keio-Shinjuku
Doi
KEIO SHIN-SEN LINE
KEIO TEITO LINE
YAMANOTE LINE
ODAKYU LINE
CHUO LINE
TO SHINJUKU CHUO KOEN (CENTRAL PARK)

you to Shinjuku Eki. You may want to stop (especially if you haven't included Akihabara on your Tōkyō itinerary) at one of the giant discount electronics stores in the area—Yodobashi and Doi are a block from the station—to get an eye- or bagful of the latest gadgets that Japan is churning out.

Or if you have energy to spare, leave the Tōkyō Tochō complex the way you came in, turn right, and walk west to Kōen-dōri, which runs along the east side of Shinjuku Chūō Kōen. Cross Kōen-dōri, turn left, and walk south about five minutes, past the end of the park (avoiding the expressway on-ramp), to the **Shinjuku Park Tower Building** ⑦⑨, at the corner of the Kōshū Kaidō (Kōshū Highway). The Park Hyatt, on the topmost floors of this building, is a good place to stop for lunch or high tea.

From the intersection turn right and walk about five minutes southwest on the Kōshū Kaidō to the **Tōkyō Opera City** ⑧⓪. There's an entrance to the Hatsudai subway station on the west side of the courtyard. Stop in at the Tower Building and see the architecture of the performance spaces of the Shin Kokuritsu Gekijō complex, and then ride the Keiō Shin-sen Line one stop back to Shinjuku Eki.

## HIGASHI-SHINJUKU

From the east exit of Shinjuku Eki, you can't miss the huge video screen on the facade of Studio Alta. Under this building begins Subnade—the most extensive underground arcade in Tōkyō, full of shops and restaurants. Studio Alta is at the northwest end of Shinjuku-dōri, which on Sunday, when the area is closed to traffic, becomes a sea of shoppers. Turn right, and as you walk southeast, Kinokuniya Bookstore looms up on your left; the sixth floor is devoted to foreign-language books, including some 40,000 titles in English. On the next block, on the same side of the street, is Isetan depāto, with a foreign customer-service counter on the fifth floor. Mitsukoshi depāto and the Marui Fashion Building are on the opposite side of Shinjuk-dōri.

At the Isetan corner, turn left onto Meiji-dōri and walk north. Cross Yasukuni-dōri, and another minute will bring you to **Hanazono Jinja** ⑧. From here you can take two different directions—indeed, to two different worlds. You can retrace your steps to Isetan depāto and the Shinjuku-san-chōme subway station, and take the Marunouchi Line one stop east to Shinjuku-Gyo-en-mae, a few steps from the north end of **Shinjuku Gyo-en National Garden** ⑧. Visit the gardens and take the subway back to Shinjuku Eki. Another option is to walk back from Hanazono Jinja as far as Yasukuni-dōri and take a right. Two blocks farther on is the south end of rough-and-tumble **Kabuki-chō** ⑧, and from here you can easily return to Shinjuku Eki on foot.

If you'd like to finish the day with a kaiseki or bentō box meal, head for Yaozen, on the 14th floor of Takashimaya Times Square.

### TIMING

Plan at least a full day for Shinjuku, if you want to see both the east and west sides. Subway rides can save you time and energy on the longer versions of these walks, but walking distances are still considerable. The Shinjuku Gyo-en National Garden is worth at least an hour, especially if you come in early April, in *sakura* (cherry blossom) time. The Tōkyō Tochō complex can take longer than you'd expect; lines for the elevators to the observation decks are often excruciatingly long. Sunday, when shopping streets are closed to traffic, makes the best day to tramp around Higashi-Shinjuku; the rainy season in late June and the sweltering heat of August are best avoided.

## What to See

⑧ **HANAZONO JINJA.** Constructed in the early Edo period, Hanazono is not among Tōkyō's most imposing shrines, but it does have one of the longest histories. Chief among the deities enshrined here is Yamatotakeru-no-Mikoto, a legendary hero, supposedly a 4th-century imperial prince, whose exploits are recounted in the earliest Japanese mythologies. His fame rests on the conquest of aboriginal tribes, which he did at the bidding of the Yamato Court. When he died, legends say, his soul took the form of a swan and flew away. Prayers offered here are believed to bring prosperity in business. The shrine is a five-minute walk north on Meiji-dōri from the Shinjuku-san-chōme subway station. *5–17–3 Shinjuku, Shinjuku-ku, tel. 03/3200–3093. Free. Daily sunrise–sunset. Subway: Marunouchi Line, Shinjuku-san-chōme Eki (Exits B2 and B3).*

**(83) KABUKI-CHŌ.** In 1872 the Tokugawa-period formalities governing geisha entertainment were dissolved, and Kabuki-chō became Japan's largest center of prostitution. Later, when vice laws got stricter, prostitution just went a bit further underground, where it remains—deeply deplored and widely tolerated.

In an attempt to change the area's image after World War II, plans were made to replace Ginza's fire-gutted Kabuki-za with a new one in Shinjuku. The plans never came to fruition—the old theater was rebuilt. But the project gave the area its present name. Kabuki-chō's own multipurpose theater is the 2,000-seat **Koma Gekijō** (1–19–1 Kabuki-chō, Shinjuku-ku). The building, which also houses several discos and bars, serves as a central landmark for the quarter.

Kabuki-chō means unrefined nightlife at its best and raunchy seediness at its worst. Neon signs flash; shills proclaim the pleasures of the places you particularly want to shun. Even when a place looks respectable, ask prices first—drinks can cost ¥5,000 or more in hostess clubs—and avoid the cheap *nomiya* (bars) under the railway tracks. All that said, you needn't be intimidated by the area: it *can* be fun, and it remains one of the least expensive areas of Tōkyō for nightlife. *JR Shinjuku Eki (Higashi-guchi/East Exit for JR lines; Exit B10, B11, B12, or B13 for Marunouchi Line).*

**77** **SEIJI TŌGŌ MUSEUM.** The painter Seiji Tōgō (1897–1978) was a master of putting on canvas the grace and charm of young maidens. More than 100 of his works from the museum collection are on display here at any given time. This is also the museum that bought Van Gogh's *Sunflowers.* Yasuda CEO Yasuo Gotō acquired the painting in 1987 for ¥5.3 billion—at the time the highest price ever paid at auction for a work of art. He later created considerable stir in the media with the ill-considered remark that he'd like the painting cremated with him when he died. The gallery has an especially good view of the old part of Shinjuku. *Yasuda Fire and Marine Insurance Bldg., 42nd floor, 1–26–1 Nishi-Shinjuku, Shinjuku-ku, tel. 03/3349–3081, www.yasuda.co.jp/ museum/museum_title_e.html. Varies depending on exhibit. Tues.–Thurs. and weekends 9:30–4:30, Fri. 9:30–6:30. Marunouchi and Toei Shinjuku subway lines (Exit A18), JR, Keiō Shin-sen and Teitō private rail lines: Shinjuku Eki (Nishi-guchi/West Exit or Exit N4 from the underground passageway).*

★ **82** **SHINJUKU GYO-EN NATIONAL GARDEN.** This lovely 150-acre park was once the estate of the powerful Naitō family of feudal lords, who were among the most trusted retainers of the Tokugawa shōguns. In 1871, after the Meiji Restoration, the family gave the grounds to the government, which—not quite ready yet to put such gems at the disposal of ordinary people—made it an imperial property. After World War II, the grounds were finally opened to the public. It's a perfect place for leisurely walks: paths wind their way through more than 3,000 kinds of plants, shrubs, and trees; artificial hills; ponds and bridges; and thoughtfully placed stone lanterns. There are different gardens in Japanese, French, and English styles as well as a greenhouse (the nation's first, built in 1885) filled with tropical plants. The best times to visit are April, when 75 different species of cherry trees—some 1,500 trees in all—are in bloom, and the first two weeks of October, during the chrysanthemum exhibition. *11 Naitō-chō, Shinjuku-ku, tel. 03/3350–0151. ¥200. Tues.–Sun. 9–4; also open Mon. 9–4 in Apr.*

*cherry-blossom season. Subway: Marunouchi Line, Shinjuku Gyo-en-mae Eki (Exit 1).*

**㊉ SHINJUKU PARK TOWER BUILDING.** The Shinjuku Park Tower has in some ways the most arrogant, hard-edged design of any of the skyscrapers in Nishi-Shinjuku, but it does provide any number of opportunities to rest and take on fuel. You might have picked a day, for example, when there's a free chamber-music concert in the atrium. Or you might have come for lunch at **Kushinobo** (tel. 03/5322–6400), on the lower level, for delicately deep-fried bamboo skewers of fish and vegetables. You might want simply to have an evening drink at the **Cafe Excelsior** (tel. 03/5322–6174). Or if you're here in the afternoon, indulge yourself and ride up to the skylighted bamboo garden of the Peak Lounge on the 41st floor of the **Park Hyatt Hotel** (tel. 03/5322–1234) for high tea and a spectacular view of the city. *3–7–1 Nishi-Shinjuku, Shinjuku-ku. JR Shinjuku Eki (Nishi-guchi/West Exit).*

**★ ㊈ TŌKYŌ TOCHŌ** (Tōkyō Metropolitan Government Office). Work on architect Kenzō Tange's grandiose city hall complex, which now dominates the western Shinjuku skyline, began in 1988 and was completed in 1991. Built at a cost of ¥157 billion, it was clearly meant to remind observers that Tōkyō's annual budget is bigger than that of the average developing country. The complex consists of a main office building, an annex, the Metropolitan Assembly building, and a huge central courtyard, often the venue of open-air concerts and exhibitions. The design has inspired a passionate controversy: Tōkyōites either love it or hate it. It's been called everything from a "fitting tribute" to a "forbidding castle." The main building soars 48 stories, splitting on the 33rd floor into two towers. On a clear day, from the observation decks on the 45th floors of both towers, you can see all the way to Mt. Fuji and to the Bōsō Peninsula in Chiba Prefecture. Several other skyscrapers in the area have free observation floors—among them the Shinjuku Center Building, the Shinjuku Nomura Building, and the Shinjuku Sumitomo Building—but city hall is the best of the lot. The Metropolitan Government Web site, incidentally, is an excellent source of information on sightseeing and current events in Tōkyō. 2–8–1 Nishi-Shinjuku, Shinjuku-ku, tel. 03/5321–1111; www.metro.tokyo.jp. Free. North and south decks both open daily 9:30–9:30. Marunouchi and Toei Shinjuku subway lines; JR; Keiō Shin-sen and Teitō private rail lines: Shinjuku Eki (Nishi-guchi/West Exit).

**⑧⓪ TŌKYŌ OPERA CITY.** Completed in 1997, this is certain to be the last major cultural project in Tōkyō for the foreseeable future. The west side of the complex is the Shin Kokuritsu Gekijō (New National Theater), consisting of the 1,810-seat Opera House, the 1,038-seat Playhouse, and an intimate performance space called the Pit, with seating for 468. Architect Helmut Jacoby's design for this building, with its reflecting pools and galleries and granite planes of wall, deserves real plaudits: the Shin Kokuritsu Gekijō is monumental and approachable at the same time.

The east side of the complex consists of a 55-story office tower—an uninspired atrium-style slab, forgettable in almost every respect—flanked by a sunken garden and art museum on one side and a concert hall on the other. The concert hall is astonishing: The sheer cost of the wood alone, polished panels of it rising tier upon tier, is staggering to consider. The amount of research involved to perfect the acoustics in its daring vertical design is even harder to imagine. 3–20–2 Nishi-Shinjuku, Shinjuku-ku, tel. 03/5353–0700 for concert hall; 03/5351–3011 for National Theater, www.tokyooperacity-cf.or.jp. Keiō Shin-sen private rail line: Hatsudai Eki (Higashi-guchi/East Exit).

## AROUND TŌKYŌ

The sheer size of the city and the diversity of its institutions make it impossible to fit all of Tōkyō's interesting sights into neighborhoods and walking tours. Plenty of worthy places—from Tōkyō Disneyland to sumō stables to the old Ōji district—fall outside the city's neighborhood repertoire. Yet no guide to Tōkyō would be complete without them. The sights below are marked on the Tōkyō Overview map at the beginning of this book.

★ **RYŌGOKU.** Two things make this working-class shitamachi neighborhood worth a special trip: this is the center of the world of sumō wrestling as well as the site of the extraordinary Edo-Tōkyō Hakubutsukan. Just five minutes from Akihabara on the JR Sōbu Line, Ryōgoku is easy to get to, and if you've budgeted a leisurely stay in the city, it's well worth a morning's expedition.

The **Edo-Tōkyō Hakubutsukan** (1–4–1 Yokoami, Sumida-ku, tel. 03/3626–9974, www.edo-tokyo-museum.or.jp) opened in 1993, more or less coinciding with the collapse of the economic bubble that had made the project possible. Money was no object in those days; much of the 30,000 square meters of the museum site is open plaza—an unthinkably lavish use of space. From the plaza the museum rises on massive pillars to the permanent exhibit areas on the fifth and sixth floors. The escalator takes you directly to the sixth floor—and back in time 300 years. You cross a replica of the Edo-period Nihombashi Bridge into a truly remarkable collection of dioramas, scale models, cutaway rooms, and even whole buildings: an intimate and convincing experience of everyday life in the capital of the Tokugawa shōguns. Equally elaborate are the fifth-floor re-creations of early modern Tōkyō, the "Enlightenment" of Japan's headlong embrace of the West, and the twin devastations of the Great Kantō Earthquake and World War II. If you only visit one nonart museum in Tōkyō, make this it.

To get to the Edo-Tōkyō Hakubutsukan, leave Ryōgoku Eki by the west exit, immediately turn right, and follow the signs. The moving sidewalk and the stairs bring you to the plaza on the third level; to request an English-speaking volunteer guide, use the entrance to the left of the stairs instead, and ask at the General Information counter in front of the first-floor Special Exhibition Gallery. The fee for the museum is ¥600; special exhibits cost extra. The museum is open Tuesday–Wednesday and weekends 10–6, Thursday–Friday 10–8 (closed December 28–January 4 and on Tuesdays when Monday is a national holiday).

Walk straight out to the main street in front of the west exit of Ryōgoku Eki, turn right, and you come almost at once to the **Kokugikan** (National Sumō Arena), with its distinctive copper-green roof. If you can't attend one of the Tōkyō sumō tournaments, you may want to at least pay a short visit to the **Sumō Hakubutsukan** (1–3–28 Yokoami, Sumida-ku, tel. 03/ 3622–0366), in the south wing of the arena. There are no explanations in English, but the museum's collection of sumō-related wood-block prints, paintings, and illustrated scrolls includes some outstanding examples of traditional Japanese fine art. Admission is free and it's open weekdays 10–4:30.

Sumō wrestlers are not free agents; they must belong to one or another of the stables officially recognized by the Sumō Association. Although the tournaments and exhibition matches take place in different parts of the country at different times, all the stables—now some 30 in number—are in Tōkyō, most of them concentrated on both sides of the Sumida-gawa near the Kokugikan. Wander this area when the wrestlers are in town (January, May, and September are your best bets) and you're more than likely to see some of them on the streets, in their wood clogs and kimonos. Come 7 AM–11 AM, and you can peer through the doors and windows of the stables to watch them in practice sessions. One of the easiest to find is the **Tatsunami Stable** (3–26–2 Ryōgoku), only a few steps from the west end of Ryōgoku Eki (turn left when you go through the turnstile and left again as you come out on the street; then walk along the station building to the second street on the right). Another, a few blocks farther south, where the Shuto Expressway passes overhead, is the **Izutsu Stable** (2–2–7 Ryōgoku).

**Sengaku-ji.** One day in the year 1701, a young provincial baron named Asano Takumi-no-Kami, serving an official term of duty at the shōgun's court, attacked and seriously wounded a courtier named Yoshinaka Kira. Kira had demanded the usual tokens of esteem that someone in his high position would expect for his goodwill; Asano refused, and Kira humiliated him in public to the point that he could no longer contain his rage.

Kira survived the attack. Asano, for daring to draw his sword in the confines of Edo Castle, was ordered to commit suicide. His family line was abolished and his fief confiscated. Headed by Kuranosuke Ōishi, the clan steward, 47 of Asano's loyal retainers vowed revenge. Kira was rich and well protected; Asano's retainers were *rōnin*—masterless samurai. It took them almost two years of planning, subterfuge, and hardship, but on the night of December 14, 1702, they stormed Kira's villa in Edo, cut off his head, and brought it in triumph to Asano's tomb at Sengaku-ji, the family temple. Ōishi and his followers were sentenced to commit suicide—which they accepted as the reward, not the price, of their honorable vendetta—and were buried in the temple graveyard with their lord.

The event captured the imagination of the Japanese like nothing else in their history. Through the centuries it has become the national epic, the last word on the subject of loyalty and sacrifice, celebrated in every medium from Kabuki to film. The temple still stands, and the graveyard is wreathed in smoke from the bundles of incense that visitors still lay reverently on the tombstones.

The story gets even better. There's a small museum on the temple grounds with a collection of weapons and other memorabilia of the event. One of these items dispels forever the myth of Japanese vagueness and indirection in the matter of contracts and formal documents. Kira's family, naturally, wanted to give him a proper burial, but the law insisted this could not be done without his head. They asked for it back, and

## Smart Sightseeings

Savvy travelers and others who take their sightseeing seriously have skills worth knowing about.

**DON'T PLAN YOUR VISIT IN YOUR HOTEL ROOM** Don't wait until you pull into town to decide how to spend your days. It's inevitable that there will be much more to see and do than you'll have time for: choose sights in advance.

**ORGANIZE YOUR TOURING** Note the places that most interest you on a map, and visit places that are near each other during the same morning or afternoon.

**START THE DAY WELL EQUIPPED** Leave your hotel in the morning with everything you need for the day—maps, medicines, extra film, your guidebook, rain gear, and another layer of clothing in case the weather turns cooler.

**TOUR MUSEUMS EARLY** If you're there when the doors open you'll have an intimate experience of the collection.

**EASY DOES IT** See museums in the mornings, when you're fresh, and visit sit-down attractions later on. Take breaks before you need them.

**STRIKE UP A CONVERSATION** Only curmudgeons don't respond to a smile and a polite request for information. Most people appreciate your interest in their home town. And your conversations may end up being your most vivid memories.

**GET LOST** When you do, you never know what you'll find—but you can count on it being memorable. Use your guidebook to help you get back on track. Build wandering-around time into every day.

**QUIT BEFORE YOU'RE TIRED** There's no point in seeing that one extra sight if you're too exhausted to enjoy it.

**TAKE YOUR MOTHER'S ADVICE** Go to the bathroom when you have the chance. You never know what lies ahead.

Ōishi—mirror of chivalry that he was—agreed. He entrusted it to the temple, and the priests wrote him a receipt, which survives even now in the corner of a dusty glass case. "Item," it begins, "One head."

Take the Toei Asakusa subway line to Sengaku-ji Eki (Exit A2), turn right when you come to street level, and walk up the hill. The temple is past the first traffic light, on the left. *2–11–1 Takanawa, Minato-ku, tel. 03/3441–5560, www.cssi.co.jp. Temple and grounds free, museum ¥200. Daily 7–6, museum daily 9–4.*

## In This Chapter

Updated by Jared Lubarsky

# eating out

**AT LAST COUNT**, there were more than 190,000 bars and restaurants in Tōkyō. In the bubble economy of the late 1980s, when money seemed to be no meaningful obstacle to anything, dining out became grotesquely expensive: it was possible to spend $1,000 on a steak dinner. The feeding frenzy is over now; wining and dining are still a major component of the Japanese way of life, but a far more sober mood prevails, and that is reflected in the range and cost of restaurants. The high end of the market, of course, has not disappeared, but Tōkyō's myriad choices also include a fair number of bargains—good cooking of all sorts that you can enjoy even on a modest budget. Food and drink, even at street stalls, are safe wherever you go.

For an international city, Tōkyō is still stubbornly provincial in many ways. Whatever the rest of the world has pronounced good, however, eventually makes its way here: French, Italian, Chinese, Indian, Middle Eastern, Latin American. It's hard to think of a cuisine of any prominence that goes unrepresented, as Japanese chefs by the thousand go abroad, hone their craft, and bring it home to this city.

Restaurants in Japan naturally expect most of their clients to be Japanese, and the Japanese are the world's champion modifiers. Only the most serious restaurateurs refrain from editing some of the authenticity out of foreign cuisines; in areas like Shibuya, Harajuku, and Shinjuku, all too many of the foreign restaurants cater to students and young office workers, who come mainly for the *fun'iki* (atmosphere). Choose a French bistro or Italian trattoria in these areas carefully, and expect to pay dearly for the real thing. That said, you can count on the fact that the city's best foreign cuisine is world-class.

A number of France's two- and three-star restaurants, for example, have established branches and joint ventures in Tōkyō, and they regularly send their chefs over to supervise. The style almost everywhere is still nouvelle cuisine: small portions, with picture-perfect garnishes and light sauces. More and more, you find interesting fusions of French and Japanese culinary traditions. Meals are served in poetically beautiful presentations, in bowls and dishes of different shapes and patterns. Recipes make imaginative use of fresh Japanese ingredients, like shimeji mushrooms and local wild vegetables.

In recent years Tōkyōites have also had more and more opportunities to experience the range and virtuosity of Italian cuisine; chances are good that a trattoria here will measure up to even Tuscan standards. Indian food here is also consistently good—and relatively inexpensive. Local versions of California-style American cooking are often admirable. Chinese food is the most consistently modified; it can be quite appetizing, but for repertoire and richness of taste, it pales in comparison to Hong Kong fare. Significantly, Tōkyō has no Chinatown.

The quintessential Japanese restaurant is the ryōtei, something like a villa, most often walled off from the bustle of the outside world and divided into a number of small, private dining rooms. These rooms are traditional in style, with tatami-mat floors, low tables, and a hanging scroll or a flower arrangement in the alcove. One or more of the staff is assigned to each room to serve the many dishes that compose the meal, pour your sake, and provide light conversation. Think of a ryōtei as an adventure, an encounter with foods you've likely never seen before and with a centuries-old graceful, almost ritualized style of service unique to Japan. Many parts of the city are proverbial for their ryōtei; the top houses tend to be in Tsukiji, Asakusa, and nearby Yanagi-bashi.

A few pointers are in order on the geography of food and drink. The farther "downtown" you go—into Shitamachi—the less likely you are to find the real thing in foreign cuisine. There is superb Japanese food all over the city, but aficionados of sushi swear (with excellent reason) by Tsukiji, where the central fish market supplies the neighborhood's restaurants with the freshest ingredients; the restaurants in turn serve the biggest portions and charge the most reasonable prices. Asakusa takes pride in its tempura restaurants, but tempura is reliable almost everywhere, especially at branches of the well-established, citywide chains. Every depāto and skyscraper office building in Tōkyō devotes at least one floor to restaurants; none of them stand out, but all are inexpensive and quite passable places to lunch. When in doubt for dinner, note that Tōkyō's top-rated international hotels also have some of the city's best places to eat and drink.

Dining out in Tōkyō does not ordinarily demand a great deal in the way of formal attire. If it's a business meal, of course, and your hosts or guests are Japanese, dress conservatively: for men, a suit and tie; for women, a dress or suit in a basic color, stockings, and a minimum of jewelry. On your own, you'll find that only a very few upscale Western venues (mainly the French and Continental restaurants in hotels) will even insist on ties for men; follow the unspoken dress codes you'd observe at home and you're unlikely to go wrong. For Japanese-style dining on tatami floors, keep two things in mind: wear shoes that slip on and off easily and presentable socks, and choose clothing you'll be comfortable in for a few hours with your legs gathered under you.

Price-category estimates for the restaurants below are based on the cost of a main Western-style course at dinner or a typical Japanese-style meal per person, excluding drinks, taxes, and service charges; a restaurant listed as $$ can easily slide up a category to $$$ when it comes time to pay the bill.

| CATEGORY | COST* |
|----------|-------|
| $$$$ | over ¥9,000 |
| $$$ | ¥6,000–¥9,000 |
| $$ | ¥2,500–¥6,000 |
| $ | under ¥2,500 |

*per person for a main course at dinner

## AOYAMA

### Japanese

$$–$$$$ **MAISEN.** You're likely to spend some time soaking in a Japanese ★ bathhouse; eating in one is a different story. Maisen was converted from a former *sentō* (public bathhouse) in 1983, and you'll find the old high ceiling, characteristic of bathing rooms built during the first quarter of the 20th century, as well as the original signs instructing bathers where to change, intact. Large bouquets of seasonal flowers help transform the large, airy space into a pleasant dining room. *Tonkatsu* (deep-fried pork cutlets) is Maisen's chef d'oeuvre. Though it's more expensive than the regular tonkatsu roast, consider trying *kuroi buta no hire* (fillet of Chinese black pork), which is very juicy and tender. Spoon a generous serving of sauce—sweet, spicy, or extra thick for black pork—over the cutlets and the shredded cabbage that comes with the sets. Miso soup and rice are also included. Or consider salmon dishes, of which the most elegant is the *oyako* set: bite-size pieces of salmon with salmon roe. There are no-smoking rooms upstairs. *4–8–5 Jingū-mae, Shibuya-ku, tel. 03/3470–0071. No credit cards. Ginza, Chiyoda, and Hanzō-mon lines, Omotesandō Eki (Exit A2).*

$–$$ **HIGO-NO-YA.** This restaurant specializes in a style called *kushi-yaki*, which refers simply to a variety of ingredients—meat, fish, vegetables—cut into bits and grilled on bamboo skewers. There's nothing ceremonious or elegant about kushi-yaki; it resembles the more familiar yakitori, except that there is more variety to it. At Higo-no-ya you can feast on such dishes as shiitake mushrooms stuffed with minced chicken; scallops wrapped in bacon; and bonito, shrimp, and eggplant with ginger. The decor here is a postmodern-traditional cross, with wood beams painted black, paper lanterns, and sliding paper screens. There's tatami, table, and counter seating. Also, a helpful English menu is available. *AG Bldg. B1, 3–18–17 Minami-Aoyama, Minato-ku, tel. 03/3423–4462. AE, V. No lunch. Subway: Ginza, Chiyoda, and Hanzō-mon lines, Omotesandō Eki (Exit A4).*

# ASAKUSA

## Japanese

**$$ TATSUMIYA.** This is a ryōtei with at least two delightfully untraditional features: it is neither inaccessible nor outrageously expensive. Most ryōtei tend to oppress the first-time visitor a little with the weight of their antiquity and the ceremonious formality of their service. Tatsumiya, which opened in 1980, takes a different attitude to the past: the rooms are almost cluttered with antique chests, braziers, clocks, lanterns, bowls, utensils, and craft work (some of which are for sale). The cuisine itself follows the kaiseki repertoire, derived from the tradition of the tea-ceremony meal. Seven courses are offered, including something raw, something boiled, something vinegared, something grilled. You must arrive before 8:30 for dinner. *1–33–5 Asakusa, Taitō-ku, tel. 03/3842–7373. Jacket and tie. No credit cards. Closed Mon. and 3rd Sun. of month. No lunch. Subway: Ginza and Toei Asakusa lines, Asakusa Eki (Exit 1 or 3).*

**$–$$ AOI-MARUSHIN.** If not the most elegant, this is surely the largest tempura restaurant in Tōkyō, with six floors of table and tatami seating. Aoi-Marushin is used to—nay, enjoys—having foreign customers and makes a visit easy with English menus. This is essentially a family restaurant; don't expect much in the way of decor—just lots of food at very reasonable prices. Asakusa is a must on any itinerary, and tempura *teishoku* (an assortment of delicately batter-fried fish, seafood, and fresh vegetables) is the specialty of the district. Aoi-Marushin's location, just a few minutes' walk from the entrance to Sensō-ji, makes it an obvious choice after a visit to the temple. 1–4–4 Asakusa, Taitō-ku, tel. 03/3841–0110. AE, MC, V. Subway: Ginza and Toei Asakusa lines, Asakusa Eki (Exit 1).

## AZABU-JŪBAN

### Korean

**$$ SANKŌ-EN.** With the embassy of the Republic of Korea a few blocks away, Sankō-en is in a neighborhood thick with barbecue joints; from the outside, not much seems to distinguish one from another. From the beginning, however, Sankō-en drew customers in droves, not just from the neighborhood but from trendy nearby Roppongi as well. It opened one branch, then another, and moved the main operation to new quarters—and customers are still lining up at all hours to get in. Korean barbecue is a smoky affair; you cook your own dinner—thin slices of beef and brisket and vegetables—on a gas grill at your table. Sankō-en also makes a great salad to go with its brisket. 1–8–7 Azabu-jūban, Minato-ku, tel. 03/3585–6306. Reservations not accepted. AE, V. Closed Wed. Subway: Namboku and Toei Ōedo Lines, Azabu-jūban Eki (Exit 7).

## DAIKANYAMA

### Contemporary

**$$–$$$ ★ TABLEAUX.** The mural in the bar depicts the fall of Pompeii, the banquettes in the restaurant are upholstered in red leather, and the walls are papered in antique gold. So with pony-tailed waiters gliding hither and yon, you suspect that somebody here really *believes* in Los Angeles. Tableaux may lay on more glitz than it really needs, but the service is cordial and professional, and the food is superb. Try *bruschetta* (toasted bread with tomato, basil, and olive oil), fettuccine with smoked salmon and sun-dried tomatoes, or grilled pork chop stuffed with chutney, onion, and garlic. Tableaux's bar is open until 1:30 AM. *Sunroser Daikanyama Bldg., basement, 11–6 Sarugaku-chō, Shibuya-ku, tel. 03/5489–2201. AE, DC, MC, V. No lunch. Tōkyū Toyoko private rail line, Daikanyama Eki (Kita-guchi/North Exit).*

## Pan-Asian

**$–$$ MONSOON CAFE.** Thanks to places like this, the demand for "ethnic" food—which by local definition means spicy and primarily Southeast Asian—continues apace in Tōkyō. The Monsoon Cafe complements its eclectic menu with an aggressively "ethnic" decor: rattan furniture, brass tableware from Thailand, colorful papier-mâché parrots on gilded stands, Balinese carvings, and ceiling fans. The best seats in the house are on the balcony that runs around the four sides of a huge atrium-style central floor space. Try the Vietnamese steamed spring rolls, the Indonesian grilled chicken with peanut sauce, or the Chinese-style beef with oyster sauce. The place stays open until 5 AM daily. *15–4 Hachiyama-chō, Shibuya-ku, tel. 03/5489–3789. AE, DC, MC, V. Tōkyū Toyoko private rail line, Daikanyama Eki (Kita-guchi/North Exit).*

## EBISU

### Eclectic

**$–$$ NINNIKUYA.** In Japanese, *ninniku* means "garlic"—an ingredient conspicuously absent from the traditional local cuisine and one that the Japanese were once supposed to dislike. Not so nowadays, if you can believe the crowds that cheerfully line up for hours to eat at this cluttered little place in the Ebisu section. Owner-chef Eiyuki Endo discovered his own passion for the savory bulb in Italy in 1976. Since then he has traveled the world for interesting garlic dishes. Endo's family owns the building, so he can give free rein to his artistry without charging a lot. There is no decor to speak of, and you may well have to share a table, but it's all good fun.

Try the littleneck clams Italian style with garlic rice, or the Peruvian garlic chicken. Ninnikuya is a little hard to find, but anybody you ask in the neighborhood can point the way. *1–26–12 Ebisu, Shibuya-ku, tel. 03/3446–5887. Reservations not accepted. No credit cards. Closed Mon. No lunch. JR and Hibiya Line, Ebisu Eki (Higashi-guchi/East Exit).*

## GINZA

### American

**$ ★** **FARM GRILL.** Tōkyō could use a few more restaurants like the Farm Grill, which specializes in innovative California-style cuisine in generous portions at truly reasonable prices. Generous also is the space, vast by any standard: there's seating at the Farm Grill for 260, at wood-block pedestal tables with rattan chairs. The focus here is on hearty salads and sandwiches, pasta and rotisserie entrées, and rich desserts—the carrot cake is pretty good, the linzertorte to die for. Try the Caesar salad, pasta Malibu (penne with chicken, mushrooms, bacon, mozzarella, and fresh herbs), or the house chili. There are more than 90 entries on the wine list, a good percentage of them at ¥1,500 or less. The all-you-can-eat dinner buffet at the Farm Grill is ¥1,900 for women, ¥2,900 for men. Can this be politically correct? Add ¥1,000 for all you can drink, and the question will probably trouble you less. *Ginza Nine 3 Gokan, 2nd floor, 8–5 Ginza, Chūō-ku, tel. 03/5568–6156. AE, DC, MC, V. No lunch. JR Yamanote Line and Ginza and Toei Asakusa subway lines: Shimbashi Eki (Exit 5).*

### Indian

**$$–$$$** **ASHOKA.** The owners of the Ashoka set out to take the high ground—to provide decor commensurate with a fashionable address. The room is hushed and spacious, incense perfumes the air, the lighting is recessed, the carpets are thick, and the waiters have spiffy uniforms. Floor-to-ceiling windows overlook Chūō-dōri, the main street in Ginza. *Thali*, a selection of curries and other specialties of the house, is served up on a figured brass tray. *Khandari nan*, a flat bread with nuts and raisins, is excellent. So is chicken *tikka*, boneless chunks marinated and cooked in the tandoor. All in all, this is a good show for the raj. *Pearl Bldg., 2nd floor, 7–9–18 Ginza, Chūō-ku, tel. 03/3572–2377. AE, DC, MC, V. Subway: Marunouchi and Ginza Lines, Ginza Eki (Exit A4).*

## Japanese

**\$\$\$–\$\$\$\$  RANGETSU.** The increase in Japan's consumption of beef over the past century has much to do with the popular appeal of shabu-shabu and sukiyaki, the house specialties here. Inside, tables for four or more people in semiprivate rooms are equipped with a tabletop stove. Only one dish can be cooked at your table, but this shouldn't stop you from trying both shabu-shabu and sukiyaki. Rangetsu is one block from the Ginza 4-chōme crossing, on the side closest to the Wako clock. *3–5–8 Ginza, Chūō-ku, tel. 03/3567–1021. AE, DC, MC, V. Subway: Marunouchi and Ginza lines, Ginza Eki (Exit A9 or A10).*

**\$\$–\$\$\$\$  ŌSHIMA.** One reason Tōkyō is such a great city for food is that it easily supports a great variety of restaurants serving the regional cuisines from all over the country. Ōshima is devoted to the cooking of Kanazawa, the city on the Sea of Japan that during the Edo period earned the nickname "Little Kyōto" for the richness of its craft traditions. Kanazawa cuisine is noted for its seafood; the grilled fresh yellowtail at Ōshima is a delight. But the specialty of the house is a stew of duck and potatoes called *jibuni*. The waitresses dress in kimonos of Kanazawa's famous Yuzen dyed silk. The exquisite table settings make use of Kutani porcelain and Wajima lacquer bowls. *Ginza Core Bldg. 9F, 5–8–20 Ginza, Chūō-ku, tel. 03/3574–8080. AE, MC, V. Subway: Ginza, Hibiya, and Marunouchi lines, Ginza Eki (Exit A5).*

# tokyo dining

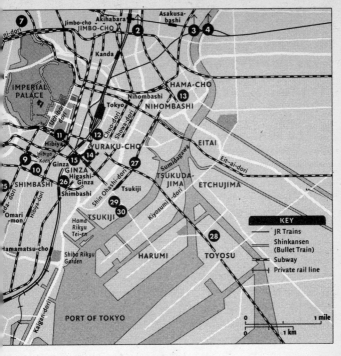

## ICHIYAGA

### Italian

**$$ RESTORANTE CARMINE.** Everybody pitched in, so the story goes, when Carmine Cozzolino opened this unpretentious little neighborhood restaurant in 1987: friends designed the logo and the interior, painted the walls (black and white), and hung the graphics, swapping their labor for meals. And they're good meals, too. For a real Italian five-course dinner, this could be the best deal in town. Specialties of the house include pasta twists with tomato and caper sauce, and veal scallopini à la marsala. The tiramisu is a serious dessert. Carmine's is not easy to find, but it's well worth the effort. When you exit the station, ask for help finding the street Ushigome-chūō-dōri. Follow the street uphill for about 10 minutes; the sign for the restaurant will be on the left. *1–19 Saiku-machi, Shinjuku-ku, tel. 03/3260–5066. No credit cards. Subway: Namboku and Yūraku-chō lines, Ichigaya Eki (Exit 5).*

### Japanese

**$$ HEALTHY KAN.** Beloved by its regular Japanese and gaijin clientele,
★ Healthy Kan serves an array of traditional vegetarian and fish dishes. The daily menu, listed on a white board, offers a complete Japanese meal that includes *haigo* (brown rice) or soba served either hot or cold depending on the season. For something different, try the tempeh set. A classic Indonesian dish, Kan's tempeh—seasoned with either soy or miso—is dressed up to look Japanese. *Komatsuna* (mustard spinach), or a comparable leafy green vegetable such as spinach or chrysanthemum leaves, in addition to tasty *hijiki* (edible algae) and pickles, is served on the side. Healthy Kan is a casual place; it's easy to linger over a glass of home-pureed vegetable juice or a piece of homemade cake (desserts run out early, so call ahead to reserve something). The menu is written in English. *Asahi Roku-ban-chō Mansion, 2nd floor, 6–4 Chiyoda-ku, tel. 03/3263–4023. No credit cards. Closed Sun. Subway: Yūraku-chō Line, Ichigaya Eki (Exit 3).*

## IKEBUKURO

### Japanese

**$$** **SASASHŪ.** This traditional-style pub is noteworthy for stocking
★ only the finest and rarest, the Latours and Mouton-Rothschilds,
of sake: these are wines that take gold medals in the annual sake
competition year after year. It also serves some of the best izakaya
food in town—and the Japanese wouldn't dream of drinking well
without eating well. Sasashū is a rambling two-story building in
traditional style, with thick beams and step-up tatami floors. The
specialty of the house is salmon steak, brushed with sake and soy
sauce and broiled over a charcoal hibachi. 2–2–6 Ikebukuro,
Toshima-ku, tel. 03/3971–6796. AE, DC, MC, V. Closed Sun. No lunch.
JR Yamanote Line; Yūraku-chō, Marunouchi and Ōedo subway lines:
Ikebukuro Eki (Exit 19).

## KYŌ-BASHI

### French

**$$$$** **CHEZ INNO.** Chef Noboru Inoue studied his craft at Maxim's in
Paris and Les Frères Troisgros in Roanne; the result is brilliant,
innovative French food. Try fresh lamb in wine sauce with truffles
and finely chopped herbs, or lobster with caviar. The main dining
room, with seating for 28, has velvet banquettes, white-stucco walls,
and stained-glass windows. A smaller room can accommodate
private parties. Across the street is the elegant Seiyō Hotel—
making this block the locus of the very utmost in Tōkyō upscale.
3–2–11 Kyō-bashi, tel. 03/3274–2020. Reservations essential. Jacket
and tie. AE, DC, V. Closed Sun. Subway: Ginza Line, Kyō-bashi Eki (Exit 2);
Yūraku-chō Line, Ginza-Itchōme Eki (Exit 7).

### Italian

**$$–$$$$** **ATTORE.** The Italian restaurant of the elegant Hotel Seiyō Ginza,
Attore is divided into two sections. The "casual" side, with seating

for 60, has a bar counter, banquettes, and a see-through glass wall to the kitchen; its comfortable decor is achieved with track lighting, potted plants, marble floors, and Indian-looking print tablecloths. The "formal" side, with seating for 40, has mauve wall panels and carpets, armchairs, and soft recessed lighting. On either side of the room, you get some of the best Italian cuisine in Tōkyō. Chef Katsuyuki Muroi trained for six years in Tuscany and northern Italy and acquired a wonderful repertoire. Try pâté of pheasant and porcini mushrooms with white-truffle cheese sauce or the walnut-smoked lamb chops with sun-dried tomatoes. The menu is simpler, and the dishes are less expensive on the casual side of the restaurant. *1–11–2 Ginza, Chūō-ku, tel. 03/3535–1111. Reservations essential for formal dining room. Jacket and tie. AE, DC, MC, V. Subway: Ginza Line, Kyō-bashi Eki (Exit 2); Yūraku-chō Line, Ginza-Itchōme Eki (Exit 7).*

## MEGURO

### Japanese

$ **TONKI.** Meguro, a neighborhood distinguished for almost nothing
★ else culinary, has the *ichiban-no* (number one) *tonkatsu ryōri* (deep-fried pork cutlet cookery) in Tōkyō. It's a family joint, with Formica-top tables and a fellow who comes around to take your order while you're waiting the requisite 10 minutes in line. And people do wait in line, every night until the place closes at 10:30. Tonki is one of those successful places that never went conglomerate; it kept getting more popular and never got around to putting frills on what it does best: pork cutlets, soup, raw cabbage salad, rice, pickles, and tea. That's the standard course, and almost everybody orders it, with good reason. *1–1–2 Shimo-Meguro, Meguro-ku, tel. 03/3491–9928. DC, V. Closed Tues. and 3rd Mon. of month. JR Yamanote Line, Meguro Eki (Nishi-guchi/West Exit).*

# Thai

**$–$$$  KEAWJAI.** Blink and you miss this little Thai restaurant, just a minute's walk or so from the east exit of Meguro Eki on Meguro-dōri. (The sign is faded, and the steps leading downstairs are barely noticeable.) But Keawjai is worth looking for: it's one of the few places in Tōkyō offering the subtle complexities of Royal Thai cuisines, and despite its size—only eight tables and four banquettes—the restaurant serves a remarkable range of dishes in different regional styles. The spicy beef salad is excellent (and *really* spicy), as are the baked rice with crabmeat served in a whole pineapple, and the red curry in coconut milk with chicken and cashews. The decor evokes Thailand with carved panels, paintings, and brass ornaments but manages to avoid clutter. The staff is all Thai, and the service is friendly and unhurried. *Meguro Kōwa Bldg. B1, 2–14–9 Kami ō saki, Meguro-ku, tel. 03/5420–7727. MC, V. Closed 2nd and 3rd Mon. of month. JR and Namboku subway line, Meguro Eki (Higashi-guchi/East Exit).*

# NIBAN-CHŌ

## Indian

**$$–$$$  ADJANTA.** About 45 years ago the owner of Adjanta came to Tōkyō to study electrical engineering and ended up opening a small coffee shop near the Indian Embassy. He started out cooking a little for his friends; now the coffee shop is one of the oldest and best Indian restaurants in town. There's no decor to speak of. The emphasis instead is on the variety and intricacy of Indian cooking—and none of its dressier rivals can match Adjanta's menu for sheer depth. The curries are hot to begin with, but you can order them even hotter. There's a small boutique in one corner, where saris and imported Indian foodstuffs are for sale. Adjanta is open 24 hours. *3–11 Niban-chō, Chiyoda-ku, tel. 03/3264–6955. AE, DC, MC, V. Subway: Yūraku-chō Line, Kōji-machi Eki (Exit 5).*

## NIHOMBASHI

### Japanese

**$ SASASHIN.** No culinary tour of Japan would be complete without a visit to an izakaya, where the food is hearty, close to home cooking, and is meant—to most of the local clientele, at least—mainly as ballast for the earnest consumption of beer and sake. Arguably one of the two or three best izakaya in Tōkyō, Sasashin spurns the notion of decor: there is a counter laden with platters of the evening's fare, a clutter of rough wooden tables, and not much else. It's noisy, smoky, crowded—and absolutely authentic. Try the sashimi, the grilled fish, or the fried tofu; you really can't go wrong by just pointing your finger to anything on the counter that takes your fancy. Sasashin is open evenings only, 5–10:30. *2–20–3 Nihombashi- Ningyōchō, Chūō-ku, tel. 03/3668–2456. Reservations not accepted. No credit cards. Closed Sun. and 3rd Sat. of month. No lunch. Subway: Hanzō-mon Line, Suitengū-mae Eki (Exit 7); Hibiya and Toei Asakusa lines, Ningyōchō Eki (Exits A1, A3).*

## OMOTESANDŌ

### French

**$$$–$$$$ LE PAPILLON DE PARIS.** This very fashion-minded restaurant is a joint venture of L'Orangerie in Paris and Madame Mori's formidable empire in couture. Muted elegance marks the decor, with cream walls, deep brown carpets, and a few good paintings. Mirrors add depth to a room that actually seats only 40. The menu, an ambitious one to begin with, changes every two weeks; the recurring salad of sautéed sweetbreads is excellent. The lunch and dinner menus are nouvelle and very pricey. This is a particularly good place to be on a late Sunday morning, for the buffet brunch (¥3,500), when you can graze through to what's arguably the best dessert tray in town. Le Papillon is on the fifth floor of the Hanae Mori Building, just a minute's walk from the Omotesandō subway station on Aoyama-dōri. *Hanae Mori Bldg., 5th floor, 3–6–*

1 Kita–Aoyama, Minato-ku, tel. 03/3407–7461. Reservations essential. AE, DC, MC, V. No dinner Sun. Subway: Ginza and Hanzō-mon lines, Omotesandō Eki (Exit A1).

# ROPPONGI

## American

**$$–$$$  SPAGO.** This was the first venture overseas by trendsetting Spago of Los Angeles, and owner-chef-celebrity Wolfgang Puck still comes periodically to Tōkyō to oversee the authenticity of his California cuisine. Will duck sausage pizza with Boursin cheese and pearl onions ever be as American as apple pie? Maybe. Meanwhile, Spago is a clean, well-lighted place, painted pink and white and adorned with potted palms. Service is smooth, and tables on the glassed-in veranda attract a fair sample of Tōkyō's gilded youth. 5–7–8 Roppongi, Minato-ku, tel. 03/3423–4025. AE, DC, MC, V. Subway: Hibiya Line, Roppongi Eki (Exit 3).

## Contemporary

**$–$$  ROTI.** Billing itself as a "modern Brasserie," Roti is basically inspired by the culinary aesthetic that emerged in the late 1960s in the United States: a creative use of simple, fresh ingredients that still lets the food speak for itself, and a fusing of Eastern and Western elements. Appetizers at Roti are more interesting than main dishes. Try the Vietnamese sea-bass carpaccio with crisp noodles and roasted garlic, or the calamari batter-fried in ale with red chili tartar sauce. Don't neglect dessert: the espresso chocolate tart is to die for. Roti stocks a fine cellar of some 60 Californian wines and has microbrewed ales from the famed Rogue brewery in Oregon as well as a selection of Cuban cigars. The best seats in the house are in fact outside, at one of the dozen tables around the big glass pyramid on the terrace. Piramide Bldg. 1F, 6–6–9 Roppongi, Minato-ku, tel. 03/5785–3671. AE, MC, V. Subway: Hibiya Line, Roppongi Eki (Exit 1).

## Indonesian

**$$ BENGAWAN SOLO.** The Japanese, whose native aesthetic demands a separate dish and vessel for everything they eat, have to overcome a certain resistance to the idea of *rijsttafel*—a kind of Indonesian smorgasbord of curries, salad, and grilled tidbits that tends to get mixed up on a serving platter. Nevertheless, Bengawan Solo has maintained its popularity with Tōkyō residents for about 40 years. The eight-course rijsttafel is spicy hot and ample. If it doesn't quite stretch for two, order an extra *gado-gado* salad with peanut sauce. An amiable clutter of batik pictures, shadow puppets, carvings, and pennants makes up the decor. The parent organization, in Jakarta, supplies periodic infusions of new staff as needed and does a thriving import business in Indonesian foodstuffs. 7–18–13 Roppongi, Minato-ku, tel. 03/3408–5698. AE, DC, MC, V. Subway: Hibiya Line, Roppongi Eki (Exit 2).

## Japanese

**$$$$ INAKAYA.** The style here is *robatayaki*, the ambience pure theater. The centerpiece is a large U-shape counter. Inside, two cooks in traditional garb sit on cushions behind the grill, with a wonderful cornucopia of food spread out in front of them: fresh vegetables, seafood, skewers of beef and chicken. Point to what you want, or tell your waiter—each speaks some English. The cook will bring it up out of the pit, prepare it, and hand it across on an 8-ft wooden paddle. Expect a half-hour wait any evening after 7. Inakaya is open from 5 PM to 5:30 AM. Reine Bldg., 1st floor, 5–3–4 Roppongi, Minato-ku, tel. 03/3408–5040. Reservations not accepted. AE, DC, MC, V. No lunch. Subway: Hibiya Line, Roppongi Eki (Exit 3).

**$$$–$$$$ SUSHI TOSHI.** This contemporary and colorful sushi shop in Roppongi caters to an eclectic clientele, all of whom can easily be seen thanks to the restaurant's U-shape counter. As in most sushi bars, a single order consists of two pieces from the superb array of the day's catch. In addition to *maguro* and *chūtoro* (both tuna, the latter coming from the middle section of the fish), kompachi (a close relative of hamachi, yellow tail) and tai (sea bream) are spectacular, and the scallops still smack of sea salt. Or if you don't see anything appealing in the glass case in front of you, ask one of the chefs to pull something from the tank. The usual pink pickled ginger, as well as kamaboko (white fish cakes) served on a haran (lily-flower) leaf, clears the palate between each "course." 5–8–3 Nakano Bldg., 1st floor, Roppongi, Minato-ku, tel. 03/3423–0333. AE, DC, MC, V. Closed Sun. No lunch. Subway: Hibiya Line, Roppongi Eki (Exit 3).

**$–$$ GANCHAN.** Although the Japanese prefer their sushi bars to be immaculately clean and light, they expect yakitori joints to be smoky, noisy, and cluttered—like Ganchan. There's counter seating only, for about 15, and you have to squeeze to get to the chairs in back by the kitchen. Festival masks, paper kites and lanterns, gimcracks of all sorts, handwritten menus, and greeting cards from celebrity patrons adorn the walls. Behind the counter, the cooks yell at each other, fan the grill, and serve up enormous schooners of beer. Try the tsukune (balls of minced chicken) and the fresh asparagus wrapped in bacon. Ganchan is open from 5:30 PM to 1 AM Monday–Saturday and until 11 PM on Sunday and holidays. 6–8–23 Roppongi, Minato-ku, tel. 03/3478–0092. V. No lunch. Subway: Hibiya Line, Roppongi Eki (Exit 1A).

# SHIBUYA

## Japanese

**$$–$$$$ TENMATSU.** The best seats in the house at Tenmatsu, as in any tempura-ya, are at the immaculate wooden counter, where your tidbits of choice are taken straight from the oil and served up immediately. You also get to watch the chef in action. Tenmatsu's brand of good-natured professional hospitality adds to the enjoyment of the meal. Here you can rely on a set menu or order à la carte delicacies like lotus root, shrimp, unagi (eel), and kisu (a small white freshwater fish). Call ahead to reserve a seat at the counter. 1–6–1 Dōgen-zaka, Shibuya-ku, tel. 03/3462–2815. DC, MC,

*V. Subway/JR: Shibuya Eki (Minami-guchi/South Exit for JR lines, Exit 3A for Ginza and Hanzō-mon subway lines).*

# SHINJUKU

## Japanese

**$$$–$$$$ YAOZEN.** On the 14th floor of Takashimaya Times Square, Yaozen has a magnificent view of the city and serves elegant kaiseki banquets for parties of three or more between the normal lunch and dinner hours (reserve in advance). Standard fare, served by kimono-clad waitresses, is a prix-fixe meal in a bentō lunch box or on elegantly lacquered trays: try the two-tiered *okusama-gozen bentō*, which includes sashimi, simmered vegetables, and grilled fish. Small desserts with *hōjicha* (parched twig tea) are popular during tea time, but with a full-course meal, it's easy to skip, since so many of the foods—in traditional Japanese style—are prepared with mirin (sweet rice wine) and sugar. *Takashimaya Times Square, 5–24–2 Sendagaya, Shibuya-ku, tel. 03/5361–1872. AE, DC, MC, V. JR/subway: Shinjuku Eki (Minami-guchi/South Exit for JR, Exit 2 for Toei Shinjuku Line).*

# SHIROKANEDAI

## Seafood

**$–$$ BLUE POINT.** The name is a bit misleading: neither the restaurant nor the bar at this chic little establishment serves oysters. What they do serve are generous portions of good seafood, at reasonable prices, in an informal trattoria-style setting—and they stay open until 3 AM on weekdays, 4 AM on weekends. Blue Point cuts corners here and there (there are processed bacon bits in the Caesar salad), but the clientele doesn't come for haute cuisine; the chief appeal, weather permitting, is to dine by candlelight at one of the 10 sidewalk tables, with their blue-and-white checkered oilcloths and the tall French windows behind them. Try the seafood risotto with saffron or the bouillabaisse. Tōkyō's well-heeled clubbers love this place. 4–19–19 Shirokanedai, Minato-ku, tel. 03/3440–3928. MC, V. Subway: Toei Mita and Namboku lines, Shirokanedai Eki (Exit 1).

## Spanish

**$$ SABADO SABADETE.** Catalonia-born jewelry designer Mañuel Benito loves to cook. For a while he indulged this passion by renting out a bar in Aoyama on Saturday nights and making an enormous paella for his friends; to keep them happy while they were waiting, he added a few tapas. Word got around: soon, by 8 it was standing room only, and by 9 there wasn't room in the bar to lift a fork. Inspired by this success, Benito found a trendy location and opened his Sabado Sabadete full-time in 1991. The highlight of every evening is still the moment when the chef, in his bright red Catalan cap, shouts out "Gohan desu yo!"—the Japanese equivalent of "Soup's on!" and dishes out his bubbling-hot paella. Don't miss the empanadas or the *escalivada* (a Spanish ratatouille with red peppers, onions, and eggplant). *Genteel Shirokanedai Bldg., 2nd floor, 5–3–2 Shirokanedai, Minato-ku, tel. 03/ 3445–9353. No credit cards. Closed Sun. Subway: Toei Mita and Namboku lines, Shirokanedai Eki (Exit 1).*

# SHŌTŌ

## French

**$$$$ CHEZ MATSUO.** Shōtō is the kind of area you don't expect Tōkyō to have—at least not so close to Shibuya Eki. It's a neighborhood of stately homes with walls half a block long, a sort of sedate Beverly Hills. Chez Matsuo opened here in 1980, in a lovely old two-story Western-style house. The two dining rooms on the first floor, and the private "Imperial Room" on the second, overlook the garden, where you can dine by candlelight on spring and autumn evenings. Owner-chef Matsuo studied as a sommelier in London and perfected his culinary finesse in Paris. His food is nouvelle; the specialty of the house is *suprême* (breast and wing) of duck. *1–23– 15 Shōtō, Shibuya-ku, tel. 03/3465–0610. Reservations essential. AE, DC,*

MC, V. Subway/JR: Shibuya Eki (Kita-guchi/North Exit for JR Yamanote Line, Ginza subway line, and private rail lines; Exit 5 or 8 for Hanzō-mon subway line).

## TORA-NO-MON

### Chinese

**$$$–$$$$** **TOH-KA-LIN.** Year after year the Hotel Okura is rated by business travelers as one of the three best hotels in the world. That judgment has relatively little to do with its architecture, which is rather understated. It has to do instead with its polish, its impeccable standards of service—and, to judge by Toh-Ka-Lin, the quality of its restaurants. The style of the cuisine here is eclectic; two stellar examples are the Peking duck and the sautéed quail wrapped in lettuce leaf. The restaurant also has a not-too-expensive midafternoon meal ($$) of assorted dim sum and other delicacies—and one of the most extensive wine lists in town. *Hotel Okura, 2–10–4 Tora-no-mon, Minato-ku, tel. 03/3505–6068. AE, DC, MC, V. Subway: Hibiya Line, Kamiya-chō Eki (Exit 4B); Ginza Line, Tora-no-mon Eki (Exit 3).*

## TSUKIJI

### Japanese

**$$–$$$$** **EDO-GIN.** In an area that teems with sushi bars, this one maintains its reputation as one of the best. Edo-Gin serves up generous slabs of fish that drape over the vinegared rice rather than perch demurely on top. The centerpiece of the main room is a huge tank, in which the day's ingredients swim about until they are required; it doesn't get any fresher than that! *4–5–1 Tsukiji, Chūō-ku, tel. 03/3543–4401. Reservations not accepted. AE, DC, MC, V. Closed Sun. Subway: Hibiya Line, Tsukiji Eki (Exit 1); Toei Ōedo Line, Tsukiji-shijō Eki (Exit A1).*

**$$ TAKENO.** Just a stone's throw from the Tōkyō central fish market, Takeno is a rough-cut neighborhood restaurant that tends to fill up at noon with the market's wholesalers and auctioneers and office personnel from the nearby Dentsu ad agency and Asahi *Shimbun* (newspaper) company. There's nothing here but the freshest and the best—big portions of it, at very reasonable prices. Sushi, sashimi, and tempura are the staple fare; prices are not posted because they vary with the costs that morning in the market. *6–21–2 Tsukiji, Chūō-ku, tel. 03/3541–8697. Reservations not accepted. No credit cards. Closed Sun. Subway: Hibiya Line, Tsukiji Eki (Exit 1); Toei Ōedo Line, Tsukiji-shijō Eki (Exit A1).*

## TSUKISHIMA

### Japanese

**$ NISHIKI.** Toss out the window any notions you might have about the delicacy and artistic presentation of Japanese food when you come to Nishiki, one of the dozens of *monjya-yaki* restaurants that line the streets of Tsukishima, a five-minute subway ride from Yūraku-chō. A close relative of the western Japanese meal-in-a-pancake innovation *okonomi-yaki*, monjya-yaki, Tōkyō residents swear, is a cuisine that's genuinely Shitamachi—old Tōkyō downtown. Unlike okonomi-yaki, however, monjya-yaki uses no eggs and less flour; this makes frying the pancakes somewhat of a challenge, but that's half the fun. The menu lists more than 20 eclectic combinations, of which the most popular are sliced potatoes and mayonnaise, *tara-ko* (cod roe), and *mochi* (rice cakes), as well as the standard mix of beef, pork, shrimp, and squid seasoned in soy sauce. *3–11–10 Tsukishima, Chūō-ku, tel. 03/3534–8697. No credit cards. Closed Tues. No lunch weekdays. Subway: Yūraku-chō and Ōedo lines, Tsukishima Eki (Exit 7).*

## UCHISAIWAI-CHŌ

### Chinese

**$$–$$$$** ★ **HEICHINROU.** This branch of one of the oldest and best restaurants in Yokohama's Chinatown is on the top floor of a prestigious office building about five minutes' walk from the Imperial Hotel, and it commands a spectacular view of Hibiya Kōen and the Imperial Palace grounds. Be sure to call ahead to reserve a table by the window. The cuisine is Cantonese; pride of place goes to the *kaisen ryōri*, an elaborate multicourse meal of steamed sea bass, lobster, shrimp, scallops, abalone, and other seafood dishes. The decor is rich but subdued, lighting is soft, and table linens are impeccable. Much of the clientele comes from the law offices, securities firms, and foreign banks on the floors below. Heichinrou has a banquet room that can seat 100 and a VIP Room with separate telephone service for power lunches. *Fukoku Seimei Bldg., 28th floor, 2–2–2 Uchisaiwai-chō, Chiyoda-ku, tel. 03/3508–0555. Jacket and tie. AE, DC, MC, V. Closed Sun. Subway: Toei Mita Line, Uchisaiwai-chō Eki (Exit A6).*

## UENO

### Japanese

**$$** ★ **SASA-NO-YUKI.** With its cross between the traditional *shōjin ryōri* (Buddhist vegetarian cuisine) and formal kaiseki dining, Sasa-no-yuki has been serving homemade silky, soft, and sensuous tofu in an array of styles for the past 300 years. The seating is on tatami, the garden has a waterfall, and the presentation of the food is truly artistic. In addition to a few nontofu à la carte items, there are three all-tofu sets, the most basic of which is a three-course meal including *ankake* tofu (bean curd in a sweet soy sauce), *kake shōyu* tofu (simmered with chicken and shiitake mushrooms), and *unsui* (a creamy tofu crepe filled with tiny morsels of sea scallops, shrimp, and minced red pepper). For the best sampling, choose the eight-course banquet, which includes yuba-kōya tofu, a delicious crepe soaked in soy milk. 2–15–10 Negishi, Taitō-ku, tel. 03/3873–1145. AE, DC, MC, V. Tues.–Sun. 11–9. Closed Mon. JR Uguisudani Eki (Kita-guchi/North Exit).

# YŪRAKU-CHŌ

## Japanese

**$$–$$$** **ROBATA.** You might find this place a little daunting at first: it's old and funky, impossibly cramped, and always packed. But chef-owner Takao Inoue, who holds forth here with an inspired version of Japanese home cooking, is also a connoisseur of pottery; he serves his own work on pieces acquired at famous kilns all over the country. There's no menu; the best thing you can do is tell Inoue-san (who speaks some English) how hungry you are and how much you want to spend, and leave the rest to him. A meal at Robata—like the pottery—is simple to the eye but subtle and satisfying. Typical dishes include steamed fish with vegetables, stews of beef or pork, and seafood salad. 1–3–8 Yūraku-chō, Chiyoda-ku, tel. 03/3591–1905. No credit cards. Closed 3rd Mon. of month. No lunch. Subway: Hibiya, Chiyoda, and Toei Mita lines, Hibiya Eki (Exit A4).

## In This Chapter

Updated by Jared Lubarsky

# shopping

**HORROR STORIES ABOUND ABOUT PRICES** in Japan—and some of them are true. Yes, a cup of coffee can cost $10, if you pick the wrong coffee shop. A gift-wrapped melon from a department-store gourmet counter can cost $100. And a taxi ride from the airport to central Tōkyō does cost about $200. Take heart: the dollar has risen quite a bit against the yen over the past few years, and with a little ingenuity and effort you can find a wide range of gifts and souvenirs at bargain prices.

Some items are better bought at home: why go all the way to Tōkyō to buy European designer clothing? Concentrate on Japanese goods that are hard to get elsewhere, especially traditional handicrafts and fabrics. Such things can be found in areas easy to reach by public transportation. If time is limited, stick to hotel arcades and depāto, or focus on one particular shopping district.

In some smaller stores and markets, prices might be given in kanji (Japanese ideographs)—but the clerk can always write the price of an item for you in Arabic numbers, or display it on a calculator.

Salespeople are invariably helpful and polite. In the larger stores they greet you with a bow when you arrive—and many of them speak at least enough English to help you find what you're looking for. There is a saying in Japan: o-kyaku-sama wa kami-sama, "the customer is a god"—and since the competition for your business is fierce, people do take it to heart.

Japan has an across-the-board 5% value-added tax (VAT) imposed on luxury goods as well as on restaurant and hotel bills. This tax can be avoided at some duty-free shops in the city (don't forget to bring your passport). It is also waived in the duty-free shops at the international airports, but because these places tend to have higher profit margins, your tax savings there are likely to be offset by the higher markups.

Stores in Tōkyō generally open at 10 AM or 11 AM and close at 8 PM or 9 PM.

## SHOPPING DISTRICTS

### Akihabara

For the ultimate one-stop display of photographic and electronic gadgetry, Akihabara is high-tech heaven. The best deals in Japan can be found here, but prices are generally comparable to those in American discount stores. West of Akihabara, in Jimbō-chō, you'll find pretty much whatever you're looking for in dictionaries and art books, rare and out-of-print editions, and prints. *For Akihabara: JR Yamanote and Sōbu lines, Akihabara Eki (Denki-gai Exit); Hibiya Line, Akihabara Eki. For Jimbō-chō: Hanzō-on, Toei Shinjuku, and Toei Mita lines, Jimbō-chō Eki.*

### Aoyama

Shopping in Aoyama can empty your wallet in no time: this is where many of the leading Japanese and Western designers have their cash-cow boutiques. European and American imports will be high, but Japanese designer clothes are usually 30%–40% lower than they are elsewhere. Aoyama tends to be a showcase, not merely of couture but of the latest concepts in commercial architecture and interior design. *Subway: Chiyoda, Ginza, and Hanzō-mon lines, Omotesandō Eki (Exits A4, A5, B1, B2, and B3); Ginza, Hanzō-mon, and Toei Ōedo lines, Aoyama-itchōme Eki.*

## Asakusa

Many of the goods here are the kind of souvenirs you would expect to find in any tourist trap, but if you look a little harder, you'll find small backstreet shops that have been making beautiful wooden combs, delicate fans, and other fine crafts for generations. The cookware shops of Kappa-bashi-dōgu-machi-dōri have everything from sushi knives to plastic lobsters. *Subway: Toei Asakusa Line, Asakusa Eki (Kaminarimon Exit); Ginza Line, Asakusa Eki (Exit 1) and Tawara-machi Eki (Exit 3).*

## Ginza

Ginza was the first entertainment and shopping district in Tōkyō, dating to the Edo period (1603–1868), and once consisted of long, willow-lined avenues. The willows have long since gone, and the streets are now lined with depāto and boutiques. The exclusive stores in this area sell quality merchandise at higher prices. *Subway: Marunouchi, Ginza, and Hibiya lines, Ginza Eki (Exits A1–A10); Yūraku-chō Line, Ginza 1-chōme stop. JR Yamanote Line, Yūraku-chō Eki.*

## Harajuku

The average shopper in Harajuku is under 20; a substantial percentage are under 16. This shopping and residential area extends southeast from Harajuku Eki along both sides of Omotesandō and Meiji-dōri; the shops that target the youngest consumers concentrate especially on the narrow street called Takeshita-dōri. Most stores focus on moderately priced clothing and accessories, with a lot of kitsch mixed in, but there are also several upscale fashion houses in the area such as Ralph Lauren. *Subway: Chiyoda Line, Meiji Jingū-mae Eki (Exits 1–5); JR Yamanote Line, Harajuku Eki.*

# tokyo shopping

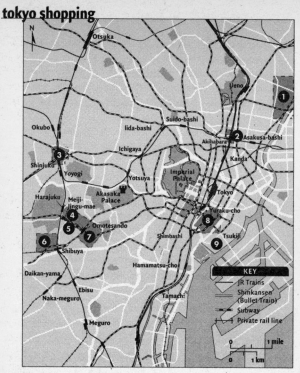

## Omotesandō

Known as the Champs-Elysées of Tōkyō, this long, wide avenue, which runs from Aoyama-dōri to Meiji Jingū, is lined with cafés and designer boutiques. There are also several antiques and print shops here, as well as one of the best toy shops in Tōkyō—Kiddyland. *Subway: Chiyoda, Ginza, and Hanzō-mon lines, Omotesandō Eki (Exits A4, A5, B1, B2, and B3).*

## Shibuya

This is primarily an entertainment district geared toward teenagers and young adults. The shopping in Shibuya also caters to these groups, with many reasonably priced smaller shops and a few depāto that are casual yet chic. *JR Yamanote Line; Tōkyū and Keiō Shinsen private rail lines; Ginza and Hanzō-mon subway lines: Shibuya Eki (Nishi-guchi/West Exit for JR, Exits 3–8 for subway lines).*

## Shinjuku

Shinjuku is not without its honky-tonk and sleaze, but it also has some of the city's most fashionable depāto. Shinjuku's merchandise reflects the crowds—young, stylish, and hip. In the station area are several discount electronics and home-appliance outlets. *JR Yamanote Line; Odakyū private rail line; Marunouchi, Toei Shinjuku, and Toei Ōedo subway lines: Shinjuku Eki.*

## Tsukiji

Best known for its daily fish-market auctions, Tsukiji also has a warren of streets that carry useful, everyday Japanese items that serve as a lens onto the lives of the Japanese. This is a fascinating area to poke around after seeing the fish auction and before stopping in the neighborhood for a fresh-as-can-be sushi lunch. *Toei Ōedo Line, Tsukiji-shijō Eki (Exit A1); Hibiya Line, Tsukiji Eki (Exit 1).*

## SPECIALTY STORES

## Books

**Bookstores of Jimbō-chō.** If you love books, put the shops on the ½-km (¼-mi:) strip of Yasukuni-dōri high on your Tōkyō itinerary. The Japanese print aesthetic and concern with paper and production quality put Japanese books in a category of their own. If you don't read Japanese, then art books, coffee-table books, and old prints make a trip here worthwhile. *Subway: Toei Mita, Toei Shinjuku, and Hanzō-mon lines, Jimbō-chō Eki (Exit A5).*

### ENGLISH-LANGUAGE BOOKSTORES

Most top hotels have a bookstore with a modest selection of English-language books. The stores below are all open daily. The best place in Tōkyō for foreign-language books and periodicals—for price if not for selection—is on the seventh floor of **Tower Records** in Shibuya (1–22–14 Jinnan, Shibuya-ku, tel. 03/3496–3661; Hanzō-mon and Ginza subway lines, Shibuya Eki [Exit6]). Unlike the "dedicated" booksellers, Tower sticks pretty much to popular titles, but it carries a wide range of newspapers from all over the world. **Jena Bookstore** (5–7–1 Ginza, Chūō-ku, tel. 03/3571–2980) carries a wide range of books and is near the Ginza and Marunouchi subway lines' exits in Ginza. For a wide selection of English and other non-Japanese-language books, try **Kinokuniya Bookstore** (3–17–7 Shinjuku, Shinjuku-ku, tel. 03/3354–0131; Marunouchi subway line, Shinkuju Eki [Exits B7, B8, B9]), which carries some 40,000 books and magazine titles. It's closed the third Wednesday of each month, except in April, July, and December. Kinokuniya also has a branch store in the **Tōkyū Plaza Building** (1–2–2 Dōgen-zaka, Shibuya-ku, tel. 03/3463–3241; JR Yamanote Line, Shibuya Eki [Minami-guchi/South Exit]), across from Shibuya Eki. **Maruzen** (2–3–10 Nihombashi, Chūō-ku, tel. 03/3272–7211), one of Japan's largest booksellers, prospers in large part on its imports—which are sold at grossly inflated rates of exchange. On the second floor you can find books in Western languages on any subject from Romanesque

# When you pack your MCI Calling Card, it's like packing your loved ones along too.

Your MCI Calling Card is the easy way to stay in touch when you travel. Use it to call to and from over 125 countries. Plus, every time you call, you can earn frequent flier miles. So wherever your travels take you, call home with your MCI Calling Card. It's even easy to get one. Just visit www.mci.com/worldphone.

## EASY TO CALL WORLDWIDE

1. Just enter the WorldPhone® access number of the country you're calling from.
2. Enter or give the operator your MCI Calling Card number.
3. Enter or give the number you're calling.

| | | | |
|---|---|---|---|
| | | Ireland | 1-800-55-1001 |
| Australia ◆ | 1-800-881-100 | Italy ◆ | 172-1022 |
| China | 108-12 | Japan ◆ | 00539-121▶ |
| France ◆ | 0-800-99-0019 | South Africa | 0800-99-0011 |
| Germany | 0800-888-8000 | Spain | 900-99-0014 |
| Hong Kong | 800-96-1121 | United Kingdom | 0800-89-0222 |

◆ Public phones may require deposit of coin or phone card for dial tone. ▶ Regulation does not permit intra-Japan calls.

# Find America
## WITH A COMPASS

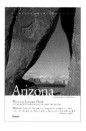
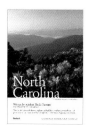
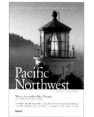

Written by local authors and illustrated throughout with spectacular color images from regional photographers, these companion guides reveal the character and culture of more than 35 of America's most spectacular destinations. Perfect for residents who want to explore their own backyards, and visitors who want an insider's perspective on the history, heritage, and all there is to see and do.

**Fodor's** COMPASS AMERICAN GUIDES

*At bookstores everywhere.*

art to embryology. There's an extensive collection here of books about Japan and also a small crafts center. The store is on Chūō-dōri south of the Tōzai and Ginza lines' Nihombashi stops. **Yaesu Book Center** (2–5–1 Yaesu, Chūō-ku, tel. 03/3281–1811), near Tōkyō Eki and the Imperial Palace, has a small selection of English books that includes popular paperbacks, business titles, and Japanese culture and travel books.

## Ceramics

It's true that pottery and fine ceramics can fill up and weigh down your luggage, but the shops will pack wares safely for travel—and they do make wonderful gifts. The Japanese have been crafting extraordinary pottery for more than 2,000 years, but this art really began to flourish in the 16th century, with the popularity and demand for tea-ceremony utensils. Feudal lords competed for possession of the finest pieces, and distinctive styles of pottery developed in regions all over the country. Some of the more prominent styles are those of Arita in Kyūshū, with painted patterns of flowers and birds; Mashiko, in Tochigi Prefecture, with its rough textures and simple, warm colors; rugged Hagi ware, from the eponymous Western Honshū city; and Kasama, in Ibaraki Prefecture, with glazes made from ash and ground rocks. Tōkyō's specialty shops and depāto carry fairly complete selections of these and other wares.

**Kisso.** This store carries an excellent variety of ceramics in modern design, made with traditional glazes, as well as a restaurant and a gift shop. *Axis Bldg., basement, 5–17–1 Roppongi, Minato-ku, tel. 03/3582–4191. Mon.–Sat. 11:30–2 and 5:30–10. Subway: Hibiya and Toei Ōedo lines, Roppongi Eki (Exit 3); Namboku Line, Roppongi-itchōme Eki (Exit 1).*

**Tachikichi.** Pottery from different localities around the country is sold here. *5–6–13 Ginza, Chūō-ku, tel. 03/3573–1986. Mon.–Sat. 11–7. Subway: Ginza, Hibiya, and Marunouchi lines, Ginza Eki (Exit B3).*

## Dolls

Many types of traditional dolls are available in Japan, each with its own charm. Kokeshi dolls are long, cylindrical, painted, and made of wood, with no arms or legs. Fine examples of Japanese folk art, they date from the Edo period (1603–1868). Daruma, papier-mâché dolls with rounded bottoms and faces, are often painted with amusing expressions. They are constructed so that no matter how you push them, they roll and remain upright. Legend has it they are modeled after a Buddhist priest who remained seated in the lotus position for so long that his arms and legs atrophied. Hakata dolls, made in Kyūshū's Hakata City, are ceramic figurines in traditional costume, such as geisha, samurai, or festival dancers.

**Kyūgetsu.** In business for more than a century, Kyūgetsu sells every kind of doll imaginable. *1–20–4 Yanagibashi, Taitō-ku, tel. 03/3861–5511. Weekdays 9:15–6, weekends 9:15–5:15. Subway: Toei-Asakusa Line, Asakusa-bashi Eki (Exit A3).*

**Sukeroku.** Come to this shop for traditional handmade Edokko dolls and models, clothed in the costumes of the Edo period. *2–3–1 Asakusa, Taitō-ku, tel. 03/3844–0577. Daily 10–5. Subway: Ginza Line, Asakusa Eki (Exit 1).*

## Electronics

The area around Akihabara Eki has more than 200 stores with discount prices on stereos, refrigerators, CD players, and anything else that plugs in or responds to digital commands. The larger of these stores have sections or floors (or even whole annexes) of goods made for export. These products come with instructions in most major languages, and if you have a tourist visa in your passport, you can purchase them duty free. The main store of **Yamagiwa** (4–1–1 Soto Kanda, Chiyoda-ku, tel. 03/3253–2111), one of the area's largest discounters, is a few minutes' walk from the Denki-gai exit of JR Akihabara Eki. Over the years it has established branches and annexes in the neighboring blocks, specializing in computers, peripherals, office equipment, and export models of consumer electronics. This branch is open daily until 7:30. **Minami** (4–3–3 Soto Kanda, Chiyoda-ku, tel. 03/3255–3730) lacks some of the variety of rival Yamagiwa but still manages to stock the major brands of every electronic gizmo you're likely to want to buy. Like most of the big discounters in the area, Minami is a few minutes' walk from the Denki-gai Exit of JR Akihabara Eki. It's open daily until 7 (7:30 on Friday and Saturday.)

**Doi** (1–18–15 Nishi-Shinjuku, Shinjuku-ku, tel. 03/3348–2241) carries a complete line of consumer electronics. It's open daily until 9 and is located within a block of Shinjuku Eki (Exit 5 for Toei Shinjuku subway line, Minami-guchi/South Exit for JR lines).

The mammoth discount camera chain **Yodobashi** (1–11–1 Nishi-Shinjuku, Shinjuku-ku, tel. 03/3346–1010) has its flagship store in Shinjuku. In addition to cameras, it sells a vast range of other products, from cellular phones and computers to DVD players and boom boxes. It's open daily until 9.

## Folk Crafts

Japanese folk crafts, called *mingei*—among them bamboo vases and baskets, fabrics, paper boxes, dolls, and toys—achieve a unique beauty in their simple and sturdy designs. Be aware, however, that simple does not mean cheap. Long hours of loving hand labor go into these objects. And every year there are fewer and fewer craftspeople left, producing their work in smaller and smaller quantities. Include these items in your budget ahead of time: The best of it—worth every cent—can be fairly expensive.

**Bingo-ya.** A complete selection of crafts from all over Japan can be found here. *10–6 Wakamatsu-chō, Shinjuku, tel. 03/3202–8778. Tues.–Sun. 10–7. Subway: Tōzai Line, Waseda Eki (Babashita-chō Exit).*

**Oriental Bazaar.** Here are three floors of just about everything you might want in a traditional Japanese (or Chinese or Korean) handicraft souvenir, from painted screens to pottery to antique chests, at fairly reasonable prices. Kimonos are downstairs. 5–9–13 Jingū-mae, Shibuya-ku, tel. 03/3400–3933. Fri.–Wed. 10–7. Subway: Chiyoda Line, Meiji Jingū-mae Eki (Exit 4).

## Foodstuffs and Wares

This hybrid category includes everything from crackers and pickled foods to standard restaurant-supply items like cast-iron kettles, paper lanterns, and essential food-kitsch like plastic sushi sets. Unless otherwise noted, shops below are centered either on Asakusa's Kappa-bashi-dōgu-machi-dōri or on the Tsukiji fish market.

**The Backstreet Shops of Tsukiji.** Between the Central Wholesale Market and Harumi-dōri, among the many fishmongers, you'll also find stores where you can buy pickles, tea, crackers, kitchen knives, baskets, and crockery. For a picture of real Japanese life, it is not to be missed. 5–2–1 Tsukiji, Chūō-ku. Subway: Toei Ōedo Line, Tsukiji-shijō Eki (Exit A1); Hibiya Line, Tsukiji Eki (Exit 1).

**Biken Kōgei.** If you want to take home an aka-chōchin (folding red-paper lantern) like the ones that hang in inexpensive bar and restaurant fronts, look no farther. 1–5–16 Nishi-Asakusa, Taitō-ku, tel. 03/3842–1646. Mon.–Sat. 9–6, Sun. 11–4 (but call in advance to confirm Sun. hrs). Subway: Ginza Line, Tawara-machi Eki (Exit 3).

**Iida Shōten.** Solid, traditional nambu ware, such as embossed cast-iron kettles and casseroles, is Iida Shōten's specialty. 2–21–6 Nishi-Asakusa, Taitō-ku, tel. 03/3842–3757. Mon.–Sat. 9:30–5:30, Sun. 10–5. Subway: Ginza Line, Tawara-machi Eki (Exit 3).

**Kondo Shōten.** If you're of the mind that your kitchen won't be complete without a bamboo tray, basket, scoop, or container of some sort, stop in at Kondo Shōten. 3–1–13 Matsugaya, Taitō-ku, tel. 03/3841–3372. Weekdays 9:30–5:30, Sat. 9:30–4:30. Subway: Ginza Line, Tawara-machi Eki (Exit 3).

**Maizuru Company.** Somebody actually has to make all that plastic food you see in restaurant windows in Japan, and real masters of the craft—the Rembrandts of counterfeit cuisine—tend to work for Maizuru. Stop in here for some of the most unusual gifts and souvenirs you're likely to find anywhere in Tōkyō. 1–5–17 Nishi-Asakusa, Taitō-ku, tel. 03/3843–1686. Daily 9–6. Subway: Ginza Line, Tawara-machi Eki (Exit 3).

**Nishimura.** This shop specializes in noren—the curtains that shops and restaurants hang to announce they're open. A typical fabric is cotton, linen, or silk, most often dyed to order for individual shops. The store also sells premade noren of an entertaining variety for your decorating pleasure. 1–10–10 Matsugaya, Taitō-ku, tel. 03/3844–9954. Mon.–Sat. 9–5. Subway: Ginza Line, Tawara-machi Eki (Exit 3).

**Tokiwa-dō.** Come here to buy some of Tōkyō's most famous souvenirs: kaminari okoshi (thunder crackers), made of rice, millet, sugar, and beans. The shop is on the west side of Asakusa's Thunder God Gate, the Kaminari-mon entrance to Sensō-ji. 1–3 Asakusa, Taitō-ku, tel. 03/3841–5656. Daily 9–8:45. Subway: Ginza Line, Asakusa Eki (Exit 1).

**Tsubaya Hōchōten.** Tsubaya sells high-quality cutlery for professionals. Its remarkable array of hōchō (knives) is designed for every imaginable use, as the art of food presentation in Japan requires a great variety of cutting implements. The best of these carry the Traditional Craft Association seal: hand-forged tools of tempered blue steel, set in handles banded with deer horn to keep the wood from splitting. 3–7–2 Nishi-Asakusa, Taitō-ku, tel. 03/3845–2005. Daily 9–5:45. Subway: Ginza Line, Tawara-machi Eki (Exit 3).

**Union Company.** Coffee paraphernaliacs, beware: roasters, grinders, beans, flasks, and filters of every shape and description will make your eyes bulge in anticipation of the caffeine ritual. Japanese kōhi (coffee) wares are ingenious. *2–22–6 Nishi-Asakusa, Taitō-ku, tel. 03/3842–4041. Mon.–Sat. 9–6, Sun. 10–5. Subway: Ginza Line, Tawara-machi Eki (Exit 3).*

**Yamamoto Noriten.** The Japanese are resourceful in their uses of products from the sea. *Nori*, the paper-thin dried seaweed used to wrap maki sushi and *onigiri* (rice balls), is the specialty here. Here's a tip if you plan to bring some home with you: buy unroasted nori and toast it yourself at home; the flavor will be far better than that of the preroasted sheets. *1–6–3 Nihombashi Muro-machi, Chūō-ku, tel. 03/3241–0261. Daily 9–6:30. Subway: Hanzō-mon and Ginza lines, Mitsukoshi-mae Eki (Exit A1).*

# Kimonos

Unless they work in traditional Japanese restaurants, Japanese women now wear kimonos mainly on special occasions, such as weddings or graduations, and like tuxedos in the United States, they are often rented instead of purchased. Kimonos are extremely expensive and difficult to maintain. A wedding kimono, for example, can cost as much as ¥1 million.

Most visitors, naturally unwilling to pay this much for a garment that they probably want to use as a bathrobe or a conversation piece, settle for a secondhand or antique silk kimono. These vary in price and quality. You can pay as little as ¥1,000 in a flea market, but to find one in decent condition, you should expect to pay about ¥10,000. However, cotton summer kimonos, called yukatas, in a wide variety of colorful and attractive designs, can be bought new, complete with sash and sandals, for ¥7,000–¥10,000.

**Hayashi.** This store specializes in ready-made kimonos, sashes, and dyed yukata. *2–1–1 Yūraku-chō, Chiyoda-ku, tel. 03/3501–4012. Mon.–Sat. 10–7, Sun. 10–6. Subway: Ginza, Hibiya, and Marunouchi lines, Ginza Eki (Exit C1).*

# Lacquerware

For its history, diversity, and fine workmanship, lacquerware rivals ceramics as the traditional Japanese craft nonpareil. One warning: lacquerware thrives on humidity. Cheaper pieces usually have plastic rather than wood underneath. Because these won't shrink and crack in dry climates, they make safer—and no less attractive—buys.

**Inachu.** Specializing in lacquerware from the town of Wajima, a famous crafts center on the Noto Peninsula, this is one of the most elegant (and expensive) crafts shops in Tōkyō. *1–5–2 Akasaka, Minato-ku, tel. 03/3582–4451. Mon.–Sat. 10–6. Subway: Marunouchi and Namboku lines, Tameike-Sannō Eki (Exit 9).*

# Miscellaneous

Handmade combs, towels, and cosmetics are other uniquely Japanese treasures to consider picking up while in Tōkyō.

**Fuji-ya.** Master textile creator Keiji Kawakami's cotton *tenugui* ("teh-*noo*-goo-ee") hand towels are collector's items, often as not framed instead of used as towels. Kawakama is also an expert on the history of this Edo-period craft. His *Tenugui Fuzoku Emaki* (roughly, *The Scroll Book of Hand Towel Customs and Usages*) is the definitive work on the hundreds of traditional towel motifs that have come down from the Edo period: geometric patterns, plants and animals, and scenes from Kabuki plays and festivals. The shop is near the corner of Dembō-in-dōri on Naka-mise-dōri. *2–2–15 Asakusa, Taitō-ku, tel. 03/3841–2283. Fri.–Wed. 10–7 Subway: Ginza Line, Asakusa Eki (Exit 6).*

**Hyaku-suke.** Hyaku-suke is the last place in Tōkyō to carry government-approved skin cleanser made from powdered nightingale droppings. Ladies of the Edo period—especially the geisha—swore by the cleanser. They mixed the powder with water and patted it on gently as a boon to their complexion. These days this 100-year-old-plus cosmetics shop sells little of the nightingale powder, but its theatrical makeup for Kabuki actors, geisha, and traditional weddings—as well as interesting things to fetch home like seaweed shampoo, camellia oil, and handmade wool cosmetic brushes bound with cherrywood—makes it a worthy addition to your Asakusa shopping itinerary. 2-2-14 Asakusa, Taitō-ku, tel. 03/3841-7058. Wed.–Mon. 11–5. Subway: Ginza Line, Asakusa Eki (Exit 6).

**Jusan-ya.** A shop selling handmade boxwood combs, this business was started in 1736 by a samurai who couldn't support himself as a feudal retainer. It has been in the same family ever since. Jusan-ya is on Shinobazu-dōri, a few doors west of its intersection with Chūō-dōri in Ueno. 2-12-21 Ueno, Taitō-ku, tel. 03/3831-3238. Mon.–Sat. 10–7. Subway: Ginza Line, Ueno Hirokō-ji Eki (Exit 6); JR Ueno Eki (Shinobazu Exit).

**Naka-ya.** If you want to equip yourself for Sensō-ji's annual Sanja Festival in May in Asakusa, this is the place to come. Best buys here are *sashiko hanten*, which are thick, woven firemen's jackets, and happi coats, cotton tunics printed in bright colors with Japanese characters—*ukiyo-e*—which are available in children's sizes. 2-2-12 Asakusa, Taitō-ku, tel. 03/3841-7877. Daily 10–7. Subway: Ginza Line, Asakusa Eki (Exit 6).

**Yono-ya.** Traditional Japanese coiffures and wigs are very complicated, and they require a variety of tools to shape them properly. Tasumi Minekawa is the current master at Yono-ya—the family line goes back 300 years—who deftly crafts and decorates a stunning array of very fine boxwood combs. Some combs are carved with auspicious motifs, such as peonies, hollyhocks, or cranes, and all are engraved with the family benchmark. 1-37-10 Asakusa, Taitō-ku, tel. 03/3844-1755. Daily 10–7. Subway: Ginza Line, Asakusa Eki (Exit 1).

# Paper

Traditional handmade *washi* (paper), which the Japanese make in thousands of colors, textures, and designs, can be fashioned into an astonishing array of useful and decorative objects.

**Kami Hyakka.** Operated by the 110-year-old Okura Sankō wholesale paper company, this showroom displays some 512 different types and colors of paper—made primarily for stationery, notes, and cards rather than as crafts material. 2–4–9 Ginza, Chūō-ku, tel. 03/3538–5025. Tues.–Sat. 10:30–7. Subway: Yūraku-chō Line, Ginza-Itchōme Eki (Exit 5).

**Kami-no-Takamura.** Specialists in washi and other papers printed in traditional Japanese designs, this shop also carries brushes, inkstones, and other tools for calligraphy. 1–1–2 Higashi-Ikebukuro, Toshima-ku, tel. 03/3971–7111. Mon.–Sat. 11–6:30. JR: Ikebukuro Eki (Exit 35).

**Kyūkyodō.** Kyūkyodō has been in business since 1663—in Ginza since 1880—selling its wonderful variety of handmade Japanese papers, paper products, incense, brushes, and other materials for calligraphy. 5–7–4 Ginza, Chūō-ku, tel. 03/3571–4429. Mon.–Sat. 10–7:30, Sun. 11–7. Subway: Ginza, Hibiya, and Marunouchi lines, Ginza Eki (Exit A2).

**Ōzu Washi.** In business since the 17th century, this shop has one of the largest washi showrooms in the city and its own gallery of antique papers. 2–6–3 Nihombashi-Honchō, Chūō-ku, tel. 03/3663–8788. Mon.–Sat. 10–6. Subway: Ginza Line, Mitsukoshi-mae Eki (Exit A4).

**Yushima no Kobayashi.** Here, in addition to shopping for paper goods, you can also tour a papermaking workshop and learn the art of origami. 1–7–14 Yushima, Bunkyō-ku, tel. 03/3811–4025. Mon.–Sat. 9–5. Subway: Chiyoda Line, Yushima Eki (Exit 5).

## Pearls

Japan remains one of the best places in the world to buy cultured pearls. They will not be inexpensive, but pearls of the same quality cost considerably more elsewhere. It's best to go to a reputable dealer, where you know that quality will be high and you will not be misled.

**Mikimoto.** Kokichi Mikimoto created his technique for cultured pearls in 1893. Since then the name Mikimoto has been associated with the best quality in the industry. Prices are high, but design and workmanship are uniformly first rate. *4–5–5 Ginza, Chūō-ku, tel. 03/3535–4611. Daily 10:30–6:30; closed 3rd Wed. of month. Subway: Ginza, Hibiya, and Marunouchi lines, Ginza Eki (Exit A9).*

**Tasaki Pearl Gallery.** Tasaki sells pearls at slightly lower prices than Mikimoto. The store has several showrooms and hosts English tours that demonstrate the technique of culturing pearls and explain how to maintain and care for them. *1–3–3 Akasaka, Minato-ku, tel. 03/5561–8881. Daily 9–6. Subway: Ginza Line, Tameike-Sannō Eki (Exit 9).*

## Toys

**Hakuhinkan** (Toy Park). This is reputedly the largest toy shop in Japan. It's on Chūō-dōri, the main axis of the Ginza shopping area. *8–8–11 Ginza, Chūō-ku, tel. 03/3571–8008. Daily 11–8. Subway: Ginza and Toei Asakusa lines, Shimbashi Eki (Exit 1).*

## ARCADES AND SHOPPING CENTERS

If you don't have the time or energy to dash about Tōkyō in search of the perfect gifts, you may want to try some of the arcades and shopping centers, which carry a wide selection of merchandise. Most of these are used to dealing with gaijin.

**Axis.** On the first floor of this Gaien-higashi-dōri complex in Roppongi, Living Motif is a home-furnishings shop with high-tech foreign and Japanese goods of exquisite design. Nuno, in the basement, sells cutting-edge fabrics of its own design and manufacture, from natural fibers like hemp and linen to high-tech metal synthetics. Be sure to look at the restaurant-store Kisso, which sells, along with lacquered chopsticks and fine baskets, an extraordinary selection of unique, modern handmade ceramics in contemporary designs, shapes, and colors. *5–17–1 Roppongi, Minato-ku. Subway: Hibiya and Toei Ōedo lines, Roppongi Eki (Exit 3); Namboku Line, Roppongi Itchōme Eki (Exit 1).*

**International Shopping Arcade.** This collection of shops in Hibiya has a range of goods—including cameras, electronics, pearls, and kimonos—and a sales staff with excellent English. The arcade is conveniently located near the Imperial Hotel, and the shops are all duty free. *1–7–23 Uchisaiwai-chō, Chiyoda-ku. Subway: Chiyoda and Hibiya lines, Hibiya Eki (Exit A13).*

**Nishi-Sandō.** This Asakusa arcade sells kimono and yukata fabrics, traditional accessories, fans, and festival costumes at very reasonable prices. It runs east of the area's movie theaters, between Rok-ku and the Sensō-ji complex. *Asakusa 2-chōme, Taitō-ku. Subway: Ginza Line, Asakusa Eki (Exit 1).*

# BOUTIQUES

Japanese boutiques pay as much attention to interior design and lighting as they do to the clothing they sell; like anywhere else, it's the image that moves the merchandise. Although many Japanese designers are represented in the major upscale depāto, you may enjoy your shopping more in the elegant boutiques of Aoyama and Omotesandō—most of which are within walking distance of one another.

**Comme Des Garçons.** This is one of the earliest and still most popular "minimalist" design houses, where you can get almost any kind of ¥7000 tank top you want, as long as it's black. 5–2–1 Minami-Aoyama, Minato-ku, tel. 03/3406–3951. Daily 11–8. Subway: Ginza, Chiyoda, and Hanzō-mon lines, Omotesandō Eki (Exit A5).

**From 1st Building.** This building houses the boutiques of several of Japan's leading designers, including Issey Miyake and Comme Ça du Mode, as well as several restaurants. "Produced" by Yasuhiro Hamano, whose atelier designs many of Tōkyō's trendiest commercial spaces, From 1st is one of the earliest and liveliest examples of the city's chic vertical malls. 5–3–10 Minami-Aoyama, Minato-ku. Subway: Ginza, Chiyoda, and Hanzō-mon lines, Omotesandō Eki (Exit A5).

**Hanae Mori Building.** This glass-mirrored structure, designed by Kenzō Tange, houses the designs of the doyenne of Japanese fashion, Mori Hanae, whose clothing has a classic look with a European influence. The café on the first floor is a good vantage point for people-watching, Harajuku's favorite sport. 3–6–1 Kita-Aoyama, Minato-ku, tel. 03/3406–1021. Daily 10:30–7. Subway: Ginza, Chiyoda, and Hanzō-mon lines, Omotesandō Eki (Exit A1).

**Koshino Junko.** Shop here for sophisticated clothing and accessories with a European accent. 6–5–36 Minami-Aoyama, Minato-ku, tel. 03/3406–7370. Mon.–Sat. 10–8. Subway: Ginza, Chiyoda, and Hanzō-mon lines, Omotesandō Eki (Exit B1).

## DEPĀTO

Most Japanese department stores are parts of conglomerates that include railways, real estate, and leisure industries. The stores themselves commonly have travel agencies, theaters, and art galleries on the premises, as well as reasonably priced restaurants on the upper or basement floors, with coffee shops strategically located in between.

Major depāto accept credit cards and provide shipping services. Some staff members speak English. If you're having communication difficulties, someone will eventually come to the rescue. On the first floor you'll invariably find a general information booth with useful maps of the store in English.

A visit to a Japanese depāto is not merely a shopping excursion—it's a lesson in Japanese culture. Plan to arrive just before it opens: promptly on the hour, two immaculately groomed young women face the customers from inside, bow ceremoniously, and unlock the doors. Walk through the store: the staff are all standing at attention, in postures of nearly reverent welcome. Notice the uniform angle of incline: many stores have training sessions to teach their new employees the precise and proper degree at which to bend from the waist.

Visit the food specialty departments on the lower levels—and be prepared for an overwhelming selection of Japanese and Western delicacies. No Japanese housewife in her right mind would shop here regularly for her groceries. A brief exploration, however, will give you a pretty good picture of what she might select for a special occasion—and the price she's prepared to pay for it. Many stalls have small samples out on the counter, and nobody will raise a fuss if you help yourself, even if you make no purchase.

Most major depāto close one or two days a month, different stores on different days of the week—but normally on Tuesday or Wednesday. These schedules vary considerably; in holiday gift-giving seasons, for example, they may be open every day. To be on the safe side, call ahead.

## Ginza/Nihombashi

**Matsuya.** The slightly frazzled presentation here is a welcome change from the generally refined and immaculately ordered shopping in the Ginza/Nihombashi area. The merchandise at

Matsuya is meant for a younger crowd, and shoppers with the patience to comb through the hordes of goods will be rewarded with many finds, particularly in women's clothing. *3–6–1 Ginza, Chūō-ku, tel. 03/3567–1211. Daily 10–8. Subway: Ginza, Marunouchi, and Hibiya lines, Ginza Eki (Exits A12 and A13).*

**Matsuzakaya.** The Matsuzakaya conglomerate was founded in Nagoya and still commands the loyalties of shoppers with origins in western Japan. Style-conscious Tōkyōites tend to find the sense of fashion here a bit countrified. *6–10–1 Ginza, Chūō-ku, tel. 03/3572–1111. Mon.–Thurs. 10:30–7:30, Fri.–Sat. 10:30–8, Sun. 10:30–7. Subway: Ginza, Marunouchi, and Hibiya lines, Ginza Eki (Exits A3 and A4).*

**Mitsukoshi.** Founded in 1673 as a dry-goods store, Mitsukoshi later played one of the leading roles in introducing Western merchandise to Japan. It has retained its image of quality and excellence, with a particularly strong representation of Western fashion designers, such as Chanel, Lanvin, and Givenchy. Mitsukoshi also stocks a fine selection of traditional Japanese goods. *1–4–1 Nihombashi Muro-machi, Chūō-ku, tel. 03/3241–3311. Daily 10–7. Subway: Ginza and Hanzō-mon lines, Mitsukoshi-mae Eki (Exits A3 and A5). 4–6–16 Ginza, Chūō-ku, tel. 03/3562–1111. Mon.–Sat. 10–8, Sun 10–7:30. Subway: Ginza, Marunouchi, and Hibiya lines, Ginza Eki (Exits A6, A7, A8).*

**Takashimaya.** The kimono department here, one of the best in Tōkyō, draws its share of brides-to-be to shop for their weddings. In addition to a complete selection of traditional crafts, antiques, and curios, Takashimaya sells very fine Japanese and Western designer goods and so has a broad, sophisticated appeal. *2–4–1 Nihombashi, Chūō-ku, tel. 03/3211–4111. Daily 10–7. Subway: Ginza Line, Nihombashi Eki (Exits B1 and B2).*

**Wako.** Deftly avoiding the classification of a mere depāto by confining itself to a limited selections of goods at the top end of the market, Wako is particularly known for its glassware, jewelry, and accessories—and for some of the handsomest, most sophisticated window displays in town. 4–5–11 Ginza, Chūō-ku, tel. 03/3562–2111. Mon.–Sat. 10:30–6. Subway: Ginza, Marunouchi, and Hibiya lines, Ginza Eki (Exits A9 and A10).

## Shibuya

**Parco.** Owned by Seibu depāto, Parco is actually not one store but four, vertical malls filled with small retail stores and boutiques, all in hailing distance of one another in the commercial heart of Shibuya. Parco Part 1 and Part 4 (Quattro) cater to a younger crowd, stocking "generic" unbranded casual clothing, crafts fabrics, and accessories from foreign climes; Quattro even has a club that hosts live music. Part 2 is devoted mainly to upmarket designer fashions, and Part 3 sells a mixture of men's and women's fashions, tableware, and household furnishings. A major overhaul of all four buildings, scheduled for completion in 2002, was under way at press time; the company plans eventually to open a fifth outlet in the area. 15–1 Udagawa-chō, Shibuya-ku, tel. 03/3464–5111. Parts 1, 2, and 3 daily 10–8:30; Quattro daily 11–9. Subway: Ginza and Hanzō-mon lines, Shibuya Eki (Exits 6 and 7).

**Seibu.** The mammoth main branch of this depāto—where even many Japanese customers get lost—is in Ikebukuro. The Shibuya branch, which still carries an impressive array of merchandise, is smaller and more manageable. Seibu is the flagship operation of a conglomerate that owns a railway line and a baseball team, the Seibu Lions. When the Lions win the pennant, prepare to go shopping: All the Seibu stores have major sales the following day (be prepared for even bigger crowds than usual). This store has an excellent selection of household goods, from furniture to china and lacquerware. 21–1 Udagawa-chō, Shibuya-ku, tel. 03/3462–0111. Mon.–Tues. and weekends 10–8, Thurs.–Fri. 10–9. Subway/JR: Shibuya Eki (Hachiko exit for JR lines, Exits 6 and 7 for Ginza and Hanzō-mon lines).

**Tōkyū.** Tōkyū's marketing strategy is apparently to harvest the spin from its Bunka-mura cultural complex next door, but this hasn't been all that successful in drawing young consumers away from rival Seibu. The store carries a good selection of imported clothing, accessories, and home furnishings, but the ambience overall is a bit conservative. 2–24–1 Dōgen-zaka, Shibuya-ku, tel. 03/3477–3111. Wed.–Mon. 10–8. Subway/JR: Shibuya Eki (Hachiko exit for JR lines, Exit 3A for Ginza and Hanzō-mon lines).

**Tōkyū Hands.** Known commonly just as "Hands," this do-it-yourself and hobby store stocks an excellent selection of carpentry tools, sewing accessories, kitchen goods, plants, and other related merchandise. The toy department is unbearably cute, and the stationery department has a comprehensive selection of Japanese papers. 12–18 Udagawa-chō, Shibuya-ku, tel. 03/5489–5111. Daily 10–8; closed 2nd and 3rd Mon. of month. Subway/JR: Shibuya Eki (Hachiko exit for JR lines, Exits 6 and 7 for Ginza and Hanzō-mon lines).

## Shinjuku

**Isetan.** Often called the Bloomingdale's of Japan—a description that doesn't quite do this store justice—Isetan has become a nearly universal favorite, with one of the most complete selections of Japanese designers in one place. If you're looking for distinctive looks without paying designer prices, this is the place for you: the store carries a wide range of knockoff brands. But expect to look long and hard for something that fits; these clothes are made specifically for the Japanese market. Ceramics, stationery, and furniture here are generally of high quality and interesting design; the folk-crafts department carries a small but good selection of fans, table mats, and other gifts. 3–14–1 Shinjuku, Shinjuku-ku, tel. 03/3352–1111. Mon.–Thurs. 10–7:30, Fri.–Sun. 10–8. Subway/JR: Shinjuku Eki (Higashi-guchi/East Exit for JR lines; Exits B2, B3, B4, and B5 for Marunouchi Line).

**Keiō.** This no-nonsense depāto has a standard but complete selection of merchandise. A me-too operation, it seems somehow to have avoided creating an image uniquely its own. *1–1–4 Nishi-Shinjuku, Shinjuku-ku, tel. 03/3342–2111. Daily 10–8. Subway/JR: Shinjuku Eki (Nishi-guchi/West Exit for JR lines, Exit A10 for Marunouchi Line).*

**Marui.** Marui is not so much a depāto as a group of specialty stores that focus on young fashions and household effects. Wildly successful for its easy credit policies, Marui is where you go when you've just landed your first job, moved into your first apartment, and need to outfit yourself presentably on the cheap. Twice a year, in February and July, prices are slashed dramatically in major clearance sales. If you're in the neighborhood, you'll know exactly when the sales are taking place: The lines will extend into the street and around the block. *3–30–16 Shinjuku, Shinjuku-ku, tel. 03/3354–0101. Thurs.–Tues. 11–8. Subway/JR: Shinjuku Eki (Nishi-guchi/West Exit for JR lines; Exits A1, A2, A3, and A4 for Marunouchi Line).*

**Odakyu.** Slightly snazzier than neighboring Keiō depāto, Odakyu is a very family-oriented store, particularly good for children's clothing. Across the street from the main building is Odakyu Halc, with a varied selection of home furnishings and interior goods on its upper floors. *1–1–3 Nishi-Shinjuku, Shinjuku-ku, tel. 03/3342–2111. Daily 10–8. Subway/JR: Shinjuku Eki (Nishi-guchi/West Exit for JR lines, Exit A10 for Marunouchi Line).*

## In This Chapter

Updated by Jared Lubarsky

# outdoor activities and sports

**JAPAN'S FERVOR FOR BASEBALL** rivals the U.S., and, with the help of legalized gambling, soccer has also made it's mark on the national landscape. If you're interested in a sport that's more *eastern*, there's always sumō wrestling. As with most big cities, unless you enjoy crowded jogging paths, staying in shape means heading indoors.

## PARTICIPANT SPORTS

### Golf

Golfing can be a daunting prospect for the casual visitor to Tōkyō: The few public courses are far from the city, and booking a tee time on even a week's notice is almost impossible. What you can do, however, if the golf bug is in your blood, is groove your swing at one of the many practice ranges in Tōkyō itself. Most driving ranges are open from 11 AM to 7 or 8 at night and will rent you a club for around ¥200. At **Golf Range Pinflag** (1–7–13 Tsukiji, Chūō-ku, tel. 03/3542–2936; Hibiya subway line, Tsukiji Eki [Exit 4]), a bucket of 24 balls costs ¥350, and you can generally get a tee without waiting very long. At the **Meguro Gorufu-jō** (5–6–22 Kami-Meguro, Meguro-ku, tel. 03/3713–2805; Tōkyū Toyoko private railway line, Nakameguro Eki), you buy a prepaid card for ¥2,000, which allows you to hit up to 142 balls. The centrally located **Shiba Gofuru-jō** (4–8–2 Shiba Kōen, Minato-ku, tel. 03/5470–1111; Toei Mita subway line, Shiba Kōen

Eki [Exit A4]) has three decks of practice tees. A bucket of only 20 balls costs ¥650 weekdays, ¥900 weekends.

## Jogging

The venue of choice for runners who work in the central wards of Chūō-ku and Chiyoda-ku is the **Imperial Palace Outer garden.** Sakurada-mon, at the west end of the park, is the traditional starting point for the 5-km (3-mi) run around the palace— though you can join in anywhere along the route. Jogging around the palace is a ritual that begins as early as 6 AM and goes on throughout the day, no matter what the weather. Almost everybody runs the course counterclockwise. Now and then you may spot someone going the opposite way, but freethinking of this sort is frowned upon in Japan.

## Swimming and Fitness

Pools and fitness centers abound in Tōkyō, but the vast majority of them are for members only. At the major international hotels, of course, you would have guest privileges at these facilities, but if your accommodations are further downscale, places to swim or work out are harder to find. The fitness center at **Big Box Seibu Sports Plaza Athletic Club** (1–35–3 Takada-no-baba, Shinjuku-ku, tel. 03/3208–7171) is open to nonmembers for ¥4,000; use of the pool, which is only available on Sunday 10–6, is an additional ¥1,500. The **Clark Hatch Fitness Center** (2–1–3 Azabu-dai, Minato-ku, tel. 03/3584–4092) has a full array of machines for mortification of the flesh and charges a guest fee of ¥2,600 for nonmembers. It does not have a pool. You don't have to be a resident to use one of the facilities operated by the various wards of Tōkyō; one of the best of these is the **Minato Ward Shiba Pool** (2–7–2 Shiba Kōen, Minato-ku, tel. 03/3431–4449), which is open Tuesday–Saturday 9:30–8 and Sunday–Monday 9:30–5. The pool charges only ¥300 for two hours of swimming.

# SPECTATOR SPORTS

## Baseball

Since 2001, when superstar Ichirō Suzuki moved to the Seattle Mariners and made the All-Star team in his first major-league season, baseball frenzy has never been greater in Japan. The game, to be sure, has been a national obsession for more than a century—but don't imagine that it's played quite the same way here as it is elsewhere. The pace and style, the fans and their worldview, are uniquely Japanese. An afternoon in the bleachers, when a despised rival like the Hanshin Tigers are in town from Ōsaka, will give you insights into the temper of everyday life available nowhere else.

The Japanese baseball season runs between April and October. Same-day tickets are hard to come by; try the **Playguide** ticket agency (tel. 03/3561–8821). **Ticket Pia** (tel. 03/5237–9999) handles mainly music and theater but can also book and sell tickets to sporting events. Depending on the stadium, the date, and the seat location, expect to pay from ¥1,900 to ¥8,000 for an afternoon at the ballpark.

Baseball fans in Tōkyō are blessed with a choice of three home teams. The Yomiuri Giants and the Nippon Ham Fighters both play at the 55,000-seat **Tōkyō Dome.** 1–3–61 Kōraku, Bunkyō-ku, tel. 03/5800–9999. Subway: Marunouchi and Namboku lines, Kōraku-en Eki (Exit 2); Ōedo and Toei Mita lines, Kasuga Eki (Exit A2); JR Suidō-bashi Eki (Nishi-guchi/West Exit).

The home ground of the Yakult Swallows is **Jingū Baseball Stadium,** in the Outer Gardens of Meiji Jingū. 13 Kasumigaoka, Shinjuku-ku, tel. 03/3404–8999. Subway: Ginza Line, Gaien-mae Eki (Exit 2).

## Soccer

Soccer is one of the marketing miracles of Japan. It was launched as a full-fledged professional sport only in 1993, and within three years—buoyed by a stunningly successful media hype—was drawing crowds of 6 million spectators a season. Much of that success was due to superstars like Gary Linaker and Dragan Stojkovic, who came to Japan to finish out their careers and train the inexperienced local teams. By 1990, the J. League had 26 teams in two divisions, and European and Latin American clubs were scouting for talented Japanese players. The popularity of soccer waned for a time but has revived again— thanks in part to Japan's successful bid to co-host the 2002 World Cup, and in part by the introduction in 2001 of legalized gambling on the results of the J. League's 13 weekly matches. (The biggest payoff in the "Toto" pools is ¥100 million.)

The original J. League marketing plan called for the fledgling soccer clubs to be sponsored by small cities in the provinces, many of them with moribund economies and declining populations; these cities would build modest stadiums for their clubs and ride the popularity of soccer back to prosperity. The plan worked, with one odd result: Tōkyō never acquired a home team. Now it has two, FC Tōkyō and Tōkyō Verde, both of which play at the 50,000-seat **Tōkyō Stadium** in Tama. The J. League season has two 15-week schedules, one beginning in mid-March and the other in mid-August; visitors to Tōkyō have a pretty fair window of opportunity to see a match. Tickets cost ¥1,000–¥6,000 and can be ordered through **Playguide** (tel. 03/3561–8821) or **Ticket Pia** (tel. 03/5237–9999). *376–3 Nishi-machi, Chōfu-shi, tel. 0424/40–0555. JR Keiō Line, Tobitakyū Eki.*

## Sumō

Sumō wrestling dates back some 1,500 years. Originally it was not merely a sport but a religious rite, performed at shrines to entertain the gods that presided over the harvest. Ritual and ceremony are still important elements of sumō matches— contestants in unique regalia, referees in gorgeous costumes, elaborately choreographed openings and closings. To the casual spectator a match itself can look like a mostly naked free-for-all. Stripped down to silk loincloths, the two wrestlers square off in a dirt ring about 15 ft in diameter and charge straight at each other; the first one to step out of the ring or touch the ground with anything but the soles of his feet loses. Other than that, there are no rules—not even weight divisions: a runt of merely 250 pounds can find himself facing an opponent twice his size.

Of the six Grand Tournaments (called *basho*) that take place during the year, Tōkyō hosts three of them: in early January, mid-May, and mid-September. The tournaments take place in the **Kokugikan**, the National Sumō Arena, in the Ryōgoku district on the east side of the Sumida-gawa. Matches go from early afternoon, when the novices wrestle, to the titanic clashes of the upper ranks at around 6 PM. The price of admission buys you a whole day of sumō; the most expensive seats, closest to the ring, are tatami-floor loges for four people, called *sajiki*. The loges are terribly cramped, but the cost (¥9,200–¥11,300) includes all sorts of food and drink and souvenirs, brought around to you by Kokugikan attendants in traditional costume. The cheapest seats cost ¥3,600 for advanced sales, ¥2,100 for same-day box office sales. For same-day box office sales you should line up an hour in advance of the tournament. You can also reserve tickets through **Playguide** (tel. 03/3561–8821) or **Ticket Pia** (tel. 03/5237–9999). *1–3–28 Yokoami, Sumida-ku, tel. 03/3622–1100. JR Sōbu Line, Ryōgoku Eki (Nishi-guchi/West Exit).*

## In This Chapter

Updated by Jared Lubarsky

# nightlife and the arts

**THE SHEER DIVERSITY** of Tōkyō's nightlife can be daunting—if not downright hazardous. Few bars and clubs have printed price lists; fewer still have lists in English. That drink you've just ordered could set you back a reasonable ¥1,000; you might, on the other hand, have wandered unknowingly into a place that charges you ¥15,000 up front for a whole bottle—and slaps a ¥20,000 cover charge on top. If the bar has hostesses, it is often unclear what the companionship of one will cost you, or whether she is there just for conversation. There is, of course, a certain amount of safe ground: hotel lounges, jazz clubs, bars, and cabarets where foreigners come out to play—and the unspoken rules of nightlife are pretty much the way they are anywhere else. But wandering off the beaten path in Tōkyō can be like shopping for a yacht: if you have to ask how much it costs, you probably can't afford it anyhow.

Few cities have as much to offer as Tōkyō does in the performing arts. It has Japan's own great stage traditions: Kabuki, Nō, Bunraku puppet drama, music, and dance. An astonishing variety of music, classical and popular, can be found here; Tōkyō is a proving ground for local talent and a magnet for orchestras and concert soloists from all over the world. Eric Clapton, Yo-Yo Ma, Winton Marsalis: whenever you visit, the headliners will be here.

## NIGHTLIFE

There are five major districts in Tōkyō that have an extensive nightlife and have places that make foreigners welcome. The *kinds* of entertainment will not vary much from one to another; the tone, style, and prices will.

**Akasaka** nightlife concentrates mainly on two streets, Tamachi-dōri and Hitotsugi-dōri, and the small alleys connecting them. The area has several cabarets and nightclubs, and a wide range of wine bars, coffee shops, late-night restaurants, pubs, and "snacks"—counter bars that will serve (and charge you for) small portions of food with your drinks, whether you order them or not. Akasaka is sophisticated and upscale, not quite as expensive as Ginza and not as popular as Roppongi. Being fairly compact, it makes a convenient venue for testing the waters of Japanese nightlife.

**Ginza** is probably the city's most well-known entertainment district, and one of the most—if not the most—expensive in the world. It does have affordable restaurants and pubs, but its reputation rests on the exclusive hostess clubs where only the highest of high rollers on corporate expense accounts can take their clients. In recent years many corporations have been taking a harder look at those accounts, and Ginza as a nightlife destination has suffered in the process.

**Roppongi** draws a largely foreign crowd and is the part of Tōkyō where Westerners are most likely to feel at home, though the area's reputation as a haunt of the rich and beautiful has taken a battering recently as petty crime and general unpleasantness dog Roppongi's once-flourishing nightlife. With the cool kids getting their kicks in Aoyama and Azabu and even the stiletto-heel brigade migrating to Shibuya, Roppongi's club scene is in decay. It's best for barhopping.

**Shibuya,** less expensive than Roppongi and not as raunchy as Shinjuku, attracts mainly students and young professionals to its many *nomiya* (inexpensive bars). There's something a bit provincial about it, in that respect, and there are few places where you can count on communicating in English, but if you know a little Japanese, this is a pleasant and inexpensive area for an evening out.

**Shinjuku's Kabuki-chō** is the city's wildest nightlife venue. The options range from the marginally respectable down to the merely sleazy to where you can almost hear the viruses mutating. Bars (straight, gay, cross-dress, S&M), nightclubs, cabarets, discos, hole-in-the-wall pubs, love-by-the-hour hotels: Kabuki-chō has it all. Just stay clear of places with English-speaking touts out front, and you'll be fine. If you're a woman unescorted, however, you probably want to stay out of Kabuki-chō after 9 PM; by then there are bound to be a few men drunk enough to make nuisances of themselves.

# Bars

**AGAVE.** Tucked away in a basement just off Roppongi's main drag, Roppongi-dōri, is the perfect place for anyone who craves mariachi and a margarita. With more than 400 types of tequila on offer at Agave, lovers of Mexican firewater won't be disappointed. You can line your stomach with a selection of nachos and other snacks before a slammer session. *Clover Bldg. B1F, 7–15–10 Roppongi, Minato-ku; tel. 03/3497–0229. Drinks from ¥800. Mon.–Thurs. 6:30 PM–2 AM, Fri. 6:30 PM–4 AM, Sat. 6 PM–4 AM. Subway: Hibiya Line, Roppongi Eki.*

**Charleston.** For years this has been the schmoozing and hunting bar for Tōkyō's single foreign community, and the young Japanese who want to meet them. It's noisy and packed until the wee small hours. *3–8–11 Roppongi, Minato-ku, tel. 03/ 3402–0372. Drinks from ¥800. Nightly 6 PM–5 AM. Subway: Hibiya Line, Roppongi Eki.*

**Den.** Launched by the mammoth beer and whiskey maker Suntory, Den is partly an exercise in corporate-image making. Meant to express the company's ecoconsciousness and its roots in traditional Japanese culture, the motif here is a confection of stones, trees, and articles of folkcraft. Den draws a fashionable crowd from the TV production, PR, and design companies in this part of town. *DST Bldg., 1st floor, 4–2–3 Akasaka, Minato-ku, tel. 03/3584–1899. Drinks from ¥800. Mon.–Thurs. 6 PM–2 AM, Fri. 6 PM–4 AM, Sat. 6 PM–11 PM. Subway: Marunouchi Line, Akasaka-mitsuke Eki (Belle Vie Akasaka Exit).*

**Ginza Inz 2.** Inside this building and one floor up is a collection of small, popular-priced bars and restaurants where people who work in the area go after hours. One such bar is the **Americana** (tel. 03/3564–1971), where drinks start at ¥800. Farther along the hallway is the **Ginza Swing** (tel. 03/3563–3757), which hosts live bands playing swing jazz. The cover varies but is usually ¥2,800; drinks start at ¥700. Ginza Inz 2 is one building east of the Kōtsū Kaikan Building; you can recognize the latter by the circular sky lounge on the roof. *2–2 Nishi-Ginza, Chūō-ku. Subway/JR: Yūraku-chō Eki (Central Exit).*

**Highlander.** The Highlander Bar in the Hotel Okura purports to stock 224 brands of Scotch whiskey, 48 of them single malts. This is a smart place to meet business acquaintances or to have a civilized drink. *Hotel Okura, 2–10–4 Tora-no-mon, Minato-ku, tel. 03/3505–6077. Drinks from ¥1,100. Mon.–Sat. 11:30 AM–1 AM, Sun. 11:30 AM–midnight. Subway: Ginza Line, Tora-no-mon Eki (Exit 3).*

**The Old Imperial Bar.** Comfortable and sedate, this is the pride of the Imperial Hotel, decorated with elements saved from Frank Lloyd Wright's earlier version of the building—alas, long since torn down. *Imperial Hotel, 1–1–1 Uchisaiwai-chō, Chiyoda-ku, tel. 03/3504–1111. Drinks from ¥1,000. Daily 11:30 AM–midnight. Subway: Hibiya Eki (Exit A13).*

**Wine Bar.** Racks and casks and dimly lighted corners: the atmosphere at this European-style bistro appeals to Japanese and gaijin. This is a good place to take a date before moving on to the dance clubs. *5–6–12 Ginza, Chuo-ku, tel. 03/3569–7211.*

Drinks from ¥600. Daily 5 PM–11:30 PM. Subway: Ginza and Hibiya lines, Ginza Eki (Ginza exit).

## Beer Halls

**Kirin City.** There's somewhat less glass-thumping and mock-Oktoberfest good cheer here than at other brewery-sponsored beer halls, but the menu of grilled chicken, fried potatoes, onion rings, and other snacks to wash down with a brew is just as good. The clientele tends to be groups of white-collar youngsters from area offices, unwinding after work. *Bunshōdo Bldg., 2nd floor, 3–4–12 Ginza, Chūō-ku, tel. 03/3562–2593. Beer ¥460. Daily 11:30–11. Subway: Ginza, Hibiya, and Marunouchi lines, Ginza Eki (Exit A13).*

**Sapporo Lion.** For a casual evening of beer and ballast—anything from yakitori to spaghetti—the Sapporo Lion is a popular and inexpensive choice. The entrance is off Chūō-dōri, near the Matsuzakaya depāto. *6–10–12 Ginza, Chūō-ku, tel. 03/3571–2590. Beer from ¥590. Mon.–Sat. 11:30–11. Subway: Ginza, Hibiya, and Marunouchi lines, Ginza Eki (Exit A3).*

**What the Dickens.** Sixteenth-century English-style pubs have been the big trend in Tōkyō in the past few years, and this is the king of them all, particularly for the gaijin crowd. In a former Aum Shinri Kyō headquarters in Ebisu (the cult held responsible for the gas attack in the Tōkyō subway), it is nearly always packed. There are live stage acts and poetry readings (first Sunday of the month), and live music starts nightly at 8:30. *1–13–3 Ebisu-Nishi, Shibuya-ku, Roob 6 Bldg., 4th floor, tel. 03/3780–2099. Sun. 5 PM–midnight, Tues.–Wed. 5 PM–1 AM, Thurs.–Sat. 5 PM–2 AM. Subway: Hibiya Line, Ebisu Eki (JR Ebisu Nishi-guchi/West Exit).*

## Dance Clubs

The club scene is alive in Tōkyō but less well than it was before the uptown crowd started to feel the pinch in its discretionary income. Dance clubs have always been ephemeral ventures, anyhow. They disappear fairly regularly, to open again with new identities, stranger names, and newer gimmicks—although the money behind them is usually the same. Even those listed here come with no guarantee they'll be around when you arrive, but it can't hurt to investigate. Where else can you work out, survey the vinyl-miniskirt brigades, and get a drink at 3 AM?

**BUL-LET'S.** Billed as an "ambient space," this club is so laid-back there are even a couple of mattresses in the middle of the room for those too tired to cut a rug. DJs spin minimal and electronica to a young and groovy crowd—a haven for lounge lizards in the maelstrom of Roppongi. B1F 1–7–11 Nishi-Azabu, Minato-ku, tel. 03/3401–4844. ¥1,000–¥2,000 (varies by event). Daily 10 PM–late (varies by event). Subway: Hibiya and Ōedo lines, Roppongi Eki.

**Geoid/Flower.** Geoid's way-after-hours (it opens at 5 AM) techno beats keep after-Roppongi party clubbers going until it closes at 1 PM—the same day. It's on Telebi Asahi-dōri, halfway between Roppongi and Hiro-o. Togensha Visiting Bldg., basement, 3–5–5 Nishi-Azabu, Minato-ku, tel. 03/3479–8161. ¥2,500 (varies by event). Sat. 5 AM–1 PM. Subway: Hibiya and Ōedo lines, Roppongi Eki.

**Luners.** At this two-story venue, barflies sit it out with a martini upstairs while hard-core dancers head for the packed dance floor in the basement. DJ offerings usually include house, trance, or a combination of the two, with monthly gay/mixed parties attracting Tōkyō's out-and-out clubbers. Fukao Bldg., 1st floor and basement, 1–4–5 Azabu-jūban, Minato-ku, tel. 03/3586–6383. ¥3,000–¥3,500 (varies by event). Fri.–Sun. 10 PM–5 AM. Subway: Ōedo Line, Azabu-jūban Eki (Exit 7).

**Maniac Love.** Known by Tōkyōites for its consistently excellent techno, garage, and ambient music, Maniac Love proves that Japanese DJs have technique to support their style. It helps that they tend to become experts in their genres by collecting even the most obscure tracks. The club also hosts regular Sunday-morning after-hours parties from 5 AM. The ¥1,000 after-hours entry fee includes free coffee. 5-10-6 Minami-Aoyama, off Kottō-dōri, tel. 03/3406–1166. ¥2,500, ¥1,000 for after-hours party. Sun.–Fri. until 5 AM (Sun. after-hours party usually ends by lunchtime); Sat. until 10 AM. Subway: Ginza and Hanzō-mon lines, Omotesandō Eki.

**Milk.** In the basement beneath What the Dickens Pub, this place is a milk bar à la *Clockwork Orange*. With tables shaped like nude women and obscene inflatable goodies, this club caters to young Tōkyōites who yearn for digital sounds, techno, or even hard rock in an erotic atmosphere. Milk hosts hip live acts and avant-garde events. DJs and the types of music change daily. 1–13–3 Ebisu-Nishi, Roob 6 Bldg., basement and 2nd-level basement, Shibuya-ku, tel. 03/5458–2826. ¥3,500, with 2 drinks. Nightly 8 PM–4 AM. JR Yamanote and Hibiya subway line: Ebisu Eki (JR Ebisu Nishi-guchi/West Exit).

**Organ Bar.** The eclectic selection at the Organ Bar, an avant-garde addition to Shibuya's nightspots, ranges from jazz to disco with a spot of poetry reading thrown in for good measure. There are no actual organs (musical or bodily) to speak of. Kuretake Bldg. 3F, 4–9 Udagawa-chō, Shibuya-ku, tel. 03/5489–5460. Sun.–Thurs. ¥1,000, Fri. and Sat. special events ¥2,000. Nightly 9 PM–4 AM. JR Yamanote and Ginza and Hanzō-mon subway lines: Shibuya Eki (Hachiko Exit).

**328 (San-ni-pa).** A fixture on the club scene since the early '90s, 328 hosts all genres of music. Across the street from Hobson's Ice Cream and next to the police box at the Nishi-Azabu intersection, 328 is often crowded due to its reputation for providing a consistently good time. It's rumored that musician Ryuichi Sakamoto and famous fashion designers sometimes stop by. 3–24–20 Nishi-Azabu, basement, Minato-ku, tel. 03/3401–4968. ¥2,500, with 2 drinks. Nightly 8 PM–5 AM. Subway: Hibiya and Ōedo lines, Roppongi Eki, then a 10-min walk; from Shibuya, take Roppongi-bound bus.

## Live Music

**Body and Soul.** Owner Kyoko Seki has been a jazz fan and an impresario for nearly 20 years. There's nothing fancy about this place—just good, serious jazz, some of it played by musicians who come in after hours, when they've finished gigs elsewhere, just to jam. *Anise Minami-Aoyama Bldg., B1 floor, 6–13–9 Minami-Aoyama, Minato-ku, tel. 03/5466–3348. Cover charge ¥3,500–¥4,000, drinks from ¥700. Mon.–Sat. 7 PM–12:30 AM. Subway: Hibiya Line, Roppongi Eki.*

**Club Quattro.** More a concert hall than a club, the Quattro hosts one show nightly, with a heavy accent on world music—especially Latin and African—by Japanese and foreign groups. Audiences tend to be young and enthusiastic. *Parco IV Bldg., 32–13 Utagawa-chō, Shibuya-ku, tel. 03/3477–8750. Cover charge ¥2,500–¥7,000. Shows usually start at 7 PM. Subway/JR: Shibuya Eki (Kita-guchi/North Exit for JR Yamanote Line and Ginza subway line; Exits 5 and 8 for Hanzō-mon subway line).*

## Skyline Lounges

**New York Bar.** All the style you would expect of one of the city's top hotels combined with superior views of Shinjuku's skyscrapers and neon-lighted streets make the New York Bar one of Tōkyō's premier nighttime venues. The price of the drinks may encourage you to sip quite slowly as you enjoy the view. And while the cover charge may be steep, the quality of the jazz on offer equals that of the view. *Park Hyatt Hotel 52F, 3–7–1–2 Nishi-Shinjuku, Shinjuku-ku, tel. 03/5322–1234. Cover charge ¥1,700 (from 8 PM Mon.–Sat., 7 PM Sun.). Drinks start at ¥800. Mon.–Sat. 5 PM–midnight, Sun. 4 PM–11 PM. Subway: Ōedo Line, Tochō-mae Eki.*

**Top of Akasaka.** On the 40th floor of the Akasaka Prince Hotel, you can enjoy some of the finest views of Tōkyō. If you can time your visit for dusk, the price of one drink gets you two views—the daylight sprawl of buildings and the twinkling lights of evening. *Akasaka Prince, 1–2 Kioi-chō, Chiyoda-ku, tel. 03/3234–1111. Drinks start at ¥1,000. Table charge ¥800 per person. Weekdays noon–2 AM, weekends noon–midnight. Subway: Ginza and Marunouchi lines, Akasaka-mitsuke Eki (Exit D).*

## THE ARTS

Tōkyō has modern theater—in somewhat limited choices, to be sure, unless you can follow dialogue in Japanese, but Western repertory companies can always find receptive audiences here for plays in English. In recent years musicals have found enormous popularity here; it doesn't take long for a hit show in New York or London to open in Tōkyō.

Japan has yet to develop any real strength of its own in ballet and has only just begun to devote serious resources to opera, but for that reason touring companies like the Metropolitan, the Bolshoi, Sadler's Wells, and the Bayerische Staatsoper find Tōkyō a very compelling venue—as well they might, when even seats at ¥30,000 or more sell out far in advance.

Film presents a much broader range of possibilities than it did in the past. The major commercial distributors bring in the movies they expect will draw the biggest receipts—horror films and Oscar nominees—but there are now dozens of small theaters in Tōkyō catering to more sophisticated audiences.

## Information and Tickets

One of the best comprehensive guides in English to performance schedules in Tōkyō is the "Cityscope" insert in the monthly *Tōkyō Journal* magazine. You can probably pick up the *Tōkyō Journal* at one of the newsstands at Narita Airport on your way into the city; if not, it's on sale in the bookstores at major international hotels. *Metropolis*, a free weekly magazine available at hotels, book and music stores, some restaurants and cafés, and other locations, lists up-to-date announcements of what's going on in the city.

Another source, rather less complete, is the *Tour Companion*, a tabloid visitor guide published every two weeks that is available free of charge at hotels and at Japan National Tourist Organization offices.

If your hotel cannot help you with concert and performance bookings, call **Ticket Pia** (tel. 03/5237–9999) for assistance in English. Be warned: this is one of the city's major ticket agencies; the lines are always busy, and it can be maddeningly difficult to get through. When phone calls fail, try the **Playguide Agency,** which has outlets in most of the depāto and in other locations all over the city, for tickets to cultural events; you can stop in at the main office (Playguide Bldg., 2–6–4 Ginza, Chūō-ku, tel. 03/3561–8821, fax 03/3567–0263; Yūraku-chō subway line, Ginza Itchōme Eki, Exit 4) and ask for the nearest counter. Note that agencies normally do not have tickets for same-day performances but only for advance booking.

## Traditional Theater

### BUNRAKU

The spiritual center of Bunraku today is Ōsaka, rather than Tōkyō, but there are a number of performances in the small hall of the Kokuritsu Gekijō. In recent years it has come into vogue with younger audiences, and Bunraku troupes will occasionally perform in trendier locations. Consult the "Cityscope" listings, or check with one of the English-speaking ticket agencies.

### KABUKI

The best place to see Kabuki is at the **Kabuki-za,** built especially for this purpose, with its *hanamichi* (runway) passing diagonally through the audience to the revolving stage. Built originally in 1925, the Kabuki-za was destroyed in an air raid in 1945 and rebuilt in the identical style in 1951. Matinees usually begin at 11 and end at 4; evening performances, at 4:30, end around 9. Reserved seats are expensive and hard to come by on short notice; for a mere ¥800 to ¥1,000, however, you can buy an unreserved ticket that allows you to see one act of a play from the topmost gallery. The gallery is cleared after each act, but there's nothing to prevent you from buying another ticket. Bring binoculars—the gallery is very far from the stage. You might also want to rent an earphone set (¥650; deposit ¥1,000) to follow the play in English, but this is really more of an intrusion than a help—and you can't use the set in the topmost galleries. *4–12–15 Ginza, Chūō-ku, tel. 03/5565–6000 or 03/3541–3131, www.shochiku.co.jp/play/kabukiza/theater. Call by 6 PM the day preceding performance for reservations. Subway: Hibiya and Toei Asakusa lines, Higashi-Ginza Eki (Exit 3).*

The **Kokuritsu Gekijō** hosts Kabuki companies based elsewhere; it also has a training program for young people who may not have one of the hereditary family connections but want to break into this closely guarded profession. Debut performances, called *kao-mise*, are worth watching to catch the stars of the next generation. Reserved seats are usually ¥1,500–¥9,000. *4–1 Hayabusa-chō, Chiyoda-ku, tel. 03/3230–3000. Subway: Hanzō-mon Line, Hanzō-mon Eki (Exit 1).*

The **Shimbashi Enbujō**, which dates to 1925, was built originally for the geisha of the Shimbashi quarter to present their spring and autumn performances of traditional music and dance. It's a bigger house than the Kabuki-za, and it presents a lot of traditional dance and conventional Japanese drama as well as Kabuki. Reserved seats commonly run ¥2,100–¥16,800, and there is no gallery. *6–18–2 Ginza, Chūō-ku, tel. 03/5565–6000. Subway: Hibiya and Toei Asakusa lines, Higashi-Ginza Eki (Exit A6).*

## NŌ

Somewhat like Kabuki, Nō is divided into a number of schools, the traditions of which developed as the exclusive property of hereditary families. The best way to see Nō is in the open air, at torchlight performances called Takigi Nō, held in the courtyards of temples. The setting and the aesthetics of the drama combine to produce an eerie theatrical experience. These performances are given at various times during the year. Consult the "Cityscope" or *Tour Companion* listings. Tickets sell out quickly and are normally available only through the temples.

Nō performances occasionally take place in public halls, like the **National Nō Theater,** but are primarily done in the theaters of the individual schools—which also teach their dance and recitation styles to amateurs. *4–18–1 Sendagaya, Shibuya-ku, tel. 03/3423–1331. JR Chūō Line, Sendagaya Eki (Minami-guchi/South Exit); Ōedo subway line, Kokuritsu-Kyōgijō Eki (Exit A4).*

Among the most important of the Nō family schools in Tōkyō is the **Kanze Nō-gakudō,** founded in the 14th century. The current *iemoto* (head) of the school is the 26th in his line. *1–16–4 Shōtō, Shibuya-ku, tel. 03/3469–5241. Subway: Ginza and Hanzō-mon lines, Shibuya Eki (Exit 3A).*

Founded in the 14th century, the Hōshō School of Nō maintains a tradition of severe, stately—nay, glacially slow—movement that may strike audiences as more like religious ritual than theater. Performances take place at the **Hōshō Nō-gakudō.** *1–5–9 Hongo, Bunkyō-ku, tel. 03/3811–4843. Subway: Toei Mita Line, Suidō-bashi Eki (Exit A1).*

Johnny-come-lately in the world of Nō is the Umewaka School, founded in 1921. Classes and performances are held at the **Umewaka Nō-gakuin.** *2–6–14 Higashi-Nakano, Nakano-ku, tel. 03/3363–7748. JR Chūō Line, Higashi-Nakano Eki (Exit 2); Marunouchi and Ōedo subway lines, Nakano-saka-ue Eki (Exit A1).*

## Modern Theater

The *Shingeki* (Modern Theater) movement began in Japan at about the turn of the 20th century, coping at first with the lack of native repertoire by performing translations of Western dramatists from Shakespeare to Shaw. It wasn't until around 1915 that Japanese playwrights began writing for the Shingeki stage, but modern drama did not really develop a voice of its own here until after World War II.

The watershed years came around 1965, when experimental theater companies, unable to find commercial space, began taking their work to young audiences in various unusual ways: street plays and "happenings"; dramatic readings in underground malls and rented lofts; tents put up on vacant lots for unannounced performances (miraculously filled to capacity by word of mouth) and taken down the next day. It was in this period that surrealist playwright Kōbō Abe found his stride and director Tadashi Suzuki developed the unique system of training that now draws aspiring actors from all over the world to his "theater community" in the mountains of Toyama Prefecture. Japanese drama today is a lively art indeed; theaters small and large, in unexpected pockets all over Tōkyō, attest to its vitality.

The great majority of these performances, however, are in Japanese, for Japanese audiences. You're unlikely to find one with program notes in English to help you follow it. Unless it's a play you already know well, and you're curious to see how it translates, you might do well to think of some other way to spend your evenings out.

Language poses no barrier to an enjoyment of the **Takarazuka**—Japan's own, wonderfully goofy all-female review. The troupe was founded in the Ōsaka suburb of Takarazuka in 1913 and has been going strong ever since; today it has not one but five companies, one of them with a permanent home in Tōkyō. Located for many years across the street from the Imperial Hotel, in Hibiya, the 2,069-seat **Tōkyō Takarazuka Theatre** was rebuilt in 2001, grander and goofier than ever. Tickets are ¥3,800–¥10,000 for regular performances, ¥2,000–¥5,000 for debut performances with the company's budding ingenues. Everybody sings; everybody dances; the sets are breathtaking; the costumes are swell. Where else but at the Takarazuka could you see Gone With the Wind, sung in Japanese, with a young woman in a mustache and a frock coat playing Rhett Butler? 1–1–3 Yūraku-chō, Chiyoda-ku, tel. 03/5251–2001. JR Yamanote Line, Yūraku-chō Eki (Hibiya-guchi Exit); Hibiya subway line, Hibiya Eki (Exit A5); Chiyoda and Toei Mita subway lines, Hibiya Eki (Exit A13).

## Music

Information in English about venues for traditional Japanese music (koto, shamisen, and so forth) can be a bit hard to find; check newspaper listings for concerts and school recitals. Western music poses no such problem: during the 1980s and early 1990s a considerable number of new concert halls and performance spaces sprang up all over the city, adding to what was already an excellent roster of public auditoriums. The following are a few of the most important.

**CASALS HALL,** the last of the fine small auditoriums built for chamber music, before the Japanese bubble economy collapsed in the early '90s, was designed by architect Arata Isozaki—justly famous for the Museum of Contemporary Art in Los Angeles. In addition to chamber music, Casals draws piano, guitar, cello, and voice soloists. 1–6 Kanda Surugadai, Chiyoda-ku, tel. 03/3294–1229. JR Chūō Line and Marunouchi subway line, Ochanomizu Eki (Exit 2).

**Iino Hall,** built before Japan fell fatally in love with marble, maintains a reputation for comfort, intelligent programming, and excellent acoustics. Chamber music and Japanese concert soloists perform here. 2–1–1 Uchisaiwai-chō, Chiyoda-ku, tel. 03/3506–3251. Subway: Chiyoda and Hibiya lines, Kasumigaseki Eki (Exit C4); Marunouchi Line, Kasumigaseki Eki (Exit B2); Ginza Line, Toranomon Eki (Exit 9); Toei Mita Line, Uchisaiwai-chō Eki (Exit A7).

**Ishi-bashi Memorial Hall's** pride is its wonderful pipe organ. Alas, it seldom schedules organ concerts but is a favorite venue for piano and violin solo recitals, string quartets, and small chamber orchestras. *4–24–12 Higashi Ueno, Taitō-ku, tel. 03/ 3843–3043. Subway: Ginza Line, Inari-chō Eki (Exit 3).*

**Nakano Sun Plaza** hosts everything from rock to Argentine tango. *4–1–1 Nakano, Nakano-ku, tel. 03/3388–1151. JR and Tōzai subway line, Nakano Eki (Kita-guchi/North Exit).*

**NHK Hall,** home base for the Japan Broadcasting Corporation's NHK Symphony Orchestra, is probably the auditorium most familiar to Japanese lovers of classical music, as performances here are routinely re-broadcast on NHK-TV. *2–2–1 Jinnan, Shibuya-ku, tel. 03/3465–1751. JR Yamanote Line, Shibuya Eki (Hachiko Exit); Ginza and Hanzō-mon subway lines, Shibuya Eki (Exits 6 and 7).*

**New National Theatre and Tōkyō Opera City Concert Hall,** with its 1,810-seat main auditorium, nourishes Japan's fledgling efforts to make a name for itself in the world of opera. *3–20–2 Nishi-Shinjuku, Shinjuku-ku, tel. 03/5353–0788; 03/5353–9999 for tickets, www.tokyooperacity-cf.or.jp. Subway: Keiō Shin-sen Line, Hatsudai Eki (Higashi-guchi/East Exit).*

**Suntory Hall,** in the Ark Hills complex, is among the most lavishly appointed of the concert auditoriums built in Japan in the past decade. It is also one of the best located for theatergoers who want to extend their evening out: there's an abundance of good restaurants and bars nearby. *1–13–1 Akasaka, Minato-ku, tel. 03/3505–1001. Subway: Ginza and Namboku lines, Tameike-Sannō Eki (Exit 13).*

**Tōkyō Bunka Kaikan** (Tōkyō Metropolitan Festival Hall) was, in the 1960s and '70s, perhaps the city's premier showcase for orchestral music and visiting soloists and still gets major bookings. *5–45 Ueno Kōen, Taitō-ku, tel. 03/3828–2111. JR Yamanote Line, Ueno Eki (Kōen-guchi/Park Exit).*

**Tōkyō Dome,** a 55,000-seat sports arena, hosts the biggest acts from abroad in rock and popular music. *1–3–61 Kōraku, Bunkyō-*

ku, tel. 03/5800–9999. Subway: Marunouchi and Namboku lines, Kōraku-en Eki (Exit 2); Ōedo and Toei Mita lines, Kasuga Eki (Exit A2); JR Suidō-bashi Eki (Nishi-guchi/West Exit).

# Dance

Traditional Japanese dance, like flower arranging and the tea ceremony, is divided into dozens of styles, ancient of lineage and fiercely proud of their differences from each other. In fact, only the aficionado can really tell them apart. They survive not so much as performing arts but as schools, offering dance as a cultured accomplishment to interested amateurs. At least once a year, teachers and their students in each of these schools hold a recital, so that on any given evening there's very likely to be one somewhere in Tōkyō. Truly professional performances are given, as mentioned previously, at the Kokuritsu Gekijō and the Shimbashi Enbujō; the most important of the classical schools, however, developed as an aspect of Kabuki, and if you attend a play at the Kabuki-za, you are almost guaranteed to see a representative example.

Ballet began to attract a Japanese following in 1920, when Anna Pavlova danced *The Dying Swan* at the old Imperial Theater. The well-known companies that come to Tōkyō from abroad perform to full houses, usually at the Tōkyō Metropolitan Festival Hall in Ueno. There are now about 15 professional Japanese ballet companies, several of which have toured abroad, but this has yet to become an art form on which Japan has had much of an impact.

Modern dance is a different story—a story that begins with a visit in 1955 by the Martha Graham Dance Company. The decade that followed was one of great turmoil in Japan; it was a period of dissatisfaction—political, intellectual, artistic—with old forms and conventions. The work of pioneers like Graham inspired a great number of talented dancers and choreographers to explore new avenues of self-expression. One of the fruits of that exploration was Butō, a movement that was at once uniquely Japanese and a major contribution to the world of modern dance.

The father of Butō was the dancer Tatsumi Hijikata (1928–86). The watershed work was his *Revolt of the Flesh*, which premiered in 1968. Others soon followed: Kazuo Ono, Min Tanaka, Akaji Marō and the Dai Rakuda Kan troupe, and Ushio Amagatsu and the Sankai Juku. To most Japanese, their work was inexplicably grotesque. Dancers performed with shaved heads, dressed in rags or with naked bodies painted completely white, their movements agonized and contorted. The images were dark and demonic, violent and explicitly sexual. Butō was an exploration of the unconscious: its gods were the gods of the Japanese village and the gods of prehistory; its literary inspirations came from Mishima, Genet, Artaud. Like many other modern Japanese artists, the Butō dancers and choreographers were largely ignored by the mainstream until they began to appear abroad—to thunderous critical acclaim. Now they are equally honored at home. Butō does not lend itself to conventional spaces (a few years ago, for example, the Dai Rakuda Kan premiered one of its new works in a limestone cave in Gunma Prefecture), but if there's a performance in Tōkyō, "Cityscope" will have the schedule. Don't miss it.

## Film

One of the best things about foreign films in Japan is that the distributors invariably add Japanese subtitles rather than dub their offerings, the way it's done so often elsewhere. The original sound track, of course, may not be all that helpful to you if the film is Polish or Italian, but the vast majority of first-run foreign films here are made in the United States. Choices are limited, however, and films take so long to open in Tōkyō that you've probably seen them all already at home. And tickets are expensive—around ¥1,800 for general admission and ¥2,500–¥3,000 for a reserved seat, called a *shitei-seki*.

The native Japanese film industry has been in a slump for more than 20 years, though it has intermittent spasms of recovery. Now and again a Japanese entry—usually by an independent producer or director—will walk off with an unexpected prize at a European film festival and then get the recognition it deserves at home. Rarely, a Japanese film (like the 1997 *Shall We Dance?*) will be a box office success abroad. The major studios, however, are for the most part a lost cause, cranking out animations, low-budget gangster movies, and sentimental comedies to keep themselves afloat.

First-run theaters that have new releases, both Japanese and foreign, are clustered for the most part in three areas: Shinjuku, Shibuya, and Yūraku-chō-Hibiya-Ginza. At most of them, the last showing of the evening starts at around 7. This is not the case, however, with the best news on the Tōkyō film scene: the handful of small theaters that take a special interest in classics, revivals, and serious imports. Somewhere on the premises will also be a chrome-and-marble coffee shop, a fashionable little bar, or even a decent restaurant. Most of these small theaters have a midnight show—at least on the weekends. The **Bunka-mura** complex in Shibuya has two movie theaters, a concert auditorium (Orchard Hall), and a performance space (Theater Cocoon); it is the principal venue for many of Tōkyō's film festivals. *2–24–1 Dōgen-zaka, tel. 03/3477–9999. JR Yamanote Line, Shibuya Eki (Hachiko Exit).*

**Chanter Cine,** a three-screen cinema complex, tends to show British and American films by independent producers but also showcases fine work by filmmakers from Asia and the Middle East. *1–2–2 Yūraku-chō, Chiyoda-ku, tel. 03/3591–1511. Subway: Hibiya, Chiyoda, and Toei Mita lines; Hibiya Eki (Exit A5).*

**Cine Saison Shibuya** occasionally gets in recent releases by award-winning directors from such countries as Iran, China, and South Korea as well as popular releases. *Prime Bldg., 2–29–5*

*Dōgen-zaka, Shibuya-ku, tel. 03/3770–1721. JR Yamanote Line, Shibuya Eki (Hachiko Exit).*

**Haiyū-za** is primarily a repertory theater, but its **Haiyū-za Talkie Nights** screens notable foreign films. *4–9–2 Roppongi, Minato-ku, tel. 03/3401–4073. Subway: Hibiya Line, Roppongi Eki (Exit 4A).*

## In This Chapter

*Updated by Jared Lubarsky*

# where to stay

**THERE ARE THREE THINGS** you can virtually take for granted when you look for a hotel in Tōkyō: cleanliness, safety, and service—impeccable almost anywhere you finally set down your bags. The factors that will probably determine your choice, then, are cost and location.

The relation between the two is not always what you'd expect. Real estate in Tōkyō is horrendously expensive; normally, the closer you get to the center of town, the more you ought to be paying for space. That's true enough for business property, but when it comes to hotels at the upper end of the market, the logic doesn't seem to apply: a night's lodging is not likely to cost you much less in Roppongi, Shinjuku, Ikebukuro, Meguro, or Asakusa than it would for a view of the Imperial Palace.

The reasons aren't complicated. A substantial number of Tōkyō's present hotels were built in the outlying subcenters during the "bubble" of the 1980s and early 1990s, when real estate speculation made prices outrageous everywhere. The bubble encouraged a "spare-no-expense" approach to hotel design: atriums, oceans of marble, interior decorators fetched in from London and New York. The cost of construction per square foot did not vary much from place to place, and that remains reflected in what you can anticipate paying for your room. Business travelers might have good reason to choose one location over another, but if you're in Tōkyō on vacation, that factor may be only marginally important. Nor should transportation be a concern: wherever you're staying, Tōkyō's subway and train system—comfortable (except in rush hours), efficient, inexpensive, and safe—will get you back and forth.

Down-market hotels, of course, provide less in the way of services and decor, but this affects the cost of accommodations—per square foot—less than you might imagine. Deluxe hotels make a substantial part of their profits from their banquet and dining facilities; they charge you more, but they can also give you more space. Farther down the scale, you pay somewhat less, but the rooms are disproportionately smaller—they can be positively tiny.

Tōkyō accommodations can be roughly divided into five categories: international (full-service) hotels, business hotels, ryokan, "capsule" hotels, and hostels.

International (full-service) hotels are exactly what you would expect; most also tend to be priced in the $$$ and $$$$ categories. Virtually all have a range of Western and Japanese restaurants, room service, direct-dial telephones, minibars, yukata (cotton bedroom kimonos), concierge services, and porters. Most have business and fitness centers. A few also have swimming pools. At least 90% of the guest rooms are Western style; the few Japanese rooms available (with tatami mats and futons) are more expensive.

Business hotels are meant primarily for travelers who need no more than a place to leave luggage, sleep, and change. Rooms are small; an individual guest will often take a double rather than suffer the claustrophobia of a single. Each room has a telephone, a small writing desk, a television (sometimes the pay-as-you-watch variety), slippers, a yukata, and a prefabricated plastic bathroom unit with tub, shower, and washbasin; the bathrooms are scrupulously clean, but if you're basketball-player size, you might have trouble coming to your full height inside. The hotel facilities are limited usually to one restaurant and a 24-hour receptionist, with no room service or porters. Business hotels are not listed below in a separate category, but entries in the $$ price category can be assumed to be of this type.

There are two kinds of ryokan. One is an expensive traditional inn, with impeccable personal service, where you are served dinner and breakfast in your room. The other is an inexpensive hostelry that offers rooms with tatami mats on the floors and futon beds; meals might be served in rooms, but more often they aren't. Tōkyō ryokan fall in the latter category. They are often family-run lodgings, where service is less a matter of professionalism than of good will. Many offer the choice of rooms with or without baths. Because they have few rooms and the owners are usually on hand to answer their guests' questions, these small, relatively inexpensive ryokan are very hospitable places to stay and especially popular with younger travelers.

Capsule hotels are literally plastic cubicles stacked one on top of another. They are used by very junior business travelers or commuters who have missed their last train home. (Very rarely, a capsule hotel will have a separate floor for women; otherwise, women are not admitted.) The capsule—marginally bigger than a coffin or a CAT scanner—has a bed, an intercom, and (in the luxury models) a TV in the ceiling. Washing and toilet facilities are shared. One such place is **Green Plaza Shinjuku** (1–29–2 Kabuki-chō, Shinjuku-ku, tel. 03/3207–4923), two minutes from Shinjuku Eki (Higashi-guchi/East Exit for JR lines; Exit B10, B11, B12, or B13 for Marunouchi Line). It is the largest of its kind, with 660 sleeping slots. Check-in starts at 3 PM; checkout in the morning is pandemonium. A night's stay in a capsule is ¥4,200.

Separate categories are provided in this section for (1) hotels near Narita Airport and (2) youth hostels and dormitory accommodations. All rooms at the hotels listed below are Western style and have private baths, unless otherwise specified.

| CATEGORY | COST* |
|----------|-------|
| $$$$ | over ¥30,000 |
| $$$ | ¥21,000–¥30,000 |
| $$ | ¥10,000–¥21,000 |
| $ | under ¥10,000 |

*All prices are for a double room, excluding service and tax.

## ASAKUSA

**$$$–$$$$  ASAKUSA VIEW HOTEL.** If you want an elegant place to stay in the heart of Tōkyō's old Asakusa area—which was actually resurrected after the World War II fire bombings—then this hotel is the only choice. Off the smart marble lobby a harpist plays in the tea lounge, and expensive boutiques line the second floor. The standard pastel guest rooms are similar to what you find in all modern Tōkyō hotels, but you also have access to communal *hinoki* (Japanese cypress) bathtubs that overlook a sixth-floor Japanese garden. Ask for rooms on the 22nd and 23rd floors, which afford a view of the Senjō-ji grounds. There are Chinese, French, Italian, and Japanese restaurants and a bar that will keep your personal bottle. *3–17–1 Nishi-Asakusa, Taitō-ku, Tōkyō-to 111-0035, tel. 03/3847–1111, fax 03/3842–2117, www.viewhotels.co.jp/asakusa/index-english.html. 333 room, 9 suites. 4 restaurants, 2 bars, coffee shop, no-smoking rooms, pool, health club, concierge floor. AE, DC, MC, V. Subway: Ginza Line, Tawara-machi Eki (Exit 3).*

**$$  RYOKAN SHIGETSU.** Just off Nakamise-dōri and inside the Sensō-ji grounds, this small inn could not be better located for a visit to the temple. Half the rooms are Japanese-style (futon bedding, tatami floors) and half are Western, plainly but comfortably furnished. All rooms have private baths, and there's also a public bath on the sixth floor with a view of the Sensō-ji pagoda. *1–31–11 Asakusa, Taitō-ku, Tōkyō-to 111-0032, tel. 03/3483–2345, fax 03/3483–2348, www.roy.hi-ho.ne.jp/shigetsu. 11 Western-style rooms, 12 Japanese-style rooms. Restaurant, Japanese baths. AE, MC, V. Subway: Ginza Line, Asakusa Eki (Exit 1/Kaminari-mon exit).*

## EBISU

**$$$$  WESTIN TŌKYŌ.** In Yebisu Garden Place, one of the last grand, pharaonic development projects to go up in Tōkyō before the real estate bubble burst in 1994, the Westin provides easy access to Mitsukoshi depāto, the Tōkyō Metropolitan Museum of Photography, an elegant concert hall, and the Taillevent-Robuchon restaurant, this last housed in a full-scale reproduction of a Louis XV château. The decor of the hotel itself is updated art nouveau, with an excess of marble and bronze. Rooms are spacious, and suites are huge by Japanese standards. *1–4 Mita 1-chōme, Meguro-ku, Tōkyō-to 153-0062, tel. 03/5423–7000, fax 03/5423–7600, www.starwood.com/westin. 445 rooms, 20 suites. 5 restaurants, 2 bars, coffee shop, no-smoking rooms, health club, shops, concierge floor, business services, travel services. AE, DC, MC, V. Subway (Hibiya Line)/JR station: Ebisu Eki (Higashi-guchi/East Exit).*

## HAKOZAKI

**$$$$  ROYAL PARK HOTEL.** This hotel would recommend itself if only for the connecting passageway to the Tōkyō City Air Terminal, where you can complete all your check-in procedures before you climb on the bus for Narita Airport. At the end of an intensive trip, there's no luxury like being able to pack, ring for the bellhop, and not have to touch your baggage again until it comes off the conveyor belt back home. Built in 1989, the 20-story Royal Park is well designed: the large, open lobby has perhaps a bit more marble than it needs, and the inevitable space-age chandelier, but this is offset by wood-paneled columns, brass trim, and lots of comfortable lounge space. Guest rooms, done in coordinated neutral grays and browns, are well proportioned; deluxe twins have handsome writing tables instead of built-in desktops. Ask for a room on one of the executive floors (16–18) with a northeast view of the Sumida-gawa. Another good option would be a room lower down (sixth–eighth floors) on the opposite side, overlooking the hotel's delightful fifth-floor Japanese garden. *2–1–1 Nihombashi, Kakigara-chō, Chūō-ku, Tōkyō-to 103-0014, tel. 03/3667–1111, fax 03/*

3667–1115, www.royalparkhotels.co.jp. 450 rooms, 9 suites. 7 restaurants, 3 bars, coffee shop, no-smoking room, shops, concierge floor, business services, travel services. AE, DC, MC, V. Subway: Hanzō-mon Line, Suitengū-mae Eki (Exit 4).

**$$**   **KAYABA-CHŌ PEARL HOTEL.** Rooms here are strictly utilitarian, but the price is low, unless you sleep late: there's a charge of 30%–50% of your room rate for late checkout (after 10 AM). The hotel is just across the bridge from Tōkyō City Air Terminal, a five-minute walk from Exit 3 or 4B of Kayaba-chō Eki on the Hibiya or Tōzai Line. 1–2–5 Shinkawa, Chūō-ku, Tōkyō-to 104-0033, tel. 03/3553–2211, fax 03/3555–1849. 262 rooms. Restaurant. AE, DC, MC, V. Subway: Kayaba-chō Eki.

## HIBIYA

**$$$$**   **IMPERIAL HOTEL.** The location of these prestigious quarters could not be better: in the heart of central Tōkyō, between the Imperial Palace and Ginza. The finest rooms, high up on the 30th floor in the New Tower, afford views of the palace grounds. The Old Imperial Bar incorporates elements from the 1922 version of the hotel, which Frank Lloyd Wright designed. The Imperial opened its doors in 1891, and from the outset the hotel has been justly proud of its Western-style facilities and Japanese service. Now, with its tower addition, the hotel is a vast complex, but it still retains its personalized service. Rooms range from standard twin size to suites that are larger than many homes. 1–1–1 Uchisaiwai-chō, Chiyoda-ku, Tōkyō-to 100-0011, tel. 03/3504–1111, fax 03/3581–9146, www.imperialhotel.co.jp. 1,005 rooms, 54 suites. 13 restaurants, 4 bars, no-smoking room, indoor pool, massage, health club, shops, concierge floor, business services, travel services. AE, DC, MC, V. Subway: Hibiya Line, Hibiya Eki (Exit 5).

## HIGASHI-GINZA

**$$$–$$$$**   **GINZA TŌBU HOTEL.** This hotel's relatively reasonable prices, friendly service, and comfortable rooms make it something of a bargain for the Ginza area. Standard rooms have blond-wood furniture and quilted bedspreads in pastel prints. The more expensive concierge floors have much larger rooms, with extras such as terry bathrobes and hair dryers; breakfast, afternoon tea, and complimentary cocktails in the lounge are part of the package. There are also French and Japanese restaurants (the excellent Muraki among the latter), as well as a 24-hour coffee shop. 6–13–10 Ginza, Chūō-ku Tōkyō-to 104-0061, tel. 03/3546–0111, fax 03/3546–8990, www.tobu.co.jp. 190 rooms, 16 suites. 2 restaurants, 2 bars, coffee shop, concierge floor, business services, travel services. AE, DC, MC, V. Subway: Hibiya and Toei Asakusa lines, Higashi-Ginza Eki (Exit A1).

## HIGASHI-GOTANDA

**$ RYOKAN SANSUISŌ.** If you're traveling on a tight budget and want to immerse yourself in Japanese culture, consider this basic ryokan near the Toei Asakusa Line's Gotanda stop. The proprietor will greet you with a warm smile and a bow and escort you to a small tatami room with a pay TV and a rather noisy heater/air-conditioner mounted in the wall. Some rooms are stuffy (you can't open a window), and only two have private baths, but the Sansuisō is clean, easy to find, and only 20 minutes on the subway from Tōkyō Eki and Ginza. The midnight curfew poses a problem for night owls. This hotel is a member of the Japanese Inn Group; the Japan National Tourist Organization (tel. 03/3201–3331) can help make reservations. 2–9–5 Higashi-Gotanda, Shinagawa-ku, Tōkyō-to 141-0022, tel. 03/3441–7475, fax 03/3449–1944. 9 rooms, 2 with bath. AE, MC, V. Subway/JR: Gotanda Eki (Exit A3 for Toei Asakusa Line, Higashi-guchi/East Exit for JR Yamanote Line).

## KUDAN-MINAMI

**$$–$$$ ★ FAIRMOUNT HOTEL.** Nostalgia buffs love the Fairmount; here's a place in relentlessly high-tech Tōkyō with pull-chain ventilators, real tile in the bathrooms, and furniture (a little chipped) that Sears & Roebuck must have phased out of its catalog in 1955. The hotel has all that and exposed water pipes—left that way even after a major renovation, neatly wrapped and painted, of course, but exposed just the same. The hotel isn't seedy, mind you, just old (it was built in 1951) and a bit set in its ways. The best thing about the seven-story Fairmount is its frontage on the park that runs along the east side of the Imperial Palace grounds; rooms facing the park afford a wonderful view of the moat and Chidorigafuchi Pond, where Tōkyō couples take rented rowboats out on summer Sunday afternoons. 2–1–17 Kudan-Minami, Chiyoda-ku, Tōkyō-to 102-0074, tel. 03/3262–1151, fax 03/3264–2476. 207 rooms, 2 suites. Restaurant, bar. AE, DC, MC, V. Subway: Hanzō-mon and Tōzai lines, Kudanshita Eki (Exit 2).

## KYŌ-BASHI

**$$$$**  **HOTEL SEIYŌ GINZA.** The muted pastels and grays of the decor, the thick pile of the carpets, and the profusion of cut flowers all combine to create an atmosphere more like an elegant private club than a hotel. Location and personalized service are the two reasons to choose the exclusive Seiyō, where double rooms start at ¥45,000. In hailing distance of Ginza, it caters to celebrities and those who require a direct line in their rooms to a personal secretary who takes care of their every need. A staff of some 220 outnumbers the guests by a considerable margin. Rooms and suites, it must be noted, are smaller than what most Westerners might expect for the price. There are four restaurants, including the Attore for Italian food and the Pastorale for French-Continental. 1–11–2 Ginza, Chūō-ku, Tōkyō-to 104-0061, tel. 03/3535–1111, fax 03/3535–1110. 51 rooms, 28 suites. 3 restaurants, bar, lounge, patisserie, health club, concierge, business services, travel services. AE, DC, MC, V. Subway: Ginza Line, Kyō-bashi Eki (Exit 2); Yūraku-chō Line, Ginza-Itchōme Eki (Exit 7).

## MARUNOUCHI

**$$$$**  **PALACE HOTEL.** The service here is extremely helpful and
**★**  professional; much of the staff has been with the hotel for more than 10 years. The location is ideal: only a moat separates the hotel

from the outer gardens of the Imperial Palace; Ginza and the financial districts of Marunouchi are both a short taxi or subway ride away. The lobby spaces are rectangular and uninspiring; an air of calm conservatism bespeaks the Palace's half century as an accommodation for the well-to-do and well connected. The tasteful, low-key guest rooms are spacious; try for one on the upper floors facing the Imperial Palace. *1–1–1 Marunouchi, Chiyoda-ku, Tōkyō-to 100-0005, tel. 03/3211–5211, fax 03/3211–6987, www.palacehotel.co.jp. 384 rooms, 6 suites. 7 restaurants, 2 bars, coffee shop, no-smoking rooms, shops, business services, travel services. AE, DC, MC, V. Subway: Chiyoda, Marunouchi, Hanzō-mon, Tōzai, and Mita lines; Ōte-machi Eki (Exit C-13B).*

**$$$ TŌKYŌ STATION HOTEL.** Kingo Tatsuno, one of Japan's first modern architects, modeled the Tōkyō Eki building on the railway station of Amsterdam. Completed in 1914, it was saved in 1990 from the wrecker's ball by a determined historical preservation movement—one of the few times, in this part of the city, that cultural values triumphed over commerce. The original charming facade remains—so far—untouched. The hotel is on the west side of the station building, on the second and third floors; the windows along the corridor look out over the station rotunda. The hotel's frosted glass and flocked wallpaper, its heavy red drapes, and its varnished wooden staircases have seen better days, but many travelers appreciate the wide corridors and high ceilings. If you're moving on from Tōkyō by train to another part of the country, the location is ideal. *1–9–1 Marunouchi, Chiyoda-ku, Tōkyō-to 100-0005, tel. 03/3231–2511, fax 03/3231–3513, www.tshl.co.jp. 58 rooms. AE, DC, MC, V. Subway/JR: Tōkyō Eki (Marunouchi Central Exit).*

**$$ GINZA MARUNOUCHI HOTEL.** Since it opened in 1976, the Ginza Marunouchi has been a popular choice for tour groups, both foreign and Japanese, for one reason: given its location—a subway stop from Ginza—the cost of accommodations here is very reasonable. Guest rooms are compact and clean, but there's nothing particularly remarkable about the decor or the service.

# tokyo lodging

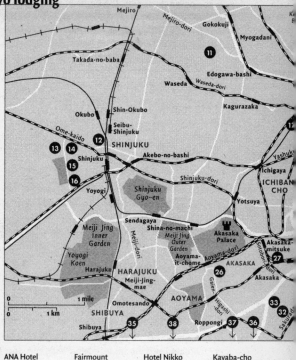

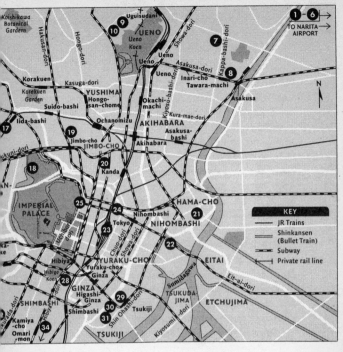

Royal Park
Hotel, 21

Ryokan
Katsutaro, 9

Ryokan
Sansuiso, 38

Ryokan
Shigetsu, 8

Sawanoya
Ryokan, 10

Shiba
Daimon Hotel, 34

Shinjuku
Washington
Hotel, 16

Star Hotel, 12

Takanawa
Tobu Hotel, 37

Tokyo Hilton
International, 14

Tokyo
International
Youth Hostel, 17

Tokyo Station
Hotel, 23

Tokyo YMCA, 20

Westin Tokyo, 35

YMCA Asia
Youth Center, 19

4-1-12 Tsukiji, Chūō-ku, Tōkyō-to 104-0045, tel. 03/3543-5431, fax 03/3543-6006. 114 rooms. Restaurant. AE, DC, MC, V. Subway: Hibiya and Toei Asakusa lines, Higashi-Ginza Eki (Exit 6).

## NAGATA-CHŌ

**$$$$ CAPITOL TŌKYŪ HOTEL.** The Tōkyū Hotel chain's flagship operation, the Capitol was built in 1963, but it feels a bit like a grand hotel of a bygone era and commands a loyal repeat clientele among foreign business travelers. It's also relatively small, even by Tōkyō standards, but with two full-time staff members to every guest, service is excellent. Guest rooms are furnished in dark wood, but shōji (sliding paper screens) on the windows create a feeling of soft warmth and light. Ask for one of the rooms that overlook the adjacent Hie Jinja. Two of the hotel's dining rooms, the Origami breakfast café and the Tea Lounge, also have views of the shrine. To the left of the lobby is a small garden with a pond. 2-10-3 Nagata-chō, Chiyoda-ku, Tōkyō-to 100-0014, tel. 03/3581-4511, fax 03/3581-5822, www.capitoltokyu.com. 440 rooms, 19 suites. 5 restaurants, 2 bars, coffee shop, no-smoking rooms, pool, massage, steam room, shops, concierge floor, business services, travel services. AE, DC, MC, V. Subway: Chiyoda and Marunouchi lines, Kokkai Gijidō-mae Eki (Exit 5); Ginza and Namboku lines, Tameike-Sannō Eki (Exit 5).

## NISHI-SHINJUKU

**$$$$ PARK HYATT TŌKYŌ.** An elevator whisks you to the 41st floor, where the hotel begins with an atrium lounge enclosed on three sides by floor-to-ceiling plate-glass windows. The panorama of Shinjuku spreads out before you; the tops of neighboring skyscrapers add to the three-dimensional spectacle. Service is so efficient and personal, the staff members seem to know your name before you introduce yourself. The mood of the hotel is contemporary and understated. Guest rooms, from the 42nd to the 50th floor, are large by any standard. King-size beds have Egyptian-cotton sheets and down-feather duvets; other appointments include pale olive-green carpets and black-lacquer cabinets. Even bathrooms have views, with tubs situated by windows. The Park Hyatt's restaurants include the Girandole (Continental cuisine), the Peak Lounge, and the very popular New York Grill, with an open kitchen that specializes in steaks and seafood. *3–7–1–2 Nishi-Shinjuku, Shinjuku-ku, Tōkyō-to 163-1090, tel. 03/5322–1234, fax 03/5322–1288, www.tokyo.hyatt.com. 155 rooms, 23 suites. 3 restaurants, 2 bars, coffee shop, no-smoking rooms, indoor pool, massage, sauna, steam room, aerobics, health club, library, business services. AE, MC, V. Subway/JR: Shinjuku Eki (Nishi-guchi/West Exit).*

**$$$$ TŌKYŌ HILTON INTERNATIONAL.** A short walk from the megalithic Tōkyō Metropolitan Government Office, the Hilton is a particular favorite of Western business travelers. When it opened in 1984, it was the largest Hilton in Asia but opted away from the prevailing atrium style in favor of more guest rooms and banquet facilities; as a result, the lobby is on a comfortable, human scale. A copper-clad spiral staircase reaching to the mezzanine floor above highlights the bar-lounge. Shōji screens instead of curtains bathe the guest rooms in soft, relaxing light. The Imari Room, with its displays of museum-quality traditional pottery, is one of Tōkyō's more elegant places to dine. *6–6–2 Nishi-Shinjuku, Shinjuku-ku, Tōkyō-to 160-0023, tel. 03/3344–5111; 0120/489–992 toll free, fax 03/3342–6094, www.hilton.com. 757 rooms, 50 suites. 5 restaurants, bar, no-smoking rooms, indoor and outdoor pool, sauna, 2 tennis courts, shops, cabaret, dance club, concierge floor, business services, travel services. AE, DC, MC, V. JR: Shinjuku Eki (Nishi-guchi/West Exit). Subway: Marunouchi Line, Nishi-Shinjuku Eki (Exit C8); Toei Ōedo Line, Tochō-mae Eki (all exits).*

**$$$–$$$$ CENTURY HYATT HOTEL.** This Hyatt has the trademark atrium-style lobby: seven stories high, with open-glass elevators soaring upward and three huge chandeliers suspended from above. Single rooms tend to be small and lack good views from their windows; larger rooms are designed to create the impression of a separate sitting area. The Hyatt emphasizes its cuisine; at any given time, there is almost sure to be a special "gourmet fair" in progress, celebrating the food of one country or another and supervised by visiting celebrity chefs. 2–7–2 Nishi-Shinjuku, Shinjuku-ku, Tōkyō-to 160-0023, tel. 03/3349–0111, fax 03/3344–5575, www.centuryhyatt.co.jp. 750 rooms, 16 suites. 5 restaurants, 2 bars, coffee shop, no-smoking room, indoor pool, shops, concierge floor, business services, travel services. AE, DC, MC, V. Subway/JR: Shinjuku Eki (Nishi-guchi/West Exit).

$$–$$$ **SHINJUKU WASHINGTON HOTEL.** This is truly a business hotel, where service is computerized as much as possible. The third-floor lobby has an automated check-in and checkout system; you are assigned a room and provided with a plastic card that opens the door and the minibar. The clerk at the counter will explain the process, but after that you're on your own. 3–2–9 Nishi-Shinjuku, Shinjuku-ku, Tōkyō-to 160-0023, tel. 03/3343–3111, fax 03/3342–2575. 1,638 rooms. 5 restaurants, bar, coffee shop, no-smoking rooms. AE, DC, MC, V. Subway/JR: Shinjuku Eki (Minami-guchi/South Exit).

$$ ★ **STAR HOTEL.** Rates at this small, friendly hotel are more reasonable than those at most other places in the area. The staff speaks only Japanese but is sympathetic to sign language. The rooms are clean but not spacious. A small, pleasant restaurant serves Japanese and Western food. Don't expect a doorman or a porter to help with your bags, but the size of the Star at least allows the people at the front desk to remember your name without the help of a computer. 7–10–5 Nishi-Shinjuku, Shinjuku-ku, Tōkyō-to 160-0023, tel. 03/3361–1111, fax 03/3369–4216. 214 rooms. 2 restaurants, bar, coffee shop, no-smoking rooms. AE, DC, MC, V. Subway/JR: Shinjuku Eki (Nishi-guchi/West Exit).

## ROPPONGI

$ **ASIA CENTER OF JAPAN.** Established mainly for Asian students and other Asian visitors on limited budgets, these accommodations have become generally popular with foreign travelers for their easy access (a 15-minute walk) to the nightlife of Roppongi. You get good value for what you pay: rooms are small, minimally furnished, and not very well soundproofed—but they are clean and comfortable. To get here, walk toward Roppongi on Gaien-higashi-dōri from the Akasaka post office on the corner of Aoyam-dōri, and take the first side street on the left. *8–10–32 Akasaka, Minato-ku, Tōkyō-to 107-0052, tel. 03/3402–6111, fax 03/3402–0738. 220 rooms, 114 with bath. Bar, cafeteria. No credit cards. Subway: Ginza and Hanzō-mon lines, Aoyama-it-chōme Eki (Exit 4).*

## SEKIGUCHI

**$$$$** **FOUR SEASONS HOTEL CHINZAN-SŌ.** Where else will you have
★ a chance to sleep in a million-dollar room? That's about what it cost, on average, to build and furnish each of the accommodations in this elegant hotel, which opened in 1992. Rooms are large by any standard; conservatory suites have their own private garden patios. Huge woolen area rugs woven in Ireland accent the Italian marble floor in the lobby. Built on what was once the estate of an imperial prince, Chinzan-sō rejoices in one of the most beautiful settings in Tōkyō; in summer the gardens are famous for their fireflies. The hotel's complimentary shuttle-bus service to the Waseda subway station (Tōzai Line) and limousine service to Tōkyō Eki make it easy to get downtown. *2–10–8 Sekiguchi, Bunkyō-ku, Tōkyō-to 112-0014, tel. 03/3943–2222, fax 03/3943–2300, www.fourseasons.com. 233 rooms, 50 suites. 4 restaurants, bar, coffee shop, lounge, no-smoking rooms, indoor pool, barbershop, hair salon, hot tub, Japanese baths, massage, gym, shops, chapel, concierge, business services, travel services. AE, DC, MC, V. Subway: Yūraku-chō Line, Edogawa-bashi Eki (Exit 1A).*

## SHIBA KŌEN

**$$** **SHIBA DAIMON HOTEL.** This moderately priced hotel a minute's walk from Zōjō-ji is popular with Japanese travelers. The staff is a bit ill at ease with guests who cannot speak Japanese but no less willing to help. The decor is unremarkable, but the rooms are reasonably spacious for the price. A good restaurant on the ground floor serves Japanese and Chinese breakfast and Chinese fare in the evening. *2–3–6 Shiba-kōen, Minato-ku, Tōkyō-to 105-0011, tel. 03/3431–3716, fax 03/3434–5177. 96 rooms. Restaurant, no-smoking room.*

AE, DC, MC, V. JR: Hamamatsu-chō Eki (Kita-guchi/North Exit). Subway: Toei Asakusa Line, Daimon Eki (Exit A3).

## SHINAGAWA

**$$$–$$$$** **HOTEL PACIFIC MERIDIEN.** Just across the street from JR Shinagawa Eki, the Pacific Meridien sits on grounds that were once part of an imperial-family estate. The decor is pastel and lilac all the way to the Sky Lounge on the 30th floor, which overlooks Tōkyō Bay. The entire back wall of the coffee lounge on the ground floor is glass, the better to contemplate a tranquil Japanese garden, sculpted with rocks and waterfalls. The hotel markets itself to convention groups and business travelers. *3–13–3 Takanawa, Minato-ku, Tōkyō-to 108-0074, tel. 03/3445–6711, fax 03/3445–5137. 913 rooms, 41 suites. 6 restaurants, 3 bars, coffee shop, no-smoking rooms, pool, shops, concierge, business services, travel services. AE, DC, MC, V. JR Yamanote Line, Shinagawa Eki (Nishi-guchi/West Exit).*

**$$$** **TAKANAWA TŌBU HOTEL.** The Takanawa Tōbu, a five-minute walk from Shinagawa Eki, provides good value for the price—particularly since the rate includes a buffet breakfast. Rooms are smallish and uninspired in decor, the bathrooms are the claustrophobic prefabricated plastic units beloved of business hotels, and there's no proper sitting area in the lobby, but the hotel atones for these shortcomings with a friendly staff (which speaks a bit of English) and a cozy bar. There's also a small Western restaurant, the Boulogne. *4–7–6 Takanawa, Minato-ku, Tōkyō-to 108-0074, tel. 03/3447–0111, fax 03/3447–0117. 190 rooms. Restaurant, bar. AE, DC, MC, V. JR Yamanote Line, Shinagawa Eki (Nishi-guchi/West Exit).*

## TORA-NO-MON

**$$$$** **ANA HOTEL TŌKYŌ.** The ANA Hotel arrived on the Tōkyō scene in 1986, and it typifies the ziggurat-atrium style that seems to have been a requirement for hotel architecture at the time. The reception floor, with its two-story fountain, is clad in enough marble to have depleted an Italian quarry. Guest rooms are airy and spacious;

those who stay on the concierge floor (35th floor) can use a separate breakfast room and a private cocktail lounge. In general, the interior designers have made skillful use of artwork and furnishings to take some of the chill off the ANA's relentless modernism. There are Chinese, French, and Japanese restaurants and three bars; the Astral Lounge on the top (37th) floor affords a superb view of the city. The hotel is a short walk from the U.S. Embassy. *1–12–33 Akasaka, Minato-ku, Tōkyō-to 107-0052, tel. 03/ 3505–1111; 0120/029–501 toll free, fax 03/3505–1155, www.anahotels.com. 872 rooms, 29 suites. 8 restaurants, 4 bars, no-smoking rooms, pool, hair salon, sauna, gym, shops, concierge floor, business services, travel services. AE, DC, MC, V. Subway: Ginza and Namboku lines, Tameike-Sannō Eki (Exit 13); Namboku Line, Roppongi-itchō Eki (Exit 3).*

**$$$$** **HOTEL OKURA.** Year after year, a poll of business travelers ranks
★ the Okura, for its exemplary service, among the best two or three hotels in Asia. The hotel opened just before the 1964 Olympics, and, understated in its sophistication, human in its scale, it remains a favorite of diplomatic visitors. The spacious guest rooms are tastefully furnished; amenities include remote-control draperies, hair dryers, and terry bathrobes. The odd-number rooms, 871–889 inclusive, overlook a small Japanese landscaped garden. The Okura Art Museum, on the hotel grounds, displays a fine collection of antique porcelain, mother-of-pearl, and ceramics; tea ceremonies take place here Monday–Saturday 11– 4 (no charge for guests of the hotel). The main building is preferable to the south wing—which you reach by an underground shopping arcade—and the Japanese-style rooms are superb. *2–10–4 Tora-no-mon, Minato-ku, Tōkyō-to 105-0001, tel. 03/3582– 0111; 0120/003–751 toll free, fax 03/3582–3707, www.okura.com. 798 rooms, 11 Japanese-style rooms, 48 suites. 8 restaurants, 3 bars, coffee shop, no-smoking rooms, indoor and outdoor pool, massage, steam room, gym, shops, chapel, concierge, business services, travel services. AE, DC, MC, V. Subway: Hibiya Line, Kamiya-chō Eki (Exit 3); Ginza Line, Tora-no-mon Eki (Exit 4B).*

## UENO

**$ RYOKAN KATSUTARŌ.** This small, simple, economical hotel is a five-minute walk from the entrance to Ueno Kōen and a 10-minute walk from the Tōkyō National Museum. The quietest rooms are in the back, away from the main street. A simple breakfast of toast, eggs, and coffee is served for only ¥500. To get here, leave the Nezu subway station by the Ike-no-hata Exit, cross the road, take the street running northeast, and turn right at the "T" intersection; Ryokan Katsutarō is 25 yards along Dōbutsuen-uramon-dōri, on the left-hand side. *4–16–8 Ike-no-hata, Taitō-ku, Tōkyō-to 110-0008, tel. 03/3821–9808, fax 03/3891–4789. 7 Japanese-style rooms, 4 with bath. Breakfast room, Japanese bath. AE, MC, V. Subway: Chiyoda Line, Nezu Eki (Exit 1/Ike-no-hata Exit).*

## YAESU

**$$ HOTEL YAESU RYŪMEIKAN.** It's hard to believe that a ryokan could still exist in the heart of the city's financial district, where the price of real estate is out of sight—but there is it, a three-minute walk from Tōkyō Eki. The Ryūmeikan hosts relatively few foreign guests in its mostly Japanese-style rooms, but a friendly, professional staff goes the extra mile to make them feel comfortable. Weekday evenings, a staff member who speaks English is usually available. Amenities are few—there are no nonsmoking rooms, for example, and a Japanese-style breakfast is served by reservation only—but for price and location this inn is hard to beat. *1–3–22 Yaesu, Chūō-ku, Tōkyō-to 103-0028, tel. 03/3271–0971, fax 03/3271–0977. 14 Japanese-style rooms, 7 Western-style rooms. Breakfast room, Japanese bath. AE, MC, V. JR and Marunouchi subway line, Tōkyō Eki (Yaesu North Exit); Tōzai subway line, Nihombashi Eki (Exit A3).*

## YANAKA

**$ SAWANOYA RYOKAN.** The residential neighborhood, in a quiet
★ area northwest of Ueno Kōen, and the hospitality of the ryokan make you feel at home in this traditional part of Tōkyō. The family

who operate this little inn truly welcome you; they'll help you plan trips and will arrange future accommodations. Two rooms have private baths, while the rest share Japanese-style common baths. No dinner is offered, but you can order a Continental (¥300) or Japanese (¥900) breakfast. Sawanoya is very popular with low-budget travelers; make a reservation by fax well before you arrive. To get here from the Nezu subway station, walk 300 yards north along Shinobazu-dōri and take the street on the right; Sawanoya is 180 yards on the right. *2–3–11 Yanaka, Taitō-ku, Tōkyō-to 110-0001, tel. 03/3822–2251, fax 03/3822–2252. 12 Japanese-style rooms. Breakfast room, Japanese baths. AE, MC, V. Subway: Chiyoda Line, Nezu Eki (Exit 1).*

## HOSTELS AND DORMITORY ACCOMMODATIONS

**$$ TŌKYŌ YMCA.** The private rooms here come with and without bath. Both men and women can stay at the hostel, which is a three-minute walk from Awaji-chō Eki (Exit B-7) on the Marunouchi Line or seven minutes from Kanda Eki (Exit 4) on the Ginza Line. *7 Kanda-mitoshiro-chō, Chiyoda-ku, Tōkyō-to 101-0052, tel. 03/3293–1919, fax 03/3293–1926. 40 rooms. No credit cards.*

**$$ YMCA ASIA YOUTH CENTER.** Both men and women can stay here, and all rooms are private and have private baths. The hostel is an eight-minute walk from Suidō-bashi Eki, which is on the JR Mita Line. *2–5–5 Saragaku, Chiyoda-ku, Tōkyō-to 101-0064, tel. 03/3233–0611, fax 03/3233–0633. 55 rooms. No credit cards.*

**$ TŌKYŌ INTERNATIONAL YOUTH HOSTEL.** In typical hostel style, you are required to be off the premises between 10 AM and 3 PM. Less typical is the fact that for an additional ¥1,200 over the standard rate, you can have breakfast and dinner in the hostel cafeteria. TIYH is a few minutes' walk from Iidabashi Eki on the JR, Tōzai, Namboku, and Yūraku-chō lines. *Central Plaza Bldg., 18th floor, 1–1 Kagura-kashi, Shinjuku-ku, Tōkyō-to 162-0823, tel. 03/3235–1107, fax 03/3267–4000. 138 bunk beds. No credit cards.*

## NEAR NARITA AIRPORT

Transportation between Narita Airport and Tōkyō proper takes—at best—about an hour. In heavy traffic, a limousine bus or taxi ride can stretch to two hours or more. A sensible strategy for visitors with early morning flights home would be to spend the night before at one of the hotels near the airport, all of which have courtesy shuttles to the departure terminals; these hotels are also a boon to visitors en route elsewhere with layovers in Narita.

**$$$ RADISSON HOTEL NARITA AIRPORT.** Set on 72 spacious acres of land, this modern hotel feels somewhat like a resort—and has Narita's largest outdoor pool. A shuttle bus runs between the Radisson and the airport every 20 minutes or so (between 1 PM and 10 PM from Terminal 1, between 12:50 PM and 9:50 PM from Terminal 2); the trip takes about 20 minutes. *650–35 Nanaei, Tomisato-machi, Inaba-gun, Chiba-ken 286-0222, tel. 0476/93–1234, fax 0476/93–4834, www.radisson.com. 496 rooms. Restaurant, no-smoking rooms, pool, 2 tennis courts, jogging, shop. AE, DC, MC, V.*

**$$–$$$ ANA HOTEL NARITA.** This 1990 hotel, like many others in the ANA chain, aspires to architecture in the grand style; expect the cost of brass and marble to show up on your bill. The amenities measure up, and the proximity to the airport (about 15 minutes by shuttle bus) makes this a good choice if you are in transit. *68 Hori-no-uchi, Narita-shi, Chiba-ken 286-0107, tel. 0476/33–1311; 0120/ 029–501 toll free, fax 0476/33–0244, www.anahotels.com. 422 rooms. 5 restaurants, bar, coffee shop, no-smoking rooms, pool, shops. AE, DC, MC, V.*

**$$–$$$ HOLIDAY INN TŌBU NARITA.** The Western-style accommodations at this hotel, a 10-minute ride by shuttle bus from the airport, provide the standard—if unremarkable—range of amenities. You can also rent one of its soundproof twin rooms for daytime-only use (11 AM–6 PM, ¥13,000). *320–1 Tokkō, Narita-shi, Chiba-ken 286-0106, tel. 0476/32–1234, fax 0476/32–0617, www.basshotels.com. 500* rooms. *2 restaurants, coffee shop, bar, no-smoking rooms, pool, barbershop, hair salon, massage, steam room, tennis court. AE, DC, MC, V.*

**$$ HOTEL NIKKŌ WINDS NARITA.** A regular shuttle bus (at Terminal 1, Bus Stop 14; Terminal 2, Bus Stop 31) makes the 10-minute trip to this modern, efficient, all-purpose hotel with one restaurant serving Japanese, French, and Chinese food. All rooms are soundproof. *560 Tokkō, Narita-shi, Chiba-ken 286-1016, tel. 0476/33–1111; 0120/582–586 toll free, fax 0476/33–1108. 321 rooms. 5 restaurants, no-smoking rooms, pool, sauna, 2 tennis courts, shops, meeting room. AE, DC, MC, V.*

**$$ NARITA VIEW HOTEL.** Boxy and uninspired, the Narita View offers no view of anything in particular but can be reached by shuttle bus from the airport in about 15 minutes. Short on charm, it tends to rely on promotional discount "campaigns" to draw a clientele. You can also rent rooms for daytime-only use from 11 to 6 for ¥6,500. *700 Kosuge, Narita-shi, Chiba-ken 286-0127, tel. 0476/32–1111, fax 0476/32–1078. 504 rooms. 4 restaurants, coffee shop, no-smoking rooms, hair salon, massage. AE, DC, MC, V.*

**$ NARITA AIRPORT REST HOUSE.** A basic business hotel without much in the way of frills, the Rest House offers the closest accommodations to the airport itself, less than five minutes away by shuttle bus. You can also rent one of its soundproof rooms for daytime-only use from 9 to 5 for about ¥5,000. *New Tōkyō International Airport, Narita-shi, Chiba-ken 286-0000, tel. 0476/32–1212, fax 0476/32–1209. 129 rooms. Restaurant, bar, coffee shop, no-smoking room. AE, DC, MC, V.*

# practical information

## Addresses

The simplest way to decipher a Japanese address is to **break the address into parts.** The following is an example of a typical Japanese address: 6-chōme 8–19, Chūō-ku, Fukuoka-shi, Fukuoka-ken. In this address the "chōme" indicates a precise area (a block, for example), and the numbers following "chōme" indicate the building within the area (buildings aren't always numbered sequentially; numbers are often assigned as buildings are erected). Only local police officers and mail carriers in Japan seem to be familiar with the area defined by the chōme. Sometimes, instead of "chōme," "machi" (town) is used.

"Ku" refers to a ward (a district) of a city, "shi" refers to a city name, and "ken" indicates a prefecture, which is roughly equivalent to a state in the United States. It's not unusual for the prefecture and the city to have the same name, as in the above address. There are a few geographic areas in Japan that are not called ken. One is Hokkaidō. The other exceptions are greater Tōkyō, which is called Tōkyō-to, and Kyōto and Ōsaka, which are followed by the suffix "-fu"—Kyōto-fu, Ōsaka-fu. Not all addresses conform exactly to the above format. Rural addresses, for example, might use "gun" (county) where cities have "ku" (ward).

Even Japanese people cannot find a building based on the address alone. If you get in a taxi with a written address, do not assume the driver will be able to find your destination. Usually, people provide very detailed instructions or maps to explain their exact locations. It's always good to **know the location of your destination in relation to a major building** or department store.

## Air Travel

### CARRIERS

The airlines of more than 50 different countries fly in and out of Tōkyō; among them, direct flights are available from hub cities in the United States, Canada, Great Britain, Australia, and New Zealand.

Japan Airlines (JAL) and United Airlines are the major carriers between North America and Narita Airport; Northwest, American Airlines, Delta Airlines, and All Nippon Airways (ANA) also link North American cities with Tōkyō. JAL, Cathay Pacific, Virgin Atlantic Airways, and British Airways fly between Narita and Great Britain; JAL, United, and Qantas fly between Narita and Australia; and JAL and Air New Zealand fly between Narita and New Zealand.

➤ **AIRLINES & CONTACTS: American** (tel. 800/433–7300; 0120/000–860 in Japan). **All Nippon Airways** (tel. 800/235–9262; 020/7355–1155 in the U.K.; 03/5489–8800 in Japan for domestic flights; 0120/5489–8800 in Japan for international flights). **British Airways** (tel. 0345/222–111 in the U.K.; 03/3593–8811 in Japan). **Canadian Airlines** (tel. 888/247–2262; 03/3281–7426 in Japan). **Continental** (tel. 800/525–0280). **Delta** (tel. 800/221–1212). **Japan Air System** (tel. 03/3438–1155 in Japan for domestic flights; 0120/511–283 in Japan for international flights). **Japan Airlines** (tel. 800/525–3663; 0345/747–700 in the U.K.; 0120/25–5931 in Japan). **Korean Air** (tel. 800/438–5000; 0800/413–000 in the U.K.; 03/5443–3311 in Japan). **Lufthansa** (tel. 0345/737–747 in the U.K.). **Northwest** (tel. 800/447–4747). **Swissair** (tel. 800/221–4750; 020/7434–7300 in the U.K.; 03/3533–6000 or 0120/120–747 in Japan). **Thai**

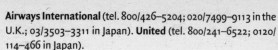

**Airways International** (tel. 800/426–5204; 020/7499–9113 in the U.K.; 03/3503–3311 in Japan). **United** (tel. 800/241–6522; 0120/114–466 in Japan).

### FLYING TIMES

Flying time to Japan is 13¾ hours from New York, 12¾ hours from Chicago, 9½ hours from Los Angeles, and 11–12 hours from the United Kingdom. Japan Airlines' GPS systems allow a more direct routing, which reduces its flight times by about 30 minutes. Your trip east, because of tailwinds, will be about 45 minutes shorter than your westbound flight.

## Airports

Tōkyō has two airports, Narita and Haneda. Narita Kūkō is 80 km (50 mi) northeast of Tōkyō and serves all international flights, except those operated by (Taiwan's) China Airways, which uses Haneda Kūkō. Narita added a new terminal building in 1992, which has somewhat eased the burden on it, but it can still be bottlenecked. In both terminals there are money exchange counters just inside the customs inspection area and just outside, in the arrivals lobby. In the shopping-restaurant area between the two wings is the Japan National Tourist Organization's Tourist Information Center, where you can get free maps, brochures, and other information. Directly across from the customs area exits at both terminals are the ticket counters for Airport Limousine Buses to Tōkyō.

Haneda Kūkō, 16 km (10 mi) southwest of Tōkyō, serves all domestic flights. At Haneda, Japan Airlines (JAL), All Nippon Airways (ANA), and Japan Air System have extensive domestic flight networks.

➤ **AIRPORT INFORMATION: Haneda Airport** (tel. 03/5757–8111). **Narita Airport** (tel. 0476/34–5000).

## AIRPORT TRANSFERS BETWEEN
## NARITA AIRPORT AND CENTER CITY

Two services, the Airport Limousine Bus, operated by Airport Transport Service Co., and the Airport Express Bus, operated by IAE Co., run from Narita to various major hotels in the $$$$ category and to the JR Tōkyō and Shinjuku stations; the fare is ¥2,400–¥3,800, depending on your destination. Even if you're not staying at one of the route's drop-off points, you can take the bus as far as the one closest to your hotel and then use a taxi for the remaining distance. Keep in mind that these buses only run every hour, and they do not run after 11 PM. The trip is scheduled for 70–90 minutes but can take two hours in heavy traffic. Ticket counters are in the arrival lobbies, directly across from the customs-area exit. Buses leave from platforms just outside terminal exits, exactly on schedule; the departure time is on the ticket.

A bus to the Tōkyō City Air Terminal (TCAT) leaves approximately every 10–20 minutes from 6:45 AM to 11 PM; the fare is ¥2,900, and you can buy tickets at the hotel bus ticket counter. TCAT is in Nihombashi in north-central Tōkyō, a bit far from most destinations, but from here you can connect directly with Suitengū Eki on the Hanzō-mon subway line, then to anywhere in the subway network. A taxi from TCAT to most major hotels will cost about ¥3,000.

Taxis are rarely used between Narita Airport and central Tōkyō— at ¥20,000 or more, depending on traffic and where you're going, the cost is prohibitive. Station-wagon taxis do exist, and the meter rates are the same as for the standard sedans, but they are not always available. Limousines are also very expensive; from Narita Airport to the Imperial Hotel downtown, for example, will set you back about ¥35,000.

Trains run every 30–40 minutes between Narita Airport Train Station and Keisei-Ueno Eki on the privately owned Keisei Line. The Keisei Skyliner takes 57 minutes and costs ¥1,920. The first

Skyliner leaves Narita for Ueno at 9:25 AM, the last at 9:58 PM; from Ueno to Narita, the first Skyliner is at 6:30 AM, the last at 5:25 PM. It only makes sense to take the Keisei, however, if your final destination is in the Ueno area; otherwise, you must change to the Tōkyō subway system or the Japan Railways loop line at Ueno (the station is adjacent to Keisei-Ueno Eki) or take a cab to your hotel.

Japan Railways trains stop at both terminals. The fastest and most comfortable is the Narita Limited Express (N'EX), which makes 23 runs a day in each direction. Trains from the airport go directly to the central Tōkyō Eki in just under an hour, then continue to Yokohama and Ōfuna. Daily departures begin at 7:43 AM; the last train is at 9:43 PM. The one-way fare is ¥2,940 (¥4,980 for the first-class "Green Car" and ¥5,380 per person for a private compartment that seats four). All seats are reserved, and you'll need to reserve one for yourself in advance, as this train fills quickly. The less elegant *kaisoku* (rapid train) on JR's Narita Line also runs from the airport to Tōkyō Eki, by way of Chiba; there are 16 departures daily, starting at 7 AM. The fare to Tōkyō is ¥1,280 (¥2,210 for the Green Car); the ride takes 1 hour and 27 minutes.

➤ **CONTACTS: Airport Transport Service Co.** (tel. 03/3665–7232 in Tōkyō; 0476/32–8080 for Terminal 1, New Tōkyō International Airport, Narita; 0476/34–6311 for Terminal 2). **IAE Co.** (tel. 0476/32–7954 for Terminal 1, New Tōkyō International Airport, Narita; 0476/34–6886 for Terminal 2). **Japan Railways** (tel. 03/3423–0111 for JR East InfoLine).

## AIRPORT TRANSFERS BETWEEN HANEDA AIRPORT AND CENTER CITY

The monorail from Haneda Airport to Hamamatsu-chō Eki in Tōkyō is the fastest and cheapest way into town; the journey takes about 17 minutes, and trains run approximately every 5 minutes; the fare is ¥470. From Hamamatsu-chō Eki, change to a JR train or take a taxi to your destination.

A taxi to the center of Tōkyō takes about 40 minutes; the fare is approximately ¥8,000.

➤ **CONTACT: Tōkyō Monorail Co., Ltd.** (tel. 03/3434–3171).

## Boat & Ferry Travel

The best ride in Tōkyō, hands down, is the *suijō basu* (river bus), operated by the Tōkyō Cruise Ship Company from Hinode Pier, from the mouth of the Sumida-gawa upstream to Asakusa. The glassed-in double-decker boats depart roughly every 20–40 minutes, weekdays 9:50–6:15, weekends and holidays 9:50–6:55 (with extended service to 7:35 July 9–September 23). The trip takes 40 minutes and costs ¥660. The pier is a seven-minute walk from Hamamatsu-chō Eki on the JR Yamanote Line.

The Sumida-gawa was once Tōkyō's lifeline, a busy highway for travelers and freight alike. The ferry service dates to 1885. Some people still take it to work, but today most passengers are Japanese tourists. On its way to Asakusa, the boat passes Tsukiji's Central Wholesale Market, the largest wholesale fish and produce market in the world; the old lumberyards and warehouses upstream; and the Kokugikan, with its distinctive green roof, which houses the sumō wrestling arena, the Sumō Museum, and headquarters of the Japan Sumō Association.

Another place to catch the ferry is at the Hama Rikyū Tei-en (Detached Palace Garden: open daily 9–4:30), a 15-minute walk from Ginza. Once part of the imperial estates, the gardens are open to the public for a separate ¥300 entrance fee. The ferry landing is inside, a short walk to the left as you enter the main gate. Boats depart every 35–45 minutes every weekday 10:25–4:10; the fare between Asakusa and Hama Rikyū is ¥620.

In addition to the ferry to Asakusa, the Tōkyō Cruise Ship Company also operates four other lines from Hinode Pier. The Harbor Cruise Line stern-wheeler makes a 50-minute circuit under the Rainbow Bridge and around the inner harbor. Departures are at 10:30, 12:30, 1:30, and 3:30 (and 4:45 in August). The fare is ¥800. If you visit in August you should definitely opt for the evening cruise; the lights on the Rainbow Bridge and neighboring Odaiba are spectacular. Two lines connect Hinode to Odaiba itself, one at 20-minute intervals from 10:10 to 6:10 to Odaiba Seaside Park and the Museum of Maritime Science at Aomi Terminal (¥400–¥520), the other every 20 minutes from 9 to 5:40 to the shopping/amusement center at Palette Town and on to the Tōkyō Big Sight exhibition grounds at Ariake (¥350). The Kasai Sealife Park Line cruise leaves Hinode hourly from 10 to 4 and travels through the network of artificial islands in the harbor to the beach and aquarium at Kasai Rinkai Kōen in Chiba; the one-way fare is ¥800. The Canal Cruise Line connects Hinode with Shinagawa Suizokukan aquarium, south along the harborside. There are nine departures daily between 10:40 and 4:40; the one-way fare is ¥600.

➤ BOAT AND FERRY INFORMATION: Tōkyō Cruise Ship Company (2–7–104 Kaigan, Minato-ku, tel. 03/3457–7830).

## Bus Travel

Because Tōkyō has no rational order bus routes are impossibly complicated. The Tōkyō Municipal Government operates some of the lines; private companies run the rest. There is no telephone number even a native Japanese can call for help. And buses all have tiny seats and low ceilings. Unless you are a true Tōkyō veteran, forget about taking buses.

## Cameras & Photography

Before departing, **register your foreign-made camera or laptop with U.S. Customs.** If your equipment is U.S. made, call the Japanese consulate to find out whether the device should be registered with local customs upon arrival.

Fluorescent lighting, which is common in Japan, gives photographs a greenish tint. You can counteract this discoloration with an FL filter.

## Car Rental

Congestion, lack of road signs in English, and the difficulty of parking make driving in Tōkyō impractical. That said, should you wish to rent a car, contact one of the following companies, with offices all around Tōkyō and Japan: Avis Rent-A-Car, Hertz Asia Pacific (Japan), Nippon Rent-A-Car Service, or Toyota Rent-A-Lease. The cost is approximately ¥15,000 per day. An international driver's license is required.

You can hire large and comfortable chauffeured cars (the Japanese call them *haiya*) for about ¥5,000 per hour for a midsize car, up to ¥18,000 per hour for a Cadillac limousine. Call Hinomaru. The Imperial, Okura, and Palace hotels also have limousine services.

➤ **LOCAL AGENCIES: Avis Rent-A-Car** (tel. 03/5550–1015). **Hertz Asia Pacific (Japan) Ltd.** (tel. 0120/489–882 toll free). **Hinomaru** (tel. 03/3505–0707). **Nippon Rent-A-Car** (tel. 03/3469–0919). **Toyota Rent-A-Lease** (tel. 03/3263–6324).

### INSURANCE
When driving a rented car you are generally responsible for any damage to or loss of the vehicle as well as for any property damage or personal injury that you may cause. Before you rent, see what coverage your personal auto-insurance policy and credit cards provide.

### REQUIREMENTS & RESTRICTIONS
In Japan your own driver's license is not acceptable. You need an international driver's permit; it's available from the American or Canadian Automobile Association, or, in the United Kingdom, from the Automobile Association or Royal Automobile Club.

## SURCHARGES

Before you pick up a car in one city and leave it in another, **ask about drop-off charges or one-way service fees,** which can be substantial. Note, too, that some rental agencies charge extra if you return the car before the time specified in your contract. To avoid a hefty refueling fee, **fill the tank just before you turn in the car,** but be aware that gas stations near the rental outlet may overcharge.

# Car Travel

It's possible for foreigners to drive in Japan with an international driver's license, and though few select this option, it is becoming more popular (to obtain a license, contact your country's major auto club). Major roads are sufficiently marked in the roman alphabet, and on country roads there is usually someone to ask for help. However, it's a good idea to **have a detailed map with town names written in** *kanji* **(Japanese characters) and** *romaji* **(romanized Japanese).**

### RULES OF THE ROAD

In Japan people **drive on the left.** Speed limits vary, but generally the limit is 80 kph (50 mph) on highways, 40 kph (25 mph) in cities.

Many smaller streets lack sidewalks, so cars, bicycles, and pedestrians share the same space. Motorbikes with engines under 50 cc are allowed to travel against automobile traffic on one-way roads. Fortunately, considering the narrowness of the streets and the volume of traffic, most Japanese drivers are technically skilled. They may not allow quite as much distance between cars as you're used to. Be prepared for sudden lane changes by other drivers. When waiting at intersections after dark, many drivers, as a courtesy to other drivers, turn off their main headlights to prevent glare.

Japan has very strict laws concerning the consumption of alcohol prior to getting behind the wheel. Given the almost zero-tolerance for driving under the influence and the occasional evening police checkpoint set up along the roads, it's wisest to avoid alcohol entirely if you plan to drive.

## Children in Japan

### BABY-SITTING

Some very expensive Western-style hotels and resorts have supervised playrooms where you can drop off your children. The baby-sitters, however, are unlikely to speak English. Child-care arrangements can also be made through your hotel's concierge, but some properties require up to a week's notice.

### LODGING

Most hotels in Japan allow children under a certain age to stay in their parents' room at no extra charge, but others charge for them as extra adults; be sure to **find out the cutoff age for children's discounts.**

### SIGHTS & ATTRACTIONS

Places that are especially appealing to children are indicated by a rubber-duckie icon (🐤) in the margin.

## Customs & Duties

When shopping, **keep receipts** for all purchases. Upon reentering the country, **be ready to show customs officials what you've bought.** If you feel a duty is incorrect or object to the way your clearance was handled, note the inspector's badge number and ask to see a supervisor. If the problem isn't resolved, write to the appropriate authorities, beginning with the port director at your point of entry.

### IN AUSTRALIA

Australian residents who are 18 or older may bring home $A400 worth of souvenirs and gifts (including jewelry), 250 cigarettes or 250 grams of tobacco, and 1,125 ml of alcohol (including wine, beer, and spirits). Residents under 18 may bring back $A200 worth of goods. Prohibited items include meat products. Seeds, plants, and fruits need to be declared upon arrival.

➤ **INFORMATION: Australian Customs Service** (Regional Director, Box 8, Sydney, NSW 2001, Australia, tel. 02/9213–2000, fax 02/9213–4000, www.customs.gov.au).

## IN CANADA

Canadian residents who have been out of Canada for at least seven days may bring home C$750 worth of goods duty-free. If you've been away fewer than seven days but more than 48 hours, the duty-free allowance drops to C$200; if your trip lasts 24–48 hours, the allowance is C$50. You may not pool allowances with family members. Goods claimed under the C$750 exemption may follow you by mail; those claimed under the lesser exemptions must accompany you. Alcohol and tobacco products may be included in the seven-day and 48-hour exemptions but not in the 24-hour exemption. If you meet the age requirements of the province or territory through which you reenter Canada, you may bring in, duty-free, 1.14 liters (40 imperial ounces) of wine or liquor or 24 12-ounce cans or bottles of beer or ale. If you are 19 or older you may bring in, duty-free, 200 cigarettes and 50 cigars. Check ahead of time with the Canada Customs Revenue Agency or the Department of Agriculture for policies regarding meat products, seeds, plants, and fruits.

You may send an unlimited number of gifts worth up to C$60 each duty-free to Canada. Label the package UNSOLICITED GIFT—VALUE UNDER $60. Alcohol and tobacco are excluded.

➤ **INFORMATION: Canada Customs Revenue Agency** (2265 St. Laurent Blvd. S, Ottawa, Ontario K1G 4K3, Canada, tel. 204/983–3500 or 506/636–5064; 800/461–9999 in Canada, www.ccra-adrc.gc.ca).

## IN JAPAN

Japan has strict regulations about bringing firearms, pornography, and narcotics into the country. Anyone caught with drugs is liable to be detained, deported, and refused reentry into Japan. Certain fresh fruits, vegetables, plants, and animals are also illegal. Nonresidents are allowed to bring in duty-free: (1) 400 cigarettes or 100 cigars or 500 grams of tobacco; (2) three bottles of alcohol; (3) 2 ounces of perfume; (4) other goods up to ¥200,000 value.

## IN NEW ZEALAND

Homeward-bound residents 17 or older may bring back $700 worth of souvenirs and gifts. Your duty-free allowance also includes 4.5 liters of wine or beer; one 1,125-ml bottle of spirits; and either 200 cigarettes, 250 grams of tobacco, 50 cigars, or a combination of the three up to 250 grams. Prohibited items include meat products, seeds, plants, and fruits.

➤ **INFORMATION: New Zealand Customs** (Custom House, 50 Anzac Ave., Box 29, Auckland, New Zealand, tel. 09/300–5399, fax 09/359–6730, www.customs.govt.nz).

## IN THE U.K.

From countries outside the European Union, including Japan, you may bring home, duty-free, 200 cigarettes or 50 cigars; 1 liter of spirits or 2 liters of fortified or sparkling wine or liqueurs; 2 liters of still table wine; 60 ml of perfume; 250 ml of toilet water; plus £145 worth of other goods, including gifts and souvenirs. If returning from outside the EU, prohibited items include meat products, seeds, plants, and fruits.

➤ **INFORMATION: HM Customs and Excise** (St. Christopher House, Southwark, London SE1 OTE, U.K., tel. 020/7928–3344, www.hmce.gov.uk).

## IN THE U.S.

U.S. residents who have been out of the country for at least 48 hours (and who have not used the $400 allowance or any part of it in the past 30 days) may bring home $400 worth of foreign goods duty-free.

U.S. residents 21 and older may bring back 1 liter of alcohol duty-free. In addition, regardless of your age, you are allowed 200 cigarettes and 100 non-Cuban cigars. Antiques, which the U.S. Customs Service defines as objects more than 100 years old, enter duty-free, as do original works of art done entirely by hand, including paintings, drawings, and sculptures.

You may also mail or ship packages home duty-free: up to $200 worth of goods for personal use, with a limit of one parcel per addressee per day (except alcohol or tobacco products or perfume worth more than $5); label the package PERSONAL USE and attach a list of its contents and their retail value. Do not label the package UNSOLICITED GIFT or your duty-free exemption will drop to $100. Mailed items do not affect your duty-free allowance on your return.

➤ **INFORMATION: U.S. Customs Service** (1300 Pennsylvania Ave. NW, Room 6.3D, Washington, DC 20229, www.customs.gov; inquiries tel. 202/354–1000; complaints c/o 1300 Pennsylvania Ave. NW, Room 5.4D, Washington, DC 20229; registration of equipment c/o Office of Passenger Programs, tel. 202/927–0530).

# Dining

The restaurants we list are the cream of the crop in each price category. Food, like many other things in Japan, is expensive. Many less expensive restaurants have plastic replicas of the dishes they serve displayed in their front windows, so you can always point to what you want to eat if the language barrier is insurmountable.

In general, Japanese restaurants are very clean (standards of hygiene are very high). The water is safe, even when drawn from a tap. Most hotels have Western-style rest rooms, but restaurants may have Japanese-style toilets, with bowls recessed into the floor, over which you must squat.

## RESERVATIONS & DRESS

Reservations are always a good idea: we mention them only when they're essential or not accepted. Book as far ahead as you can, and reconfirm as soon as you arrive. We mention dress only when men are required to wear a jacket or a jacket and tie.

# Disabilities & Accessibility

Japan has a long way to go before accessibility throughout the country equals that in the West. Though wheelchair navigation is not an impossibility and elevators are everywhere, the sheer number of people in Tōkyō is likely to frustrate even the most determined disabled traveler. Such disadvantages may be countered, of course, by the amazing helpfulness of strangers and by their eagerness to extend even the smallest kindness.

## SIGHTS & ATTRACTIONS

Many shrines and temples are set on high ground, with steep steps, so people with mobility problems may have difficulty visiting them.

# Electricity

To use electric-powered equipment purchased in the United States or Canada, **bring a converter and adapter.** The electrical current in Japan is 100 volts, 50 cycles alternating current (AC) in eastern Japan; the United States runs on 110-volt, 60-cycle AC current. Wall outlets in Japan accept plugs with two flat prongs, like in the United States, but do not accept U.S. three-prong plugs.

If your appliances are dual-voltage, you'll need only an adapter. Don't use 110-volt outlets marked FOR SHAVERS ONLY for high-wattage appliances such as blow-dryers. Most laptops operate equally well on 110 and 220 volts and so require only an adapter.

# Embassies

➤ **AUSTRALIA: Australian Embassy and Consulate** (2–1–14 Mita, Minato-ku, tel. 03/5232–4111; subway: Toei Mita Line, Shiba-Kōen Eki [Exit A2]; Toei Ōedo and Namboku lines, Azabu-jūban Eki [Exits 2 and 4]).

➤ **CANADA: Canadian Embassy and Consulate** (7–3–38 Akasaka, Minato-ku, tel. 03/5412–6200; subway: Hanzō-mon and Ginza lines, Aoyama-itchōme Eki [Exit 4]).

➤ **NEW ZEALAND: New Zealand Embassy** (20–40 Kamiyama-chō, Shibuya-ku, tel. 03/3467–2270; subway: Chiyoda Line, Yoyogi-kōen Eki [Minami-guchi/South Exit]).

➤ **UNITED KINGDOM: British Embassy and Consulate** (1 Ichiban-chō, Chiyoda-ku, tel. 03/3265–5511; subway: Hanzō-mon Line, Hanzō-mon Eki [Exit 4]).

➤ **UNITED STATES: U.S. Embassy and Consulate** (1–10–5 Akasaka, Minato-ku, tel. 03/3224–5000; subway: Namboku Line, Tameike-Sannō Eki [Exit 13]).

# Emergencies

## DOCTORS AND DENTISTS

The International Catholic Hospital (Seibō Byōin) accepts emergencies and takes regular appointments Monday–Saturday 8 AM–11 AM; outpatient services are closed the third Saturday of the month. The International Clinic also accepts emergencies. Appointments there are taken weekdays 9–noon and 2:30–5 and on Saturday 9–noon. St. Luke's International Hospital is a member of the American Hospital Association and accepts emergencies. Appointments are taken weekdays 8:30 AM–11 AM. The Tōkyō Medical and Surgical Clinic takes appointments weekdays 9–5 and Saturday 9–noon.

The Yamauchi Dental Clinic, a member of the American Dental Association, is open weekdays 9–12:30 and 3–5:30, Saturday 9–noon.

➤ **CONTACTS: International Catholic Hospital** (Seibō Byōin; 2–5–1 Naka Ochiai, Shinjuku-ku, tel. 03/3951–1111; subway: Seibu Shinjuku Line, Shimo-Ochiai Eki [Nishi-guchi/West Exit]). **International Clinic** (1–5–9 Azabu-dai, Roppongi, Minato-ku, tel. 03/3582–2646 or 03/3583–7831; subway: Hibiya Line, Roppongi Eki [Exit 3]). **St. Luke's International Hospital** (9–1 Akashi-chō, Chūō-ku, tel. 03/3541–5151; subway: Hibiya Line, Tsukiji Eki [Exit 3]; Yūraku-chō Line, Shintomichō Eki [Exit 6]). **Tōkyō Medical and Surgical Clinic** (32 Mori Bldg., 3–4–30 Shiba Kōen, Minato-ku, tel. 03/3436–3028; subway: Toei Mita Line, Onarimon Eki [Exit A1]; Hibiya Line, Kamiyachō Eki [Exit 1]; Toei Ōedo Line, Akabane-bashi Eki). **Yamauchi Dental Clinic** (Shirokanedai Gloria Heights, 1st floor, 3–16–10 Shirokanedai, Minato-ku, tel. 03/3441–6377; JR Yamanote Line, Meguro Eki [Higashi-guchi/East Exit]; subway: Namboku and Toei Mita lines, Shirokanedai Eki [Exit 1]).

## EMERGENCY SERVICES

Assistance in English is available 24 hours a day on the Japan Helpline. The Tōkyō English Life Line (TELL) is a telephone service available daily 9 AM–4 PM and 7 PM–11 PM for anyone in distress who cannot communicate in Japanese. The service will relay your emergency to the appropriate Japanese authorities and/or will serve as a counselor.

➤ **CONTACTS: Ambulance and Fire** (tel. 119). **Japan Helpline** (tel. 0120/461–997 toll free). **Police** (tel. 110). **Tōkyō English Life Line** (TELL; tel. 03/5774–0992).

## LATE-NIGHT PHARMACIES

No drugstores in Tōkyō are open 24 hours a day. The American Pharmacy stocks American products. It's near the Tourist Information Center and is open Monday–Saturday 9:30–8:30

and Sunday 10–6:30. Note that grocery stores frequently carry such basics as aspirin.

Nagai Yakkyoku is open Wednesday–Monday 10–7 and will mix a Chinese and/or Japanese herbal medicine for you after a consultation. You can't have a doctor's prescription filled here, but you can find something for a headache or stomach pain. A little English is spoken.

➤ **CONTACTS: American Pharmacy** (Hibiya Park Building, 1–8–1 Yūraku-chō, Chiyoda-ku, tel. 03/3271–4034; Hibiya subway line, Hibiya Eki [Exit A3]). **Nagai Yakkyoku** (1–8–10 Azabu-jūban, Minato-ku, tel. 03/3583–3889; Namboku and Toei Ōedo subway lines, Azabu-jūban Eki [Exit 7]).

## Etiquette & Behavior

Propriety is an important part of Japanese society. Many Japanese expect foreigners to behave differently and are tolerant of faux pas, but they are pleasantly surprised when people acknowledge and observe their customs. The easiest way to ingratiate yourself with the Japanese is to **take time to learn and respect Japanese ways.**

It is customary to **bow upon meeting someone.** The art of bowing is not simple; the depth of your bow depends on your social position in respect to that of the other person. Younger people, or those of lesser status, must bow deeper in order to indicate their respect and acknowledge their position. You're not expected to understand the complexity of these rules, and a basic nod of the head will suffice. Many Japanese are familiar with Western customs and will offer a hand for a handshake.

Don't be offended if you're not invited to someone's home. Most entertaining among Japanese is done in restaurants or bars. It's an honor when you are invited to a home; this means your host feels comfortable and close to you. If you do receive an invitation, bring along a small gift—a souvenir from your country makes the best present, but food and liquor or anything that can be consumed (and not take up space in the home) is also appreciated. Upon entering a home, **remove your shoes in the foyer and put on the slippers that are provided**; in Japan shoes are for wearing outdoors only. Be sure your socks or stockings are in good condition.

Japanese restaurants often provide a small hot towel called an *oshibori*. This is to wipe your hands but not your face. You may see some Japanese wiping their faces with their oshibori, but sometimes this is considered to be bad form. If you must use your oshibori to remove forehead perspiration, wipe your face first, then your hands. When you are finished with your oshibori, do not just toss it back onto the table, but fold or roll it up. If you're not accustomed to eating with chopsticks, ask for a fork instead. When taking food from a shared dish, do not use the part of the chopsticks that has entered your mouth to pick up a morsel. Instead, use the end that you have been holding in your hand. **Never leave your chopsticks sticking upright in your food**; this is how rice offerings at funerals are arranged. Instead, rest chopsticks on the edge of the tray, bowl, or plate between bites and at the end of the meal.

## BUSINESS ETIQUETTE

Although many business practices are universal, certain customs remain unique to Japan. It's not necessary to observe these precepts, but the Japanese always appreciate it if you do.

In Japan, *meishi* (business cards) are mandatory. Upon meeting someone for the first time, it is common to bow and to proffer your business card simultaneously. Although English will suffice on your business card, it's best to have one side printed in Japanese (there are outfits in Japan that provide this service in 24 hours). In a sense, the cards are simply a convenience. Japanese sometimes have difficulty with Western names, and referring to the cards is helpful. Also, in a society where hierarchy matters, Japanese like to know job titles and rank, so it's useful if your card indicates your position in your company. Japanese often place the business cards they have received in front of them on a table or desk as they conduct their meetings. Follow suit and do not simply shove the card in your pocket.

The concept of being fashionably late does not exist in Japan; it is extremely important to **be prompt for both social and business occasions.** Japanese addresses tend to be complicated, and traffic is often heavy, so allow for adequate travel time. Most Japanese are not accustomed to using first names in business circumstances. Even coworkers of 20 years' standing use surnames. Unless you are sure that the Japanese person is extremely comfortable with Western customs, it is best to **stick to last names and use the honorific word -san after the name,** as in *Tanaka-san* (Mr. or Mrs. Tanaka). Also, respect the hierarchy, and as much as possible address yourself to the most senior person in the room.

Don't be frustrated if decisions are not made instantly. Rarely empowered to make decisions, individual businesspeople must confer with their colleagues and superiors. Even if you are annoyed, **don't express anger or aggression.** Losing one's temper is equated with losing face in Japan.

A separation of business and private lives remains sacrosanct in Japan, and it is best not to ask about personal matters. Rather than asking about a person's family, **stick to neutral subjects in conversation.**

Because of cramped housing, again, many Japanese entertain in restaurants or bars. It is not customary for Japanese businessmen to bring wives along. If you are traveling with your spouse, do not assume that an invitation includes both of you. You may ask if it is acceptable to bring your spouse along, but remember that it is awkward for a Japanese person to say no. You should pose the question carefully, such as "Will your [wife or husband] come along, too?" This eliminates the need for a direct, personal refusal.

Usually, entertaining is done over dinner, followed by an evening on the town. Drinking is something of a national pastime in Japan. If you would rather not suffer from a hangover the next day, do not refuse your drink—sip, but keep your glass at least half full. Because the custom is for companions to pour drinks for each other, an empty glass is nearly the equivalent of requesting another drink. Whatever you do, **don't pour your own drink, and if a glass at your table happens to be empty, show your attentiveness by filling it for your companion.**

A special note to women traveling on business in Japan: remember that although the situation is gradually changing, many Japanese women do not have careers. Many Japanese businessmen do not yet know how to interact with Western businesswomen. They may be uncomfortable, aloof, or patronizing. Be patient and, if the need arises, gently remind them that, professionally, you expect to be treated as any man would be.

## Gay & Lesbian Travel

It is no small feat to orient yourself as a gay or lesbian traveler to Japan's gay nightlife. Forget about gay restaurants, cafés, even bookstores that sell more than "adult" books. Because Japan does not have the religious opposition to homosexuality that the West does, the major barrier that continues to suppress gay lifestyle in Japan is the Confucian duty to continue the family line, to bring no shame to the family, and to fit into Japanese society. So gay and lesbian travelers aren't likely to stumble upon many establishments that cater to a gay clientele.

There *are* bars, karaoke lounges, discos, "snacks" (a type of bar), hostess bars, host bars, and drag king/queen bars—the trick is finding them. Even the gay district of Shinjuku 2-chōme (a 15-minute walk west of Shinjuku Station) leaves you wondering if you've found the place. When you get there, look for people who live in the area, particularly Westerners, and approach them. The Japanese would never broach the subject except, perhaps, at the end of a night of drinking. In fact, it is a bad idea to broach the subject with a Japanese: it will cause much awkwardness, and the response will be nowhere near as sophisticated as it has become in the West. All of this said, homosexuality (as an interest but not a life choice) is more accepted in the realm of human expression than it is in the West. This may sound quite discouraging, but in actuality, Japan can prove to be an outlet of immense freedom for gays if you are successful in making friends in Tōkyō.

International Gay Friends is a gay meeting group in Tōkyō. Occur Help Line sets aside different days of the month for women and men. Out in Japan magazine is available at Tower Records.

➤ CONTACTS & INFORMATION: International Gay Friends (tel. 03/5693–4569). Occur Help Line (tel. 03/3380–2269).

## Health

Tap water everywhere is safe. It may be difficult to buy the standard over-the-counter remedies you're used to, so it's best to bring with you any medications (in their proper packaging) you may need. Medical treatment varies from highly skilled and professional treatment at major hospitals to somewhat less advanced procedures in small neighborhood clinics. At larger hospitals you have a good chance of encountering English-speaking doctors who have been partly educated in the West.

## Holidays

As elsewhere, peak times for travel in Japan tend to fall around holiday periods. You'll want to avoid traveling during the few days before and after New Year's; during Golden Week, which follows Greenery Day (April 29); and in mid-July and mid-August, at the time of Obon festivals, when many Japanese return to their hometowns (Obon festivals are celebrated July or August 13–16, depending on the location). Note that when a holiday falls on a Sunday, the following Monday is a holiday.

January 1 (*Ganjitsu*, New Year's Day); the second Monday in January (*Senjin-no-hi*, Coming of Age Day); February 11 (*Kenkoku Kinen-no-bi*, National Foundation Day); March 20 or 21 (*Shumbun-no-hi*, Vernal Equinox); April 29 (*Midori-no-hi*, Greenery Day); May 3 (*Kempo Kinen-bi*, Constitution Day); May 5 (*Kodomo-no-hi*, Children's Day); September 15 (*Keiro-no-hi*, Respect for the Aged Day); September 23 or 24 (*Shubun-no-hi*, Autumnal Equinox); the second Monday in October (*Taiiku-no-hi*, Sports Day); November 3 (*Bunka-no-hi*, Culture Day); November 23 (*Kinro Kansha-no-hi*, Labor Thanksgiving Day); December 23 (*Tennō Tanjobi*, Emperor's Birthday).

## Language

Communicating in Japan can be a challenge. This is not because the Japanese don't speak English but because most of us know little, if any, Japanese. Take some time before you leave home to **learn a few basic words,** such as where (*doko*), what time (*nan-ji*), bathroom (*o-te-arai*), thank you (*arigatō gozaimasu*), excuse me (*sumimasen*), and please (*onegai shimasu*).

English is a required subject in Japanese schools, so most Japanese study English for nearly a decade. This does not mean everyone *speaks* English. Schools emphasize reading, writing, and grammar. As a result, many Japanese can read English but can speak only a few basic phrases. Furthermore, when asked, "Do you speak English?" many Japanese, out of modesty, say no, even if they do understand and speak a fair amount of it. It is usually best to simply ask what you really want to know slowly, clearly, and as simply as possible. If the person you ask understands, he or she will answer or perhaps take you where you need to go.

Although a local may understand your simple question, he or she cannot always give you an answer that requires complicated instructions. For example, you may ask someone on the subway how to get to a particular stop, and he may direct you to the train across the platform and then say something in Japanese that you do not understand. You may discover too late that the train runs express to the suburbs after the third stop; the person who gave you directions was trying to tell you to switch trains at the third stop. To avoid this kind of trouble, **ask more than one person for directions every step of the way.** You can avoid that trip to the suburbs if you ask someone on the train how to get to where you want to go. Also, remember that politeness is a matter of course in Japan and that the Japanese won't want to lose face by saying that they don't know how to get somewhere. If the situation gets confusing, bow, say *arigatō gozaimashita* ("thank you" in the past tense), and ask someone else. Even though you are communicating on a very basic level, misunderstandings can happen easily.

Traveling in Japan can be problematic if you don't read Japanese. Before you leave home, **buy a phrase book** that shows English, English transliterations of Japanese (*romaji*), and Japanese characters (*kanji* and *kana*). You can read the romaji to pick up a few Japanese words and match the kanji and kana in the phrase book with characters on signs and menus. When all else fails, ask for help by pointing to the Japanese words in your book.

The most common system of writing Japanese words in Roman letters is the modified Hepburn system, which spells out Japanese words phonetically and is followed in this book.

# Lodging

The Japanese Inn Group is a nationwide association of small ryokan and family-owned tourist hotels. Because they tend to be slightly out of the way and provide few amenities, these accommodations are priced to attract budget-minded travelers. The association has the active support of the Japan National Tourist Organization. The best way to get information about the member inns in Tōkyō and throughout Japan—and arrange bookings on the spot—is to visit the JNTO Tourist Information Center (open weekdays 9–5, Saturday 9–noon) on the lower level of the Tōkyō International Forum.

➤ **CONTACT: JNTO Tourist Information Center** (Tōkyō International Forum B1, 3–5–1 Marunouchi, Chiyoda-ku, tel. 03/3201–3331; subway: Yūraku-chō Line, Yūraku-chō Eki [Exit A-4B]).

## LODGING PRICES

Assume that hotels operate on the **European Plan** (EP, with no meals) unless we specify that they use the **Continental Plan** (CP, with a Continental breakfast), **Modified American Plan** (MAP, with breakfast and dinner), or the **Full American Plan** (FAP, with all meals).

## HOME VISITS

Through the home visit system, travelers can get a sense of domestic life in Japan by visiting a local family in their home. The program is voluntary on the home owner's part, and there is no charge for a visit. To make a reservation, **apply in writing for a home visit at least a day in advance** to the local tourist information office of the place you are visiting. Contact the Japan National Tourist Organization before leaving for Japan for more information on the program.

## HOSTELS

No matter what your age, you can **save on lodging costs by staying at hostels.** They run about ¥3,000–¥4,000 per night.

➤ **ORGANIZATIONS: Japan Youth Hostels, Inc.** (Suido-bashi Nishiguchi Kaikan, 2–20–7 Misaki-chō, Chiyoda-ku, Tōkyō 101–0061, tel. 03/3288–1417).

## Mail & Shipping

The Japanese postal service is very efficient. Air mail between Japan and the United States takes between five and eight days. Surface mail can take anywhere from four to eight weeks. Express service is also available through post offices.

Most hotels have stamps and will mail your letters and postcards; they will also give you directions to the nearest post office. The main International Post Office is on the Imperial Palace side of JR Tōkyō Eki. For cables, contact the KDD International Telegraph Office.

The Japanese postal service has implemented use of three-numeral-plus-four postal codes, but its policy is similar to that in the United States regarding ZIP-plus-fours; that is, addresses with the three-numeral code will still arrive at its destination, albeit perhaps one or two days later. Mail to rural towns may take longer.

➤ **MAJOR SERVICES: International Post Office** (2–3–3 Ōte-machi, Chiyoda-ku, tel. 03/3241–4891; Tōkyō Eki). **KDD International Telegraph Office** (2–3–2 Nishi-Shinjuku, Shinjuku-ku, tel. 03/3344–5151; Tōei Ōedo subway line, Tochō-mae Eki [any exit]).

### POSTAL RATES
It costs ¥110 to send a letter by air to North America and Europe. An airmail postcard costs ¥70. Aerograms cost ¥90.

### RECEIVING MAIL
To get mail, have parcels and letters sent "poste restante" at the central post office in major cities; unclaimed mail is returned after 30 days.

# Money Matters

Japan is expensive, but there are ways to cut costs. This requires, to some extent, an adventurous spirit and the courage to stray from the standard tourist paths. One good way to hold down expenses is to avoid taxis (they tend to get stuck in traffic anyway) and try the inexpensive, efficient subway and bus systems; instead of going to a restaurant with menus in English and Western-style food, go to places where you can rely on your good old index finger to point to the dish you want, and try food that the Japanese eat.

A cup of coffee costs ¥350–¥600; a bottle of beer, ¥350–¥1,000; a 2-km (1-mi) taxi ride, ¥660; a McDonald's hamburger, ¥340; a bowl of noodles, ¥700; an average dinner, ¥2,500; a double room in Tōkyō, ¥11,000–¥45,000.

Prices throughout this guide are given for adults. Substantially reduced fees are almost always available for children, students, and senior citizens.

## ATMS
All major branch offices of the post office have ATM machines that accept Visa, MasterCard, American Express, Diners Club, and Cirrus cards. You can also use cards on the Cirrus network at Citibank ATMs. Banking hours are weekdays 9–3.

## CREDIT CARDS
MasterCard and Visa are the most widely accepted credit cards in Japan. Throughout this guide, the following abbreviations are used: **AE,** American Express; **DC,** Diners Club; **MC,** MasterCard; and **V,** Visa.

➤ **REPORTING LOST CARDS: American Express** (tel. 03/3220–6100). **Diners Club** (tel. 03/3499–1181). **MasterCard** (tel. 0031/113–886). **Visa** (tel. 0120/133–173).

## CURRENCY

The unit of currency in Japan is the yen (¥). There are bills of ¥10,000, ¥5,000, ¥2,000, and ¥1,000. Coins are ¥500, ¥100, ¥50, ¥10, ¥5, and ¥1. Japanese currency floats on the international monetary exchange, so changes can be dramatic. Some vending machines will not accept the newly introduced ¥2,000 bill or the new version of the ¥500 coin, but these older machines are gradually being replaced. At press time the exchange rate was about ¥121 to the U.S. dollar, ¥78 to the Canadian dollar, and ¥175 to the pound sterling.

## CURRENCY EXCHANGE

Most hotels will change both traveler's checks and notes into yen. However, their rates are always less favorable than at banks. Because Japan is largely free from street crime, you can safely consider changing even hefty sums into yen at any time; three places that may be familiar to you are American Express International and Citibank. The larger branches of most Japanese banks have foreign exchange counters where you can do this as well; the paperwork will be essentially the same.

➤ CONTACTS: **American Express International** (4–30–16 Ogikubo, Suginami-ku, tel. 03/3220–6100; JR Chuo Line, Ogikubo Eki [Higashi-guchi/East Exit]). **Citibank** (Ōte Center Bldg. 1F, 1–1–3 Ōte-machi, Chiyoda-ku, tel. 0120/110–330 toll free for members; 03/3215–0051 for nonmembers; Chiyoda, Marunouchi, Hanzō-mon, Tōzai, and Mita subway lines; Ōte-machi Eki [Exit C-13B]).

# Packing

To avoid customs and security delays, carry medications in their original packaging. Don't pack any sharp objects in your carry-on luggage, including knives of any size or material, scissors, manicure tools, and corkscrews, or anything else that might arouse suspicion.

Pack as you would for any American or European city. At more expensive restaurants and nightclubs, men usually need to wear a jacket and tie, and women need a dress or skirt. Make sure to bring comfortable clothing that isn't too tight to wear in traditional Japanese restaurants, where you may need to sit on tatami-matted floors. Wear conservative-color clothing at business meetings. Casual clothes are fine for sightseeing. Jeans are as popular in Japan as they are in the United States and are perfectly acceptable for informal dining and sightseeing.

Japanese do not wear shoes in private homes or in any temples or traditional inns. Having shoes you can quickly slip in and out of is a decided advantage. Take some wool socks along to help you through those shoeless occasions during the winter.

If you're a morning coffee addict, **take along packets of instant coffee.** All lodgings provide a thermos of hot water and bags of green tea in every room, but for coffee you'll either have to call room service (which can be expensive) or buy very sweet coffee in a can from a vending machine. If you're staying in a Japanese inn, they probably won't have coffee.

Although sunglasses, sunscreen lotions, and hats are readily available, you're better off buying them at home, because they're much more expensive in Japan. It's a good idea to carry a couple of plastic bags to protect your camera and clothes during sudden cloudbursts.

Take along small gift items, such as scarves or perfume sachets, to thank hosts (on both business and pleasure trips), whether you've been invited to their home or out to a restaurant.

## Passports & Visas

When traveling internationally, **carry your passport** even if you don't need one (it's always the best form of I.D.) and **make two photocopies of the data page** (one for someone at home and another for you, carried separately from your passport). If you lose your passport, promptly call the nearest embassy or consulate and the local police.

**ENTERING JAPAN**
Visitors from the United States, Canada, Great Britain, Australia, and New Zealand can enter Japan for up to 90 days with a valid passport; no visa is required.

## Rest Rooms

The most hygienic rest rooms are found in hotels and department stores and are usually clearly marked with international symbols. You may encounter Japanese-style toilets, with bowls recessed into the floor, over which you squat facing the hood. This may take some getting used to, but it's completely sanitary as you don't come into direct contact with the facility.

In many homes and Japanese-style public places, there will be a pair of slippers at the entrance to the rest rooms. Change into these before entering the room, and change back when you exit.

## Safety

Even in its major cities, Japan is a very safe country with one of the lowest crime rates in the world. You should avoid Ura-Kabuki-chō in the Shinjuku district and some of the large public parks at nighttime.

## Subway Travel

Thirteen subway lines serve Tōkyō; nine of them are operated by the Rapid Transportation Authority (Eidan) and four by the Tōkyō Municipal Authority (Toei). Maps of the system, bilingual signs at entrances, and even the trains are color-coded for easy identification. Japan Travel Phone can provide information in English on subway travel. Subway trains run roughly every five minutes from about 5 AM to midnight; except during rush hours, the intervals are slightly longer on the newer Toei lines.

The network of interconnections (subway to subway and train to subway) is particularly good. One transfer—two at most—will take you in less than an hour to any part of the city you're likely to visit. At some stations—such as Ōte-machi, Ginza, and Iidabashi—long underground passageways connect the various lines, and it does take time to get from one to another. Directions, however, are clearly marked. Less helpful is the system of signs that tell you which of the 15 or 20 exits (exits are often numbered and alphabetized) from a large station will take you aboveground closest to your destination; only a few stations have such signs in English. Exit names or numbers have been included in the text where they'll be most useful. You can also try asking the agent when you turn in your ticket; she or he may understand enough of your question to come back with the exit number and letter (such as A3 or B12), which is all you need.

Subway fares begin at ¥160. Toei trains are generally a bit more expensive than Eidan trains, but both are competitive with JR lines. From Ueno across town to Shibuya on the old Ginza Line (orange), for example, is ¥190; the ride on the JR Yamanote Line will cost you the same. The Eidan (but not the Toei) has inaugurated an electronic card of its own, called Metrocard. The denominations are ¥1,000, ¥3,000, and ¥5,000. Automatic card dispensers are installed at some subway stations. Remember to hold onto your ticket during your trip; you'll need it again to exit the station turnstile.

➤ **CONTACT: Japan Travel Phone** (tel. 03/3201–3331).

## Taxes

### HOTEL
A 5% national consumption tax is added to all hotel bills. Another 3% local tax is added to the bill if it exceeds ¥15,000.

You may save money by paying for your hotel meals separately rather than charging them to your bill.

At first-class, full-service, and luxury hotels, a 10% service charge is added to the bill in place of individual tipping. At the more expensive ryokan, where individualized maid service is offered, the service charge is usually 15%. At business hotels, minshuku, youth hostels, and economy inns, no service charge is added to the bill.

### SALES

There is an across-the-board, nonrefundable 5% consumer tax levied on all sales. Since the tax was introduced in 1989, vendors have either been absorbing the tax in their quoted retail prices or adding it on to the sale. Before you make a major purchase, inquire if tax is extra. A 5% federal consumer tax is added to all restaurant bills. Another 3% local tax is added to the bill if it exceeds ¥7,500. At the more expensive restaurants, a 10%–15% service charge is added to the bill. Tipping is not customary.

## Taxis

In spite of the introduction of ¥340 initial-fare cabs, Tōkyō taxi fares remain among the highest in the world. Most meters start running at ¥660 and after the first 2 km (1 mi) tick away at the rate of ¥80 every 274 meters (about ⅙ mi). Keep in mind that the ¥340 taxis (which are a very small percentage of those on the street) are only cheaper for trips of 2 km (1 mi) or less; after that the fare catches up with the ¥660 cabs. The ¥340 taxis have a sticker on the left-rear window.

There are also smaller cabs, called *kogata*, that charge ¥640 and then ¥80 per 290 meters (⅕ mi). If your cab is caught in traffic—hardly an uncommon event—the meter registers another ¥80 for every 1½ minutes of immobility. Between 11 PM and 5 AM, a 30% surcharge is added to the fare.

You do get very good value for the money, though. Taxis are invariably clean and comfortable. The doors open automatically for you when you get in and out. Drivers take you where you want to go by the shortest route they know and do not expect a tip. Tōkyō cabbies are not, in general, a sociable species (you wouldn't be either if you had to drive for 10–12 hours a day in Tōkyō traffic), but you can always count on a minimum standard of courtesy. And if you forget something in the cab—a camera, a purse—your chances of getting it back are almost 100% (☞ Lost and Found, *above*).

Hailing a taxi during the day is seldom a problem. You would have to be in a very remote part of town to wait more than five minutes for one to pass by. In Ginza, drivers are allowed to pick up passengers only in designated areas; look for short lines of cabs. Elsewhere, you need only step off the curb and raise your arm. If the cab already has a fare, there will be a green light on the dashboard, visible through the windshield; if not, the light will be red.

Night, when everyone's been out drinking and wants a ride home, changes the rules a bit. Don't be astonished if a cab with a red light doesn't stop for you: the driver may have had a radio call, or he may be heading for an area where a long, profitable fare to the suburbs is more likely. (Or the cab driver may simply not feel like coping with a passenger in a foreign language. Refusing a fare is against the law—but it's done all the time.) Between 11 PM and 2 AM on Friday and Saturday nights, you have to be very lucky to get a cab in any of the major entertainment districts; in Ginza it is almost impossible.

## Telephones

### AREA & COUNTRY CODES

The country code for Japan is 81. When dialing a Japanese number from outside of Japan, drop the initial o from the local area code. The country code is 1 for the United States and Canada, 61 for Australia, 64 for New Zealand, and 44 for the United Kingdom.

## DIRECTORY & OPERATOR ASSISTANCE

For directory information on Tōkyō telephone numbers, dial 104; for elsewhere in Japan, dial 105. These services are only in Japanese, but the NTT Information Customer Service Centre, open weekdays 9–5, has service representatives who speak English, French, Spanish, Portuguese, Korean, and Chinese.

➤ **CONTACT: NTT Information Customer Service Centre** (tel. 0120/364–463 toll-free).

## INTERNATIONAL CALLS

Many gray, multicolor, and green phones have gold plates indicating, in English, that they can be used for international calls. Three Japanese companies provide international service: KDDI (001), Japan Telecom (0041), and IDC (0061). Dial the company code + country code + city/area code and number of your party. KDD offers the clearest connection but is also the most expensive. Telephone credit cards are especially convenient for international calls. For operator assistance in English on long-distance calls, dial 0051.

## PUBLIC PHONES

Pay phones are one of the great delights of Japan. Not only are they conveniently located in hotels, restaurants, and on street corners, but at ¥10 for three minutes, they have to be one of the few remaining bargains in Japan.

Telephones come in various colors, including pink, red, and green. Most pink and red phones, for local calls, accept only ¥10 coins. Green and gray phones accept ¥10 and ¥100 coins as well as prepaid telephone cards. Domestic long-distance rates are reduced as much as 50% after 9 PM (40% after 7 PM). Green phones take coins and accept telephone cards—disposable cards of fixed value that you use up in increments of ¥10. Telephone cards, sold in vending machines, hotels, and a variety of stores, are tremendously convenient because you will not have to search for the correct change.

## Time

Tōkyō is 9 hours ahead of Greenwich Mean Time and 14 hours ahead of U.S. Eastern Standard Time. Daylight saving time is not observed.

## Tipping

Tipping is not common in Japan. It's not necessary to tip taxi drivers, or at hair salons, barbershops, bars, or nightclubs. A chauffeur for a hired car usually receives a tip of ¥500 for a half-day excursion and ¥1,000 for a full-day trip. Porters charge fees of ¥250–¥300 per bag at railroad stations and ¥200 per piece at airports. It's not customary to tip employees of hotels, even porters, unless a special service has been rendered. In such cases, a gratuity of ¥2,000 or ¥3,000 should be placed in an envelope and handed to the staff member discreetly.

## Tours & Packages

Because everything is prearranged on a prepackaged tour or independent vacation, you spend less time planning—and often get it all at a good price.

### BOOKING WITH AN AGENT

Travel agents are excellent resources. But it's a good idea to collect brochures from several agencies as some agents' suggestions may be influenced by relationships with tour and package firms that reward them for volume sales. If you have a special interest, **find an agent with expertise in that area**; the American Society of Travel Agents (ASTA; ☞ Travel Agencies, *below*) has a database of specialists worldwide.

Make sure your travel agent knows the accommodations and other services of the place being recommended. Ask about the hotel's location, room size, beds, and whether it has a pool, room service, or programs for children, if you care about these. Has your agent been there in person or sent others whom you can contact?

Do some homework on your own, too: local tourism boards can provide information about lesser-known and small-niche operators, some of which may sell only direct.

➤ TOUR-OPERATOR RECOMMENDATIONS: **American Society of Travel Agents** (☞ Travel Agencies, *below*). **National Tour Association** (NTA; 546 E. Main St., Lexington, KY 40508, tel. 859/ 226–4444 or 800/682–8886, www.ntaonline.com). **United States Tour Operators Association** (USTOA; 342 Madison Ave., Suite 1522, New York, NY 10173, tel. 212/599–6599 or 800/468–7862, fax 212/599–6744, www.ustoa.com).

## Train Travel

Japan Railways (JR) trains in Tōkyō are color-coded, making it easy to identify the different lines. The Yamanote Line (green or silver with green stripes) makes a 35-km (22-mi) loop around the central wards of the city in about an hour. The 29 stops include the major hub stations of Tōkyō, Yūraku-chō, Shimbashi, Shinagawa, Shibuya, Shinjuku, and Ueno.

The Chūō Line (orange) runs east to west through the loop from Tōkyō to the distant suburb of Takao. During the day, however, these are limited express trains that don't stop at most of the stations inside the loop. For local cross-town service, which also extends east to neighboring Chiba Prefecture, you have to take the Sōbu Line (yellow).

The Keihin Tōhoku Line (blue) goes north to Ōmiya in Saitama Prefecture and south to Ōfuna in Kanagawa, running parallel to the Yamanote Line between Tabata and Shinagawa. Where they share the loop, the two lines usually use the same platform—Yamanote trains on one side and Keihin Tōhoku trains, headed in the same direction, on the other. This requires a little care. Suppose, for example, you want to take the loop line from Yūraku-chō around to Shibuya, and you board a blue train instead of a green one; four stops later, where the lines branch, you'll find yourself on an unexpected trip to Yokohama.

JR Yamanote Line fares start at ¥130; you can get anywhere on the loop for ¥260 or less. Most stations have a chart in English somewhere above the row of ticket vending machines, so you can check the fare to your destination. If not, you can simply buy the cheapest ticket and pay the difference at the other end. In any case, hold on to your ticket: you'll have to turn it in at the exit. Tickets are valid only on the day you buy them, but if you plan to use the JR a lot, you can save time and trouble with an Orange Card, available at any station office. The card is electronically coded; at vending machines with orange panels, you insert the card, punch the cost of the ticket, and that amount is automatically deducted. Orange Cards come in ¥1,000 and ¥3,000 denominations.

Shinjuku, Harajuku, and Shibuya are notorious for the long lines that form at ticket dispensers. If you're using a card, make sure you've lined up at a machine with an orange panel; if you're paying cash and have no change, make sure you've lined up at a machine that will change a ¥1,000 note—not all of them do.

Yamanote and Sōbu Line trains begin running about 4:30 AM and stop around 1 AM. The last departures are indicated at each station—but only in Japanese. Bear in mind that 7 AM–9:30 AM and 5 PM–7 PM trains are packed to bursting with commuters; avoid the trains at these times, if possible. During these hours smoking is not allowed in JR stations or on platforms.

➤ **CONTACT: Japan Railways** (tel. 03/3423–0111).

## RESERVATIONS

Many travelers assume that rail passes guarantee them seats on the trains they wish to ride. Not so. If you're using a rail pass, there's no need to buy individual tickets, but you should **book seats ahead.** This guarantees you a seat and is also a useful reference for the times of train departures and arrivals. You can reserve up to two weeks in advance or just minutes before the train departs. If you fail to make a train, there is no penalty, and you can reserve again.

Most clerks at train stations know a few basic words of English and can read roman script. Moreover, they are invariably helpful in plotting your route. The complete railway timetable is a mammoth book written only in Japanese; however, you can **get an English-language train schedule from the Japan National Tourist Organization (JNTO;** ☞ Visitor Information, *below*) that covers the Shinkansen and a few of the major JR Limited Express trains. JNTO's booklet *The Tourist's Handbook* provides helpful information about purchasing tickets in Japan.

## Travel Agencies

A good travel agent puts your needs first. Look for an agency that has been in business at least five years, emphasizes customer service, and has someone on staff who specializes in your destination. In addition, **make sure the agency belongs to a professional trade organization.** The American Society of Travel Agents (ASTA)—the largest and most influential in the field with more than 26,000 members in some 170 countries—maintains and enforces a strict code of ethics and will step in to help mediate any agent-client disputes if necessary. ASTA (whose motto is "Without a travel agent, you're on your own") also maintains a Web site that includes a directory of agents. (If a travel agency is also acting as your tour operator, *see* Buyer Beware in Tours & Packages, *above*.)

➤ **LOCAL AGENT REFERRALS: American Society of Travel Agents** (ASTA; 1101 King St., Suite 200, Alexandria, VA 22314, tel. 800/965–2782 24-hr hot line, fax 703/739–7642, www.astanet.com). **Association of British Travel Agents** (68–71 Newman St., London W1T 3AH, tel. 020/7637–2444, fax 020/7637–0713, www.abtanet.com). **Association of Canadian Travel Agents** (130 Albert St., Suite 1705, Ottawa, Ontario K1P 5G4, tel. 613/237–3657, fax 613/237–7052, www.acta.net). **Australian Federation of Travel Agents** (Level 3, 309 Pitt St., Sydney NSW 2000, tel. 02/9264–3299, fax 02/9264–1085, www.afta.com.au). **Travel Agents' Association of New Zealand** (Level 5, Paxus House, 79 Boulcott St., Box 1888, Wellington 10033, tel. 04/499–0104, fax 04/499–0827, www.taanz.org.nz).

## Visitor Information

The Tourist Information Center (TIC) in the Tōkyō International Forum, at the north end of the lower concourse, is an extremely useful source of free maps and brochures. The center also advises on trip planning in Japan. Make a point of dropping by early in your stay in Tōkyō; it's open weekdays 9–5, Saturday 9–noon.

The Asakusa Tourist Information Center, opposite Kaminari-mon, has some English-speaking staff and plenty of maps and brochures; it's open daily 9:30–8.

A taped recording in English on festivals, performances, and other events in the Tōkyō area operates 24 hours a day and is updated weekly. Two free weekly magazines, the *Tour Companion* and *Metropolis*, available at hotels, book and music stores, some restaurants and cafés, and other locations, carry up-to-date announcements of what's going on in the city. The better of the two is *Metropolis*, which breaks its listings down in separate sections for Art & Exhibitions, Movies, TV, Music, and After Dark. *Tōkyō Journal* (¥600), available at newsstands in Narita Airport and at many bookstores that carry English-language books, is a monthly magazine with similar listings. The *Japan Times*, a daily English-language newspaper, is yet another resource for entertainment reviews and schedules.

NTT (Japanese Telephone Corporation) can help you find information (in English), such as telephone numbers, museum openings, and various other information available from its databases. It's open weekdays 9–5.

➤ **JAPAN NATIONAL TOURIST ORGANIZATION (JNTO): Canada:** (165 University Ave., Toronto, Ontario M5H 3B8, tel. 416/366–7140). **Japan:** (2–10–1 Yūrakuchō 1-chōme, Chiyoda-ku, Tōkyō, tel. 03/3502–1461; Kyōto Tower Bldg., Higashi-Shiokoji-chō, Shimogyo-ku, Kyōto, tel. 075/371–5649). **United Kingdom:** (Heathcoat House, 20 Savile Row, London W1X 1AE, tel. 020/7734–9638). **United States:** (1 Rockefeller Plaza, Suite 1250, New York, NY 10020, tel. 212/757–5640; 401 N. Michigan Ave., Suite 770, Chicago, IL 60611, tel. 312/222–0874; 1 Daniel Burnham Court, San Francisco, CA 94109, tel. 415/292–5686; 515 S. Figueroa St., Suite 1470, Los Angeles, CA 90071, tel. 213/623–1952).

➤ **TOURIST INFORMATION: Asakusa Tourist Information Center** (2–18–9 Kaminari-mon, Taitō-ku, tel. 03/3842–5566; subway: Ginza Line, Asakusa Eki [Exit 2]). **Metropolis** (tel. 03/3423–6931, www.metropolis.co.jp). **NTT** (tel. 0120/36–4463 toll free). **Tourist Information Center** (TIC; Tōkyō International Forum, 3–5–1 Marunouchi, Chiyoda-ku, tel. 03/3201–3331; subway: Yūraku-chō Line, Yūraku-chō Eki [Exit A-4B]).

## When to Go

The best seasons to travel to Japan are spring and fall, when the weather is at its best. In the spring, the country is warm, with only occasional showers, and flowers grace landscapes in both rural and urban areas. The first harbingers of spring are plum blossoms in early March; *sakura* (cherry blossoms) follow, beginning in Kyūshū and usually arriving in Tōkyō by mid-April. Summer brings on the rainy season, with particularly heavy rains and humidity in July. Fall is a welcome relief, with clear blue skies and glorious foliage. Occasionally a few surprise typhoons occur in early fall, but the storms are usually as quick to leave as they are to arrive. Winter is gray and chilly, with little snow in most areas. Temperatures rarely fall below freezing.

## CLIMATE

The following is a list of average daily maximum and minimum temperatures for Tōkyō.

➤ **FORECASTS: Weather Channel Connection** (tel. 900/932–8437), 95¢ per minute from a Touch-Tone phone.

## TŌKYŌ

| Jan. | 46F | 8C | May | 72F | 22C | Sept. | 78F | 26C |
|------|-----|-----|------|-----|-----|-------|-----|-----|
|      | 29  | −2  |      | 53  | 12  |       | 66  | 19  |
| Feb. | 48F | 9C  | June | 75F | 24C | Oct.  | 70F | 21C |
|      | 30  | −1  |      | 62  | 17  |       | 56  | 13  |
| Mar. | 53F | 12C | July | 82F | 28C | Nov.  | 60F | 16C |
|      | 35  | 2   |      | 70  | 21  |       | 42  | 6   |
| Apr. | 62F | 17C | Aug. | 86F | 30C | Dec.  | 51F | 11C |
|      | 46  | 8   |      | 72  | 22  |       | 33  | 1   |

# WORDS AND PHRASES

Japanese sounds and spellings differ in principle from those of the West. We build words letter by letter, and one letter can sound different depending where it appears in a word. For example, we see *ta* as two letters, and *ta* could be pronounced three ways, as in *tat*, *tall*, and *tale*. For the Japanese, *ta* is one character, and it is pronounced one way: *tah*.

The *hiragana* and *katakana* (tables of sounds) are the rough equivalents of our alphabet. There are four types of syllables within these tables: the single vowels *a*, *i*, *u*, *e*, and *o*, in that order; vowel-consonant pairs like *ka*, *ni*, *hu*, or *ro*; the single consonant *n*, which punctuates the upbeats of the word for bullet train, *Shinkansen* (shee-n-ka-n-se-n); and compounds like *kya*, *chu*, and *ryo*. Remember that these compounds are one syllable. Thus *Tōkyō*, the capital city has only two syllables—*tō* and *kyō*—not three. Likewise pronounce Kyōtō *kyō-tō*, not *kee-oh-to*.

Japanese vowels are pronounced as follows: *a*–ah, *i*–ee, *u*–oo, *e*–eh, *o*–oh. The Japanese *r* is rolled so that it sounds like a bounced *d*.

**No diphthongs.** Paired vowels in Japanese words are not slurred together, as in our words *coin*, *brain*, or *stein*. The Japanese separate them, as in *mae* (ma-eh), which means in front of; *kōen* (ko-en), which means park; *byōin* (byo-een), which means hospital; and *tokei* (to-keh-ee), which means clock or watch.

**Macrons.** Many Japanese words, when rendered in *romaji* (roman letters), require macrons over vowels to indicate correct pronunciation, as in Tōkyō. When you see these macrons, double the length of the vowel, as if you're saying it twice: *to-o-kyo-o*. Likewise, when you see double consonants, as in the city name Nikkō, linger on the Ks—as in "bookkeeper"—and on the O.

**Emphasis.** Some books state that the Japanese emphasize all syllables in their words equally. This is not true. Take the words *sayōnara* and *Hiroshima*. Americans are likely to stress the downbeats: sa-yo-*na*-ra and hi-ro-*shi*-ma. The Japanese actually emphasize the second beat in each case: sa-*yō*-na-ra (note the macron) and hi-*ro*-shi-ma. Metaphorically speaking, the Japanese don't so much stress syllables as pause over them or race past them: Emphasis is more a question of speed than weight. In the vocabulary below, we indicate emphasis by italicizing the syllable that you should stress.

Three interesting pronunciations are in the vocabulary below. The word *desu* roughly means "is." It looks like it has two syllables, but the Japanese race past the final u and just say "dess." Likewise, some verbs end in -*masu*, which is pronounced "mahss." Similarly, the character *shi* is often quickly pronounced "sh," as in the phrase meaning "pleased to meet you:" ha-ji-me-*mash*(i)-te. Just like *desu* and -*masu*, what look like two syllables, in this case, *ma* and *shi*, are pronounced *mahsh*.

**Hyphens.** Throughout the book, we have hyphenated certain words to help you recognize meaningful patterns. This isn't conventional; it is practical. For example, Eki-*mae*-dōri, which literally means "Station Front Avenue," turns into a blur when rendered Ekimaedōri.

**Chapter glossaries.** In the same spirit, we have added glossaries to each chapter to signal important words that appear in the city or region in question. From studying the Japanese language, we have found that knowing these few words and suffixes adds meaning to reading about Japan and makes asking directions from Japanese people a whole lot more productive.

## Basics　基本的表現

| | | |
|---|---|---|
| Yes/No | *ha-i/ii-e* | はい／いいえ |
| Please | o-ne-*gai* shi-masu | お願いします |
| Thank you (very much) | (*dō*-mo) a-*ri*-ga-to go-*zai*-ma su | （どうも）ありがとうございます |
| You're welcome | *dō* i-ta-shi-ma-shi-te | どういたしまして |
| Excuse me | su-mi-ma-*sen* | すみません |
| Sorry | *go*-men na-*sai* | ごめんなさい |
| Good morning | o-*ha*-yō *go*-zai-ma-su | お早うございます |
| Good day/afternoon | kon-*ni*-chi-wa | こんにちは |
| Good evening | kom-*ban*-wa | こんばんは |
| Good night | o-*ya*-su-mi na-*sai* | おやすみなさい |
| Goodbye | sa-*yō*-na-ra | さようなら |
| Mr./Mrs./Miss | -san | 一さん |
| Pleased to meet you | *ha*-ji-me-*mashi*-te | はじめまして |
| How do you do? | *dō*-zo yo-*ro*-shi-ku | どうぞよろしく |

## Numbers　数

The first reading is used for reading numbers, as in telephone numbers, and the second is often used for counting things.

| | | | | | |
|---|---|---|---|---|---|
| 1 | *i*-chi / hi-*to*-tsu | 一／一つ | 17 | *jū*-shi-chi | 十七 |
| 2 | ni / fu-*ta*-tsu | 二／二つ | 18 | *jū*-ha-chi | 十八 |
| 3 | san / *mit*-tsu | 三／三つ | 19 | *jū*-kyū | 十九 |
| 4 | shi / *yot*-tsu | 四／四つ | 20 | *ni*-jū | 二十 |
| 5 | go / i-*tsu*-tsu | 五／五つ | 21 | *ni*-jū-i-chi | 二十一 |
| 6 | *ro*-ku / *mut*-tsu | 六／六つ | 30 | *san*-jū | 三十 |
| 7 | *na*-na / na-*na*-tsu | 七／七つ | 40 | yon-jū | 四十 |
| 8 | *ha*-chi / *yat*-tsu | 八／八つ | 50 | go-jū | 五十 |
| 9 | kyū / ko-ko-no-*tsu* | 九／九つ | 60 | *ro*-ku-jū | 六十 |
| 10 | jū / tō | 十／十 | 70 | na-na-jū | 七十 |
| 11 | *jū*-i-chi | 十一 | 80 | *ha*-chi-jū | 八十 |
| 12 | *jū*-ni | 十二 | 90 | kyū-jū | 九十 |
| 13 | *jū*-san | 十三 | 100 | *hya*-ku | 百 |
| 14 | *jū*-yon | 十四 | 1000 | sen | 千 |
| 15 | *jū*-go | 十五 | 10,000 | *i*-chi-man | 一万 |
| 16 | *jū*-ro-ku | 十六 | 100,000 | *jū*-man | 十万 |

## Days of the Week 曜日

| Sunday | *ni*-chi *yō*-bi | 日曜日 |
| Monday | *ge*-tsu *yō*-bi | 月曜日 |
| Tuesday | *ka* *yō*-bi | 火曜日 |
| Wednesday | *su*-i *yō*-bi | 水曜日 |
| Thursday | *mo*-ku *yō*-bi | 木曜日 |
| Friday | *kin* *yō*-bi | 金曜日 |
| Saturday | *dō* *yō*-bi | 土曜日 |
| Weekday | hei-*ji*-tsu | 平日 |
| Weekend | Shū-ma-tsu | 週末 |

## Months 月

| January | *i*-chi *ga*-tsu | 一月 |
| February | *ni* ga-tsu | 二月 |
| March | *san* ga-tsu | 三月 |
| April | *shi* ga-tsu | 四月 |
| May | *go* ga-tsu | 五月 |
| June | *ro*-ku *ga*-tsu | 六月 |
| July | *shi*-chi *ga*-tsu | 七月 |
| August | *ha*-chi *ga*-tsu | 八月 |
| September | *ku* ga-tsu | 九月 |
| October | *jū* ga-tsu | 十月 |
| November | *jū*-i-chi *ga*-tsu | 十一月 |
| December | *jū*-ni *ga*-tsu | 十二月 |

## Useful Expressions, Questions, and Answers よく使われる表現

| Do you speak English? | *ei*-go ga wa-*ka*-ri-ma-su *ka* | 英語が。わかりますか |
| I don't speak Japanese. | *ni*-hon-go ga wa-*ka*-ri-ma-*sen* | 日本語が わかりません。 |
| I don't understand. | wa-*ka*-ri-ma-*sen* | わかりません。 |
| I understand. | wa-*ka*-ri-ma-shi-*ta* | わかりました。 |
| I don't know. | *shi*-ri-ma-*sen* | 知りません。 |
| I'm American (British). | wa-*ta*-shi wa a-*me*-ri-ka (i-*gi*-ri-su) jin *desu* | 私はアメリカ (イギリス) 人 です。 |
| What's your name? | o-*na*-ma-e wa *nan* desu *ka* | お名前は何ですか。 |
| My name is . . . | . . . to *mo*-shi-*ma*-su | .....と申します。 |
| What time is it? | *i*-ma *nan*-ji desu *ka* | 今何時ですか。 |

| | | |
|---|---|---|
| How? | *dō* yat-te | どうやって。 |
| When? | *i*-tsu | いつ。 |
| Yesterday/today/<br>tomorrow | ki-*nō*/kyō/*ashi*-ta | きのう／きょう／<br>あした |
| This morning | *ke*-sa | けさ |
| This afternoon | *kyō* no *go*-go | きょうの午後 |
| Tonight | kom-*ban* | こんばん |
| Excuse me, what? | su-*mi*-ma-*sen, nan*<br>desu *ka* | すみません、<br>何ですか。 |
| What is this/that? | *ko*-re/*so*-re wa *nan*<br>desu *ka* | これ／<br>それは何ですか。 |
| Why? | *na*-ze desu *ka* | なぜですか。 |
| Who? | *da*-re desu *ka* | だれですか。 |
| I am lost. | *mi*-chi ni<br>ma-yo-i-*mash*-ta | 道に迷いました。 |
| Where is [place] | [place] wa *do*-ko<br>desu *ka* | .....はどこですか。 |
| Train station? | e-ki | 駅 |
| Subway station? | chi-*ka*-te-tsu-no eki | 地下鉄の駅 |
| Bus stop? | *ba*-su *no*-ri-*ba* | バス乗り場 |
| Taxi stand? | *ta*-ku-shi-i *no*-ri-*ba* | タクシー乗り場 |
| Airport? | kū-kō | 空港 |
| Post office? | *yū*-bin-*kyo*-ku | 郵便局 |
| Bank? | *gin*-kō | 銀行 |
| the [name] hotel? | [name] ho-*te*-ru | ホテル |
| Elevator? | e-re-bē-tā | エレベーター |
| Where are the<br>restrooms? | *to*-i-re wa *do*-ko<br>desu *ka* | トイレは<br>どこですか。 |
| Here/there/over there | *ko*-ko/*so*-ko/*a*-so-ko | ここ／そこ／あそこ |
| Left/right | hi-*da*-ri/*mi*-gi | 左／右 |
| Straight ahead | mas-*su*-gu | まっすぐ |
| Is it near (far)? | chi-*ka*-i (*to*-i) desu *ka* | 近い（遠い）ですか。 |
| Are there any rooms? | *he*-ya *ga* a-ri-masu *ka* | 部屋がありますか。 |
| I'd like [item] | [item] ga ho-*shi*-i no<br>desu ga | .....がほしいの<br>ですが。 |
| Newspaper | *shim*-bun | 新聞 |
| Stamp | *kit*-te | 切手 |

| | | |
|---|---|---|
| Key | *ka*-gi | 鍵 |
| I'd like to buy [item] | [item] o kai-*ta*-i no desu ke do | .....を買いたいの ですけど。 |
| a ticket to [event] | [event] *ma*-de no *kip*-pu | .....までの切符 |
| Map | *chi*-zu | 地図 |
| How much is it? | i-*ku*-ra desu ka | いくらですか。 |
| It's expensive (cheap). | ta-*ka*-i (ya-*su*-i) de su *ne* | 高い (安い) ですね。 |
| A little (a lot) | su-*ko*-shi (*ta*-ku-san) | 少し (たくさん) |
| More/less | *mot*-to o-ku/ su-ku-*na*-ku | もっと多く／少なく |
| Enough/too much | *jū*-bun/o-su-*gi*-ru | 十分／多すぎる |
| I'd like to exchange . . . | . . . *ryō*-ga e shi-*te* i-*ta*-da-ke-masu ka | .....両替して 頂けますか。 |
| dollars to yen | *do*-ru o *en* ni | ドルを円に |
| pounds to yen | *pon*-do o *en* ni | ポンドを円に |
| How do you say . . . in Japanese? | ni-*hon*-go de . . . wa *dō* i-i-masu ka | 日本語で.....は どう言いますか。 |
| I am ill/sick. | wa-*ta*-shi wa *byō*-ki desu | 私は病気です。 |
| Please call a doctor. | *i*-sha o *yon*-de ku-da-sa-*i* | 医者を呼んで 下さい。 |
| Please call the police. | *ke*-i-sa-tsu o *yon*-de ku-da-*sa*-i | 警察を 呼んで下さい。 |
| Help! | *ta*-su-*ke*-te | 助けて！ |

# Restaurants　レストラン
## Basics and Useful Expressions　よく使われる表現

| | | |
|---|---|---|
| A bottle of . . . | . . . *ip*-pon | .....一本 |
| A glass/cup of . . . | . . . *ip*-pai | .....一杯 |
| Ashtray | ha-i-*za*-ra | 灰皿 |
| Plate | *sa*-ra | 皿 |
| Bill/check | kan-*jō* | かんじょう |
| Bread | pan | パン |
| Breakfast | *chō*-sho-ku | 朝食 |
| Butter | ba-*tā* | バター |
| Cheers! | kam-*pai* | 乾杯！ |

| Chopsticks | *ha*-shi | 箸 |
| Cocktail | *ka*-ku-*te*-ru | カクテル |
| Dinner Does that include... | *yū*-sho-ku *ga tsu-ki-ma-su-ka* | 夕食が付きますか。 |
| Excuse me! | su-mi-ma-*sen* | すみません |
| Fork | *fō*-ku | フォーク |
| I am diabetic. | wa-*ta*-shi wa tō-*nyō*-byō de su | 私は糖尿病です。 |
| I am dieting. | *da*-i-et-to *chū* desu | ダイエット中です。 |
| I am a vegetarian. | sa-i-*sho*-ku *shū*-gi-sha de-su | 菜食主義者です。 |
| I cannot eat [item] | [item] wa *ta*-be-ra-re-ma-*sen* | .....は食べられません。 |
| I'd like to order. | *chū*-mon o shi-*tai* desu | 注文をしたいです。 |
| I'd like [item] | [item] o o-ne-*gai*-shi-ma su | .....をお願いします。 |
| I'm hungry. | o-na-ka ga *su*-i-te i-*ma* su | お腹が空いています。 |
| I'm thirsty. | *no*-do ga ka-*wa*-i-te i-*ma* su | 喉が渇いています。 |
| It's tasty (not good) | o-i-shi-i (ma-*zu*-i) desu | おいしい（まずい）です。 |
| Knife | *na*-i-fu | ナイフ |
| Lunch | *chū*-sho-ku | 昼食 |
| Menu | me-nyū | メニュー |
| Napkin | *na*-pu-*kin* | ナプキン |
| Pepper | ko-*shō* | こしょう |
| Please give me [item] | [item] o ku-da-*sa*-i | .....を下さい。 |
| Salt | *shi*-o | 塩 |
| Set menu | *te*-i-sho-ku | 定食 |
| Spoon | su-*pūn* | スプーン |
| Sugar | sa-to | 砂糖 |
| Wine list | *wa*-i-n *ri*-su-*to* | ワインリスト |
| What do you recommend? | o-su-su-me *ryō*-ri wa *nan* desu *ka* | お勧め料理は何ですか。 |

## Meat Dishes　　肉料理

| | | |
|---|---|---|
| 焼き肉 | yaki-niku | Thinly sliced meat is marinated then barbecued over an open fire at the table. |
| すき焼き | suki-yaki | Thinly sliced beef, green onions, mushrooms, thin noodles, and cubes of tōfu are simmered in a large iron pan in front of you. These ingredients are cooked in a mixture of soy sauce, mirin (cooking wine), and a little sugar. You are given a saucer of raw egg to cool the suki-yaki morsels before eating. Using chopsticks, you help yourself to anything on your side of the pan and dip it into the egg and then eat. Best enjoyed in a group. |
| しゃぶしゃぶ | shabu-shabu | Extremely thin slices of beef are plunged for an instant into boiling water flavored with soup stock and then dipped into a thin sauce and eaten. |
| 肉じゃが | niku-jaga | Beef and potatoes stewed together with soy sauce. |
| ステーキ | sutēki | steak |
| ハンバーグ | hambāgu | Hamburger pattie served with sauce. |
| トンカツ | tonkatsu | Breaded deep-fried pork cutlets. |
| しょうが焼 | shōga-yaki | Pork cooked with ginger. |
| 酢豚 | subuta | Sweet and sour pork, originally a Chinese dish. |
| からあげ | kara-age | deep-fried without batter |
| 焼き鳥 | yaki-tori | Pieces of chicken, white meat, liver, skin, etc., threaded on skewers with green onions and marinated in sweet soy sauce and grilled. |
| 親子どんぶり | oyako-domburi | Literally, "mother and child bowl"—chicken and egg in broth over rice. |
| 他人どんぶり | tanin-domburi | Literally, "strangers in a bowl"—similar to oyako domburi, but with beef instead of chicken. |

| ロール・キャベツ | rōru kyabetsu | Rolled cabbage; beef or pork rolled in cabbage and cooked. |
| はやしライス | hayashi raisu | Beef flavored with tomato and soy sauce with onions and peas over rice. |
| カレーライス | karē-raisu | Curried rice. A thick curry gravy typically containing beef is poured over white rice. |
| カツカレー | katsu-karē | Curried rice with tonkatsu. |
| お好み焼き | okonomi-yaki | Sometimes called a Japanese pan-cake, this is made from a batter of flour, egg, cabbage, and meat or seafood, griddle-cooked then covered with green onions and a special sauce. |
| シュウマイ | shūmai | Shrimp or pork wrapped in a light dough and steamed. |
| ギョウザ | gyōza | Pork spiced with ginger and gar-lic in a Chinese wrapper and fried or steamed. |

## Seafood Dishes　　魚貝類料理

| 焼き魚 | yaki-zakana | broiled fish |
| 塩焼 | shio-yaki | Fish sprinkled with salt and broiled until crisp. |
| さんま | samma | saury pike |
| いわし | iwashi | sardines |
| しゃけ | shake | salmon |
| 照り焼き | teri-yaki | Fish basted in soy sauce and broiled. |
| ぶり | buri | yellowtail |
| 煮魚 | nizakana | soy-simmered fish |
| さばのみそ煮 | saba no miso ni | Mackerel stewed with soy-bean paste. |
| 揚げ魚 | age-zakana | deep-fried fish |
| かれいフライ | karei furai | deep-fried breaded flounder |
| 刺身 | sashimi | Very fresh raw fish. Served sliced thin on a bed of white radish with a saucer of soy sauce and horseradish. Eaten by dipping fish into soy sauce mixed with horseradish. |

| まぐろ | maguro | tuna |
| --- | --- | --- |
| あまえび | ama-ebi | sweet shrimp |
| いか | ika | squid |
| たこ | tako | octopus |
| あじ | aji | horse mackerel |
| さわら | sawara | Spanish mackerel |
| しめさば | shimesaba | Mackerel marinated in vinegar. |
| かつおのたたき | katsuo no tataki | Bonito cooked just slightly on the surface. Eaten with cut green onions and thin soy sauce. |
| どじょうの 柳川なべ | dojo no yanagawa nabe | Loach cooked with burdock root and egg in an earthen dish. Considered a delicacy. |
| うな重 | una-jū | Eel marinated in a slightly sweet soy sauce is charcoal-broiled and served over rice. Considered a delicacy. |
| 天重 | ten-jū | Deep-fried prawns served over rice with sauce. |
| 海老フライ | ebi furai | Deep-fried breaded prawns. |
| あさりの酒蒸し | asari no sakamushi | Clams steamed with rice wine. |

## Sushi  寿司

| 寿司 | sushi | Basically, sushi is rice, fish, and vegetables. The rice is delicately seasoned with vinegar, salt, and sugar. There are basically three types of sushi: nigiri, chirashi, and maki. |
| --- | --- | --- |
| にぎり寿司 | nigiri zushi | The rice is formed into a bite-sized cake and topped with various raw or cooked fish. The various types are usually named after the fish, but not all are fish. Nigiri zushi is eaten by picking up the cakes with chopsticks or the fingers, dipping the fish side in soy sauce, and eating. |

| ちらし寿司 | chirashi zushi | In chirashi zushi, a variety of seafood is arranged on the top of the rice and served in a bowl. |
| 巻き寿司 | maki zushi | Raw fish and vegetables or other morsels are rolled in sushi rice and wrapped in dried seaweed. Some popular varieties are listed here. |
| まぐろ | maguro | tuna |
| とろ | toro | fatty tuna |
| たい | tai | red snapper |
| さば | saba | mackerel |
| こはだ | kohada | gizzard shad |
| しゃけ | shake | salmon |
| はまち | hamachi | yellowtail |
| ひらめ | hirame | flounder |
| あじ | aji | horse mackerel |
| たこ | tako | octopus |
| あなご | anago | conger eel |
| えび | ebi | shrimp |
| 甘えび | ama-ebi | sweet shrimp |
| いか | ika | squid |
| みる貝 | miru-gai | giant clam |
| あおやぎ | aoyagi | round clam |
| 卵 | tamago | egg |
| かずのこ | kazunoko | herring roe |
| かに | kani | crab |
| ほたて貝 | hotate-gai | scallop |
| うに | uni | sea urchin |
| いくら | ikura | salmon roe |
| 鉄火巻 | tekka-maki | tuna roll |
| かっぱ巻 | kappa-maki | cucumber roll |
| 新香巻 | shinko-maki | shinko roll (shinko is a type of pickle) |
| カリフォルニア巻 | kariforunia-maki | California roll, containing crab-meat and avocado. This was in- |

| | | vented in the U.S. but was re-exported to Japan and is gaining popularity there. |
|---|---|---|
| うに | uni | Sea urchin on rice wrapped with seaweed. |
| いくら | ikura | Salmon roe on rice wrapped with seaweed. |
| 太巻 | futo-maki | Big roll with egg and pickled vegetables. |

## Vegetable Dishes　野菜料理

| | | |
|---|---|---|
| おでん | oden | Often sold by street vendors at festivals and in parks, etc., this is vegetables, octopus, or egg simmered in a soy fish stock. |
| 天ぷら | tempura | Vegetables, shrimp, or fish deep-fried in a light batter. Eaten by dipping into a thin sauce containing grated white radish. |
| 野菜サラダ | yasai sarada | vegetable salad |
| 大学いも | daigaku imo | fried yams in a sweet syrup |
| 野菜いため | yasai itame | stir-fried vegetables |
| きんぴらごぼう | kimpira gobō | Carrots and burdock root, fried with soy sauce. |
| 煮もの | nimono | vegetables simmered in a soy- and sake-based sauce |
| かぼちゃ | kabocha | pumpkin |
| さといも | satoimo | taro root |
| たけのこ | takenoko | bamboo shoots |
| ごぼう | gobō | burdock root |
| れんこん | renkon | lotus root |
| 酢のもの | sumono | Vegetables seasoned with ginger. |
| きゅうり | kyūri | cucumber |
| 和えもの | aemono | Vegetables dressed with sauces. |
| ねぎ | tamanegi | onions |
| おひたし | o-hitashi | Boiled vegetables with soy sauce and dried shaved bonito or sesame seeds. |

| ほうれん草 | hōrenso | spinach |
| --- | --- | --- |
| 漬物 | tsukemono | Japanese pickles. Made from white radish, eggplant or other vegetables. Considered essential to the Japanese meal. |

## Egg Dishes　卵料理

| ベーコン・エッグ | bēkon-eggu | bacon and eggs |
| --- | --- | --- |
| ハム・エッグ | hamu-eggu | ham and eggs |
| スクランブル・エッグ | sukuramburu eggu | scrambled eggs |
| ゆで卵 | yude tamago | boiled eggs |
| 目玉焼 | medama-yaki | fried eggs, sunny-side up |
| オムレツ | omuretsu | omelet |
| オムライス | omuraisu | Omelet with rice inside, often eaten with ketchup. |
| 茶わんむし | chawan mushi | Vegetables, shrimp, etc., steamed in egg custard. |

## Tōfu Dishes　豆腐料理

Tōfu, also called bean curd, is a white, high-protein food with the consistency of soft gelatin.

| 冷やっこ | hiya-yakko | Cold tōfu with soy sauce and grated ginger. |
| --- | --- | --- |
| 湯どうふ | yu-dōfu | boiled tōfu |
| あげだしどうふ | agedashi dōfu | Lightly fried plain tōfu dipped in soy sauce and grated ginger. |
| マーボーどうふ | mābō dōfu | Tōfu and ground pork in a spicy red sauce. Originally a Chinese dish. |
| とうふの田楽 | tōfu no dengaku | Tōfu broiled on skewers and flavored with miso. |

## Rice Dishes　ごはん料理

| ごはん | gohan | steamed white rice |
| --- | --- | --- |
| おにぎり | onigiri | Triangular balls of rice with fish or vegetables inside and wrapped in a type of seaweed. |

| おかゆ | okayu | rice porridge |
| チャーハン | chāhan | Fried rice; includes vegetables and pork. |
| ちまき | chimaki | A type of onigiri made with sweet rice. |
| パン | pan | Bread, but usually rolls with a meal. |

## Soups 汁もの

| みそ汁 | miso shiru | Miso soup. A thin broth containing tōfu, mushrooms, or other morsels in a soup flavored with miso or soy-bean paste. The morsels are taken out of the bowl and the soup is drunk straight from the bowl without a spoon. |
| すいもの | suimono | Soy sauce flavored soup, often including fish and tofu. |
| とん汁 | tonjiru | Pork soup with vegetables. |

## Noodles 麺類

| うどん | udon | Wide flour noodles in broth. Can be lunch in a light broth or a full dinner called *nabe-yaki udon* when meat, chicken, egg, and vegetables are added. |
| そば | soba | Buckwheat noodles. Served in a broth like udon or, during the summer, cold on a bamboo mesh and called *zaru soba*. |
| ラーメン | rāmen | Chinese noodles in broth, often with *chashu* or roast pork. Broth is soy sauce, miso or salt flavored. |
| そう麺 | sōmen | Very thin wheat noodles, usually served cold with a tsuyu or thin sauce. Eaten in summer. |

# index

## FODOR'S POCKET TŌKYŌ

**EDITORS:** Carissa Bluestone, Deb Kaufman

**Editorial Contributors:** Jared Lubarsky, James Vardaman

**Editorial Production:** Taryn Luciani

**Maps:** David Lindroth, *cartographer*; Bob Blake and Rebecca Baer, *map editors*

**Design:** Fabrizio La Rocca, *creative director*; Tigist Getachew, *art director*; Melanie Marin, *photo editor*

**Production/Manufacturing:** Angela L. McLean

**Cover Photograph:** Glen Allison/Mira

2nd Edition

ISBN 0-679-00892-6

ISSN 1527-4926

## IMPORTANT TIP

Although all prices, opening times, and other details in this book are based on information supplied to us at press time, changes occur all the time in the travel world, and Fodor's cannot accept responsibility for facts that become outdated or for inadvertent errors or omissions. So **always confirm information when it matters,** especially if you're making a detour to visit a specific place.

## SPECIAL SALES

Fodor's Travel Publications are available at special discounts for bulk purchases for sales promotions or premiums. Special editions, including personalized covers, excerpts of existing guides, and corporate imprints, can be created in large quantities for special needs. For more information, contact your local bookseller or write to Special Markets, Fodor's Travel Publications, 280 Park Avenue, New York, NY 10017. Inquiries from Canada should be directed to your local Canadian bookseller or sent to Random House of Canada, Ltd., Marketing Department, 2775 Matheson Boulevard East, Mississauga, Ontario L4W 4P7. Inquiries from the United Kingdom should be sent to Fodor's Travel Publications, 20 Vauxhall Bridge Road, London SW1V 2SA, England.

PRINTED IN THE UNITED STATES OF AMERICA

10 9 8 7 6 5 4 3 2 1